JOURNEY
TO THE
END
OF
ISLAM

JOURNEY TO

THE END OF ISLAM

Michael Muhammad Knight

Soft Skull Press
New York

BOOKS BY MICHAEL MUHAMMAD KNIGHT
The Taqwacores
Blue-Eyed Devil
The Five Percenters
Impossible Man
Osama Van Halen
Journey to the End of Islam

* * *

Copyright © 2009 by Michael Muhammad Knight. All rights reserved under International and Pan-American Copyright Conventions.

Peace to Sonia Pabley, Phyllis Wender, and Lynn Hyde at the Gersh Agency.

Peace to Denise Oswald, Anne Horowitz, Carrie Deringer, Adam Krefman, and everyone at Soft Skull Press.

Peace to Richard Nash.

This manuscript was completed during a residency at Headlands Center for the Arts; peace to Holly Blake.

Peace and love to Azreal.

Library of Congress Cataloging-in-Publication Data is available.

ISBN: 978-1-59376-246-9

Cover design by Brett Yasko
Interior design by Neuwirth & Associates
Printed in the United States of America

Soft Skull Press
An Imprint of Counterpoint LLC
2117 Fourth Street
Suite D
Berkeley, CA 94710

www.softskull.com
www.counterpointpress.com

Distributed by Publishers Group West

10 9 8 7 6 5 4 3 2 1

Dedicated to

Master Fard Muhammad

and

Sadaf Khatri

BOOK 1

We must pray that when your head's finished turning,
your face is to the front again.

—**ROBERT BOLT,** *A Man for All Seasons*

Homeless in the Ummah

1.

Real pilgrimage, I thought on the plane, might be like *Fantastic Voyage* (the Isaac Asimov novel, not the Coolio song). The story's premise is more famous than the actual book or 1966 movie, having been spoofed and redone in a thousand cartoons—*The Simpsons, Family Guy, Aqua Teen Hunger Force, Sealab 2021, Dexter's Laboratory, Futurama, Ren & Stimpy, SpongeBob SquarePants, Rugrats, Muppet Babies, Transformers*: a team of scientists have to shrink down to subatomic size and pilot a nanosubmarine through some guy's carotid artery to destroy a blood clot in his brain. Pilgrimage would be like that, but you're not only the microscopic explorers; you're also the body being explored. After making your way through the circulatory system and reaching the end of your mission, turns out it was just a journey to the center of *you*.

When they dimmed the lights for us to sleep, I imagined that outside this green and white Pakistan International Airlines airbus was a blood vessel instead of a starry night—we were flying up the carotid canal into my head, a subatomic cruise to knowledge of self. That's what Pakistan meant to me.

The first time I went to Pakistan, I was seventeen years old, a senior at my Catholic high school, a born-again convert to Islam, and insane. I spent two months at Faisal Mosque in

Islamabad, doing the madrassa thing and considering jihad in Chechnya. That trip was a decade and a half ago, and I hadn't been back since. This time, I was flying to Lahore to take part in a documentary and hang out with Pakistan's first punk rock band.

The Indian-American Muslim girl I left behind worried about what her family would think of my awful books, but they were always nice to me. The week of our engagement party, Sadaf's mom had given me a miniature Qur'an in a little box, each page only the size of my thumbnail but every verse was there. "Who has the eyes to read it?" she asked me, but the baby Qur'an wasn't meant to be read, functioning more as a talisman like dashboard Virgin Marys. I wouldn't have known what it said anyway, all in God's language. That Qur'an was in my hand when the plane took off. I kissed it and let it be magic.

2.

Before heading to Toronto to fly out with the film crew, I was in Brooklyn, walking down Bushwick Avenue while on the phone with another producer from Hollywood.

"You know what's great about your novel?"

"No," I said.

"It's such an *American* story! We can always argue about religion, you know—I'm Christian, you're Muslim, we can fight over who's saved and who's going to hell—but we're all free to practice whatever religion we want to, and no one will ever say, 'You're not an American.'"

"Actually, Ron . . ."

I helped him through some history: Mother Ann, leader of the Shakers, jailed for opposing war during the American Revolution; Elijah Muhammad and his son locked up on the same charge nearly two centuries later; the Sun Dance, central act of Lakota religious life, banned by the federal government for fifty years; Reed Smoot's election to the Senate in 1902 challenged on the grounds that he was a Mormon; Five Percenters in South Carolina prisons thrown into solitary confinement until they renounced their beliefs; the Department of Veterans Affairs refusing to allow Wiccan symbols in military graveyards; Sikh police officers dismissed for wearing turbans while on duty; the ATF turning Waco into a new Karbala. There has never been a shortage of religions that failed to qualify, at one time or another, as sufficiently "American."

Sometimes, Allah just throws the answer at you. Two days later, I found the street littered with pages from a book whose binding had given out. Deciding to get religious about it—since I'm a traveler and real travelers have to believe that things come to them for a reason—I picked up a page.

There was no trace of the cover or any page with the title or author's name, so I can't properly cite the text besides that it's pages 137 and 138 of something; apologies to someone:

> Regarded as a foreign body that ought to be expelled from the national organism, and as the agent of a foreign power, the Church had to fight to establish its Americanism. Catholic laymen who took pride in their religious identity responded to the American milieu with militant self-assertion whenever they could, and Church spokesmen seemed to feel that it was not scholarship but vigorous polemicism which was needed. The Church thus took on a militant stance that ill accorded with reflection; and in our time, when the initial prejudice against it has been largely surmounted, its members persist in what Monsignor Ellis calls a "self-imposed ghetto mentality" . . . [remainder of sentence obscured by dried mud].
>
> Catholicism was, moreover, the religion of the immigrant. To American Catholics, the true Church seemed to be in Europe . . .

Catholics had come a long way from whenever that book was written—probably before America had a Catholic president. The random page had me thinking that the producer might have been right, at least partly: under a constitution that defined religion as a personal choice, theoretically uninvolved with the state, every religion had the chance to *become* American—if it was willing to negotiate. As early as the 1820s, American Jews were petitioning their rabbis for sermons in English, shorter services, and new prayers that spoke to their own lives. These changes led to the rise of Reform Judaism, today's largest denomination of Jews in the United States, a direct offspring of the Jewish American experience.

The Church of Latter-Day Saints (LDS) was an indigenous American religion, but still had to "become" American in terms of the larger society. The process began with abandoning polygamy, which opened the door for their Utah theocracy to fully enter the Union as a state, and continued with a revelation to shave off their long beards. The Mormon Tabernacle Choir purged its hymns of LDS-specific heresies like golden plates and Joseph Smith to focus on normative Judeo-Christianity, Moses and Noah and such, eventually becoming Christian enough and American enough to perform at Ronald Reagan's inauguration.

To most Americans today, Buddhism looks harmless, the religion of smiling happy monks in orange and saffron, but it wasn't always that way. During World War II, patriots like Alan Hynd, author of *Betrayal from the East: The Inside Story of Japanese Spies in America*, revealed the danger of Buddhist temples as "frequently the locations of secret meetings in the hours before dawn when engineers known to have been engaged in the construction of scale models of bridges, water-supply systems, naval bases, and other such strategic locations unquestionably taught sabotage tactics to those in attendance." It was in 1944, at an internment camp in Utah, that imprisoned

Japanese-Americans first organized as the Buddhist *Churches* of America, with Christianized rituals and services in English. Must have seemed like a good move at the time.

It all had me considering my Muslim community, and how American Islam might look after these strange years.

ON THE PLANE I skimmed through 582 pages printed from a free-download PDF: *Obama's Planet of the Apes*, by Dr. Michael Sunstar. Perhaps you've seen the author's previous work, the 447-page *How Barack Obama Fits the Profile of Being the Buraq Winged Horse of the 20-Year Plan of Islamic 'Change' for Islamic Democracy in America*. His main point was that Obama, determined to "avenge the enslavement of his Islamic African peoples," would use "gorilla warfare" to turn the USA into the "United Islamic African States of Islamic African America." Sunstar was nuts, but the mainstream media wasn't much better, discussing photos of Obama in Africa with a turban on his head, speculating on possible secret Muslim-ness and what that would mean for the free world—without any hard look at the meaning of the question itself, that Islam was now a political slur.

The conservative wiki site "Conservapedia" offered a list of proofs that if Obama won the election, he would be our first Muslim president: his middle name referenced Husayn, the Prophet Muhammad's grandson; he described the adhan as "one of the prettiest sounds on Earth at sunset" and could recite the opening lines with a "first-class [Arabic] accent"; he cited Malcolm X's autobiography as a personal inspiration and took part in Louis Farrakhan's Million Man March; he converted to Christianity only after becoming "politically ambitious"; he pronounced "Pakistan" the "Muslim Pakistani" way, rather than the "common American one." Even Obama's denials could be contextualized within Islam, the site argued, since "the Islamic doctrine of *taqiyya* encourages adherents to deny they are Muslim if it advances the cause of Islam."

Obama's father was a Muslim, everyone said. While Barack Sr. had a Muslim name, he was actually an atheist, which wouldn't make him any more electable in American politics. Even Obama's Christianity became a nightmare for white Christians who knew nothing of black churches, liberation theology, or the Bible as read by those who God had failed to save. After Obama's pastor supposedly cursed America, the talking heads asked whether churches were appropriate places to even discuss politics. Reverend Wright showed up on Fox News and calmly whipped Sean Hannity's ass, leaving Hannity with nothing but to plead for tolerance and love "in the spirit of Dr. King"—who himself had said, during the Vietnam War, that God would break the back of an arrogant empire.

I watched Obama's Philadelphia speech, regarded by many as the most important American statement on race since King's letter from a Birmingham jail. For all of the honesty and pain as he navigated between black grievances and white grievances, he still established his patriotism by shitting on Muslims—disowning the "profoundly distorted view" that "sees the conflicts in the Middle East as rooted primarily in the actions of stalwart allies like Israel, instead of emanating from the perverse and hateful ideologies of radical Islam." After Farrakhan spoke of my Islamo-American saint from 1930, Master Fard Muhammad, as the son of a black man and white woman, adding that perhaps in 2008 the savior could again be the son of a black man and white woman, I watched Hillary Clinton grill Obama to renounce the minister. Obama managed to escape Farrakhan's endorsement and ultimately win the Democratic nomination—within a week of Dunkin' Donuts pulling an ad with Rachael Ray because she wore what *looked* like an Arab scarf that now symbolized "murderous Palestinian jihad." While I struggled to define Islam in my own life, it was also Islam's turn to be the un-American religion, maybe the most un-American religion in our whole history . . .

Which I found amusing, because I understood Islam in such a thoroughly American way that it all but cut me off from the rest of the Muslim world.

MY MOTHER WAS an Irish Catholic. My father's father was a Pentecostal preacher descended from the Pennsylvania Dutch, Anabaptists who came in search of religious freedom before there was any such thing as the United States of America. I was their Muslim son, but what did that mean in the American desert—the desert that was empty because it overflowed, a desert that meant nothing because it had the capacity to mean anything? People say that America has no religion, but it's the opposite: America has every religion, all the old ones, and produces more new ones than anywhere else on earth. America's religious life is like the photo mosaic in which a thousand little images add up to one big picture, except there's no big picture, just a blob of unrelated and unrelatable images, texts, and poses, the freedom to take what you want from a religion and reject the rest and be lonely, standing outside the warm shelters of temples with your own goon god that no one else can understand. I was homeless in Islam, my practice coming from no family or national identity, no tribe or Islamic Republic.

For some converts, it's easier to latch onto a readymade community and become Arab, become Turkish or Persian, whichever template fits best. I've gone through that with Pakistani Islam and African American Islam and now preferred to mix and match; in New York I could sneak across borders without leaving the city. In downtown Manhattan I visited a Sufi order; uptown, in Harlem, I built with the Five Percenters, who taught that the black man was Allah and his name stood for "Arm Leg Leg Arm Head." In Brooklyn my Islam became Indian with Sadaf buying me CDs of *qawwalis*. She wore a Qur'anic verse on her necklace, which was a common practice in South Asia, but discouraged in Saudi Arabia by the religious police. Her Islam was as social as it was spiritual, the Islam of aunties and uncles, *Qur'an khanis*, sparkly outfits for Eid parties, and huge wedding celebrations. We talked about ours for the next summer. Her family was Sunni, but at Ashura time I'd mourn with the Shi'as in Jamaica, Queens.

"Are you Shi'a?" Sadaf asked over dinner.

"I think I just love Ali and Husayn," I told her. "What does it mean to be Shi'a?"

"I don't know. Do you pray like a Shi'a?"

"No, I pray Sunni, that's how I was taught."

"You can love Ali and Husayn without being Shi'a. My mom fasts on Ashura."

"What does it mean to be Sunni?"

"I don't know."

"If you don't know, I don't know."

When I prayed in a mosque that wouldn't allow women into the main prayer halls, she waited on the street for me; but in that same city, I have also prayed side by side with women, even behind a woman imam at a Friday jum'aa that made headlines around the world, and I struggled to appreciate what a radical act it had been. My relationship to Islam could fly only in America with no apostasy laws or religious police to enforce the sect of the rulers and ban the rest. I'd rather be a Shi'a in New York than in Cairo, or a Sunni in New York than in Tehran. I'd rather be an Ahmadi in New York than in Lahore, and I'd rather be a Sufi in New York than in Mecca; is that a shitty thing to say? I didn't want to surrender anything to Ron the producer, since he said it in such a foolish flag-waving way, but America might have been the most truly Islam-friendly nation in the world.

MY PLANE LANDED in the afternoon. After what felt like a spot of rough turbulence, I looked out the window and saw that we were already on the ground, and then realized the true gravity of travel. I was in Pakistan. Going up the ramp to customs, neither the passengers nor security guards said anything. It was just a long walk in silence to absorb the new country: *Yes, you're here; this is Pakistan.* I sought some familiar feeling, any proof that I knew this place and had been here before.

Basim and Shahjehan, Pakistan's new punk rock heroes, were waiting outside. Omar the documentary filmmaker asked me to wait fifteen minutes before leaving the airport, so his crew could have time to set up and film the big reunion. Last time I had seen Basim and Shahj was a year ago in Boston, after serving as driver for their band, the Kominas (the name's Punjabi for the "low-borns"), in the States. A bunch of dirty taqwacore kids piled into a green school bus that I bought on eBay, and we took it six thousand miles. Then Basim went back to Pakistan, where he met some musicians and started another band, the Dead Bhuttos. The name turned out to be a bad idea, and the band didn't last. Then Shahjehan followed Basim to Lahore to start a new band.

I stood by the baggage claim, watched people, walked around, went to the bathroom, and waited for the clock on the wall to let me go outside and see my friends. I took a seat and pulled out my notepad to see if something would come, reflecting on what it meant that I was here again.

All I wrote was "Noble Drew." Basim and Shahj's new band, the first punk band in the history of Pakistan. It was named after a man who was too black to be fully American in his time, and too American to be fully Muslim.

Prophet Noble Drew Ali was born Timothy Drew in 1886, to runaway slaves in South Carolina. Adopted and raised by Cherokees, he later claimed to visit the Great Pyramid of Cheops and then Mecca, receiving secret initiations and returning to America with his own scripture, popularly known as the *Circle 7 Koran*. Google it, the whole text now lives online.

In the 1920s, while America was inundated with new European

identities—Irish, Polish, Italian, etc.—black people were only "Negroes," second-class citizens with no nationality of their own. Noble Drew Ali understood it as his sacred mission to restore African-Americans to their true status: "You are not Negroes or Colored," he said, but Moors, the heirs to empires in the East. According to Moorish Science legend, he arrived at the White House and demanded that Woodrow Wilson return their stolen flag; the president and the prophet descended into the basement, where Wilson opened a safe and searched through piles of flags until Noble Drew Ali found it, Morocco's red flag with the five-pointed green star.

Noble Drew Ali taught some heresies, first that Allah and the Devil existed within us as our higher and lower selves. Moorish Science didn't relate much to "Islam" in any traditional sense of the word, and Noble Drew Ali's claim to prophethood earned him a fatwa of condemnation from the most prestigious Islamic institution in the world, Al-Azhar University in Cairo. But it stirred up the memory of an Islam brought to America with African slaves and formed the first mutation of a new Islam for the new world. Noble Drew Ali's new Islam even spoke to the old Islam, now finding its way to Pakistan with two brown Sunni kids from white Boston suburbs who came to reclaim their own flag. And then there was me, the white devil sitting at Qaid-e-Azam International Airport wearing a thirty-year-old black satin Nation of Islam jacket (also purchased on eBay). We blew that Clash of Civilizations mess out of the water.

3.

I left *Obama's Planet of the Apes* in the garbage and threw my backpack over my shoulder. That was all I had, no checked baggage or anything. I brought only the jeans that I was wearing; in my backpack I had a dozen or so rolled-up boxers and T-shirts, all chosen because they could be left behind, and a couple notebooks.

I walked outside and Basim and Shahjehan tackled me, which, along with the film crew's camera and boom mic, made for a big scene of attention around us. As men stood and stared, I hugged Basim and Shahj and met their new bandmates, Asif and Mamoon. Both of them had also lived in the States. There was a whole subculture of kids, Asif told me, who had spent time in the US or the UK and returned for whatever reasons—sometimes because coming to Pakistan meant a move up to the rich class.

Not far from our little circle, a bigger scene was developing: crowds of protesters for the Lahore portion of the Long March, a cross-country caravan to Islamabad demanding the reinstatement of Pakistan's judiciary and impeachment for Musharraf. Driving out of the airport's parking lot, we passed flatbed trailers full of young men waving green and red flags.

"What's with the green and red?" I asked the film's production manager, a nineteen-year-old named Ammar. He said that the green Islamists and red Marxists had temporarily united against Musharraf; but according to Basim, Ammar was a Communist who read his preferred revolutionary symbolism into everything.

"Musharraf's time is running out," Ammar told me. He broke down Pakistan's political situation for me. There were two parties calling themselves the Pakistan Muslim League: Musharraf's party—the PML-Q (the Q for Qaid-e-Azam, boasting lineage from Pakistan's founder Mohammad Ali Jinnah) and PML-N (the N for Nawaz Sharif, who would call for Musharraf's hanging)—and the Pakistan People's Party (PPP), the party of dead Benazir Bhutto, now headed by her twenty-year-old son. The PPP's red, black, and green flag looked like the black nationalist flag of Marcus Garvey, who had his own PPP (People's Political Party) almost a century ago in Jamaica. The Bhutto PPP still used the slogan championed by the first dead Bhutto, Benazir's father Zulfikar Ali Bhutto (*roti, kapda, aur makaan*: "food, clothing, and shelter") and claimed socialism, which made it the lesser of two evils for Ammar and his mom—an avowed communist who had fled to Russia years ago, but had since returned and now displayed portraits of Benazir in her home.

BASIM AND SHAHJEHAN'S punk flat looked like Lal Masjid after Musharraf bombed the place. Both of the couches were broken in the middle; empty bottles and piles of dirty clothes lay scattered everywhere; and someone hung a dirty, tattered Pakistan flag found outside on a standing lamp. In the middle of the living room, between the two busted couches and surrounded by miscellaneous garbage, sat a *haandi*, a ritual urn that Basim and Shahj used for ashes and nail clippings. It came from the ruins at Taxila, Basim told me, and must have been more than two thousand years old.

"How'd you get it?" I asked him.

"There's a big government smuggling operation there, and H— showed up pretending to be a high-ranking official and just walked out with it."

The characters in Noble Drew's taqwacore life started showing up: Arieb, a bandana-wearing world traveler who had lived in Croatia for years before returning to Lahore with his guitar; the Malang Party, a band of shaggy-haired stoners with Che Guevara tattoos who had come from Islamabad to play at Noble Drew's upcoming first gig; and Basim's girlfriend, Zaynab, who did volunteer work with abused and battered women. For an example of the fucked-up shit that filled her head all day, she told us about a baby less than a year old who had been raped to death by its father. Everyone gathered around the haandi and smoked up. Whiskey had come from somewhere and they shared it.

"Isn't alcohol illegal?" I asked Basim.

"Only for Muslims," he answered. "Christians are allowed to drink, which leads to an interesting bootlegging network." I don't drink, so Basim's servant Ramazan-bhai made me a mango shake.

4.

I updated the boys on life back home. My books had earned me academic credits through the University Without Walls program at Skidmore College, which meant that I could actually get a degree and even think about grad school. My friend Laury Silvers, a serious Muslim feminist and Skidmore professor on sabbatical, had moved to Toronto but still had six months left on her lease; so I headed to Saratoga Springs, lived at her empty house, and bummed around on campus. It all fell together at the right time, since I was getting married and would need a more consistent source of income than this writing hustle.

Basim and Shahj and I shared a laugh about the nonsense we left in the States, getting sued by the pillars of the American Muslim community. It started when maniacal Brooklyn imam Siraj Wahhaj was quoted as saying that if there was ever a gay-friendly mosque, he'd burn it down himself. Basim mocked Wahhaj in "Rumi was a Homo (Siraj Wahhaj You're a Fag)," praising Rumi as a hero of queer-positive Islam while homoerotically baiting the homophobe ("You can light my minaret on fire anytime you want").

Wahhaj had also made statements about establishing a caliphate in the United States, testified on behalf of the blind shaykh Omar Abdel-Rahman, and was named as a potential unindicted coconspirator in the first attack on the World Trade Center. The Kominas had a good time mocking him in "Rumi

was a Homo," but he wasn't the one who sued. The song also
attacked the other end of the spectrum; the verse, "You give
better hand jobs than Asma Hasan" took on a Republican
author and commentator and daughter of millionaires who
founded a group called Muslims for Bush. Hasan's brother was
running for Colorado state senate, and the Rumi song gave
her family a chance to temporarily silence a few critical voices;
so a week after the brother filed as a candidate, Asma filed
her defamation suit. Asma's complaint mentioned my book
Blue-Eyed Devil as portraying her as "wealthy, self-absorbed,
insensitive, and acutely uniformed," which she claimed had
inspired the Kominas to make fun of her in a song. I was sued
for being friends with the band.

The cost of our friendship went both ways. In Pakistan
Basim lost his previous social circle over me; even a former
member of the Dead Bhuttos had taken back his amp and said
he never wanted to speak to Basim again.

The reason: my Wikipedia page.

Commenting on woman-led prayer at his ProgressiveIslam.org
blog, Knight wrote, "If the Prophet wouldn't have liked it, then
in 2005 the Prophet is wrong, shit on him. La ilaha illa Allah."
The comment caused numerous Muslim scholars and thinkers
to withdraw from the site, refuse participation, or demand that
Knight be removed.

The comment was a response to progressive Muslim types
who reached so desperately to reconcile Western liberalism and
Islamic tradition that they embarrassed themselves and their
cause. I couldn't see how they expected to be taken seriously by
conservatives—or by me, for that matter. To the conservatives,
these feminists were heretics and deviants; I just thought that
they were wimps with good intentions but no spirit. We had
some genuine rottenness in our religion, like any religion that's

old in the modern world, and the only thing that worked for me was to stare it in the face and admit to it. If the Prophet showed up in this day and age advocating domestic violence, I wouldn't follow him. I didn't need to wrestle a dead man into agreeing with me.

I could have said it better, which occurred to me after learning that Article 295(c) of Pakistan's penal code called for life imprisonment or execution for anyone who defiled the name of the Prophet. Muhammad was even more legally protected than the Qur'an, the desecration of which called for a life sentence but did not carry the death penalty. In the course of my pinballing in and out of faith, I've been guilty of both offenses; and now, for the first time since even considering this trip to Pakistan, I realized that I would be a criminal here, that I had smuggled in a brain full of contraband.

> I personally am more inclined to religions in which the mediator appears to be less essential or almost tuned out.
> —RAINER MARIA RILKE

Me too. Some of the original Muslims refused to accept that Muhammad could die; after he passed, Umar swung his sword around, threatening to kill anyone who implied such blasphemy. Abu Bakr answered him: "If you worship Muhammad, Muhammad is dead; if you worship Allah, know that Allah is alive and cannot die." Or, as I put it, "shit on him." I saw my defecation on the Prophet as inherently Islamic, more committed to *tawhid*—the Absolute Oneness of Allah—than these mosques with Muhammad's name next to God's on the walls and these borderline polytheists who believed that Muhammad would intercede for them on the Day of Judgment like a Catholic "Holy Mary, Mother of God, pray for us sinners." If *la ilaha illa Allah*—there is no god but God—then what's everything else? One of the earliest Sufi saints, an

Iraqi woman named Rabi'a, was visited by Muhammad in a vision; when he asked her if she loved him, Rabi'a replied, "I love Allah so much, I have no room for you." The name of her religion wasn't Muhammadism. In medieval Japan poets like Ummon used to call the Buddha a "dried shit-stick," and some Zen lunatics even burned Buddhist scriptures. They were devout Buddhists who only wanted to bring the holy down to earth, kicking out the crutches of empty worship. I wished that we could do that in Islam, that the voices like Rabi'a hadn't been completely erased from our heritage.

Basim warned that people wouldn't be interested in discussing the nuance and possible readings of "The Prophet is wrong, shit on him."

"In Karachi," he said, "they killed a doctor for saying that Muhammad wasn't circumcised."

"*Was* he circumcised?" I asked. "Who circumcised him?" This seemed to be a real crisis for some, which could explain the legend that prophets are born without foreskins.

Basim showed me a friend's text message declaring that people weren't so keen on this "Mike Knight and gigging thing." It didn't help that Shahj and Basim's new band was named after a man who claimed to be a prophet. Basim insisted that his former friends got drunk and even said their own blasphemies, but the thought of doing it on a stage and having my name attached scared them off. One of them had warned him, "Everyone becomes a mullah when they leave this apartment." Basim could only guess at how to take that.

I pleaded my case to Arieb, that I wasn't saying *shit on the Prophet* even when I said *shit on the Prophet*, that I was a real Muslim or at least trying to learn what it meant to be one. After an ugly first encounter with Islam, I told him, I needed to deconstruct my religion before building it back up. Arieb just shrugged at the whole issue; the word *Muslim* meant nothing to him.

"Religion paralyzes people with fear," he said; "religion divides people, religion hurts people." But when he spoke, he sounded religious to me—like he had the real faith of a character who had wandered the earth for thousands of years, watching religions come and go while he clung only to the eternal cores. He drew up some wisdom from Bulleh Shah, the Punjabi Sufi poet who shit on religion all the time but in such a way that still looked deeply religious, rejecting the vain mullahs and getting to the religion of love and humanity. Arieb said one of those standard lines about all religions simply being paths up the same mountain, or rivers emptying into the same sea, whichever, a statement that made for terrible scholarship but great religion.

Even these drunks and heretics wouldn't go where I had gone, since a convert could walk in and out of religion and burn every bridge with Muslims on a whim. The community had nothing on me. My future wife didn't have that freedom, juggling her conscience and family—which was now, or would soon be, my family. What would that mean for my grimy books? I'd be forfeiting all convert privileges and joining the desi immigrant community, and I didn't know what to do about that, especially as my own heart changed. My real sisters and brothers in Islam were the ones outside the mosque, like the fourteen-year-old girl who wrote to say that *The Taqwacores* was her new Qur'an (Astaghfur'Allah)—but I also loved the ones who would be heartbroken, my sisters and aunties in *dupattas* and bearded brothers who cried for the Prophet and could never understand me. I owed them something too. I found an unoccupied corner of the room, lay on my back, and listened to a conversation about "Khuda hafiz" vs. "Allah hafiz." The two phrases both meant the same thing—"God is the Protector"—but *Khuda* was the Persian word for God and had started to lose out to *Allah*, since the Arabic language made anything more Islamically legitimate. People were saying that they didn't hear Khuda hafiz anymore; it was all Allah hafiz now. Things like that pissed me off to no end, but I fell asleep. When I woke up, the lights were out. "Load shedding," they called it, when the government shut down everyone's power several times throughout the day. With the room illuminated by someone's cell phone, Arieb played guitar and lead sing-alongs of the qawwali "Mast Qalandar," about the Sufi saint Lal Shahbaz Qalandar and his love for Ali that transgressed all limits, but carry on merry Qalandar: *Dum mast Qalandar, mast mast, Dum mast Qalandar, mast mast, Dum mast Qalandar, mast mast, Dum mast Qalandar, mast mast.* From there Arieb went into "Ring of Fire," and at first I was just happy to be hearing Johnny Cash at a punk flat in Lahore, but then I really got it: the song was another *ghazal*, as though Johnny Cash had come from this tradition of Divine Love veiled in songs of earthly love, Johnny Cash secretly a Qalandar Sufi singing drunken ecstatic passion for the One. *Love is a burning thing, and it makes a fiery ring/bound by wild desire, I fell into a ring of fire* sounded like Rumi to me. I stayed where I was in my far corner of the room, not joining in but just listening and feeling thankful.

5.

The next morning I couldn't get anyone to wake up, but shook Basim enough for him to give me directions to Jail Road and then left him passed out. Outside a dog staggered down the street with lean face, teats hanging slack, tongue wagging, and eyes beady and desperate, looking like something besides a dog . . . perhaps a transition between a dog and a more serious wild animal. The dog had a nationality, it belonged to Pakistan, and any animal in Pakistan could kill the shit out of its American equivalent: the dogs were hungrier and friendless, the birds bigger and mean. It seemed worth looking into the idea that you could learn about a society by the condition of its animals.

Later we went to Food Street in Gawalmandi and found a man selling freedom for little yellow birds bouncing around in a big cage under his arm—for every ten rupees you gave him, he'd let one go. Zaynab told me that the birds had been injured so that as soon as we left the scene, he'd scoop them back up and put them back in the cage.

6.

Noble Drew's first gig was on the thirteenth. I told Asif about the Five Percenters and demonstrated how we'd manifest the date in their righteous algebra, the Supreme Mathematics. 1 expressed the attribute of Knowledge, and 3 meant Understanding. 1 + 3 = 4, and 4 represented Culture.

"So Culture comes from how we Understand our Knowledge," I said. "Muslims all have the same Knowledge, but they Understand it in different ways, so we have different Cultures." The Five Percenters had come out of the Nation of Islam, so I had to tell Asif about Master Fard, whose sacred text—the Supreme Wisdom Lessons, a series of his questions with the answers provided near exact by his student Elijah Muhammad—spoke of the "Poor Righteous Teachers," who comprised a mere 5 percent of society and rejected the lies of the ruling 10 percent. "The Ten Percenters oppose the Five Percenters," I told him. "The Ten Percenters are holding onto their power with religion, but the Five Percenters say fuck that, all the divine power is within you, you don't need to follow a priest or imam or anyone." The Five Percenters were like Roddy Piper's character in *They Live*, in which he finds special sunglasses (the lessons) that enable him to identify the skull-faced aliens and see through their lies.

Asif asked about the remaining 85 percent. The deaf, dumb, and blind, I answered, reciting the lessons, *slaves to mental death and power*, the ones who still need parents to keep them safe in the crib.

THE GIG WAS in the parking lot of a museum. We rode there crowded in the back of a pickup truck, Basim and Asif and Mamoon discussing the original ideas behind Pakistan's formation.

"It was secular," said Mamoon. "It wasn't about going hardcore religious, at least not in the beginning. Zia fucked it all up."

I was flipping through my wad of rupees, different sizes and colors, blue, pink and red, orange and red, green, burgundy, with landmarks on the backs and the same design on all the fronts: Qaid-e-Azam, Great Leader, Muhammad Ali Jinnah in his Jinnah cap and determined glare into the future that no one could see. But he couldn't see it either, I was pretty sure. We hit a bump in the road and I almost lost my money.

The rupees bore a hadith from the Prophet Muhammad on the backs, translated in Urdu: "Seeking honest livelihood is worship of God."

IT COST SEVENTY rupees to get into the show, a little more than a dollar. The place was filled with rich kids in jeans and T-shirts.

"Why are they sitting down?" I asked Basim.

"We have to reeducate the audience," he said. It wasn't going to happen in one night. Asif was dancing around the stage in a traditional groom's outfit, screaming into a megaphone. I loved it on an Andy Kaufman level, but Kaufman liked to piss off his audience. Before the set was over, half the people were gone.

*   *   *

They'd try again with a show in Islamabad. Omar and the crew got a hotel room somewhere, and the rest of us stayed with Basim's friend Imran, another kid who had grown up in America and came back. Imran's place was covered in American posters, Radiohead and Weezer, and a wall hanging of the Ka'ba. He was in Pakistan for medical school and played in a band, the Fatsumas.

While the band smoked up, I went to Imran's bedroom to use his computer. He followed me in and asked if we could talk.

"So you're Michael *Muhammad Knight*," he said. "When you first got here, I had no idea. I thought you were just Mike."

I didn't know how he felt about that. We built a little on the book. An adolescent tantrum, I called it.

"It's like when you're a little kid," I told him, "and you think your parents are superheroes who can do no wrong. But when you're a teenager, you wake up to their bullshit, and it hurts, so you start fights and storm out of the house. Then you get older, and you gain a little wisdom. Yes, your parents were human beings and made mistakes and whatever, but you've reached a place in life where you can better understand them."

"So that's where you're at with Islam?"

"Yeah, maybe. I'm still trying to figure it out."

"It's hard to know what's real," he said. From there we went into a deep build about how humans make religion and the starting point can be so clean and straight from God but then the little men muddy it up and turn it into something else. I've had that conversation with a few Muslims, always timid at first; but once you make the first move and open up, you'd be surprised at how many people are relieved to hear it.

The show was up in the mountains surrounding Islamabad, and on the long drive up I could catch glimpses of Faisal Mosque—it was miles away but still overwhelmed the landscape with its big stone pyramid dome and four tall smooth minarets like missiles. After all the crumbling onion-domed village mosques we had passed on the long train ride, with crenellates like forts, I could recognize that Faisal didn't look like a Pakistani mosque at all—because it wasn't. Designed by a Turkish architect and built with riyals, Faisal Mosque was a gift from Saudi Arabia's King Faisal to the new Islamic Republic.

The show turned out just like the other one. The rich kids sat on the ground and never moved. They seemed to enjoy Malang Party, who played Hendrix covers and engaged in masturbatory jamming. The defining moment of the night for me was lost on everyone: Basim screaming the Kominas song "9,000 Miles," which came from Master Fard:

Can the Devil fool a Muslim?

Not nowadays.

Do you mean that the Devil fooled them 379 years ago?

Yes, the Trader made an interpretation that they receive gold for their labor, more than they were earning in their own country.

Did they receive more gold?

No. The Trader disappeared and there was no one that could speak their language.

Then what happened?

Well, they wanted to go back home, but they could not swim 9,000 miles.

7.

Faisal Mosque looked more like a stadium than a house of worship, and driving up to it felt as though we were on our way to an event, heading to Rich Stadium to see the Buffalo Bills. Like Rich Stadium, it felt like a sad place.

I walked slow and kept my head down. The courtyard was

so big that I had to take off my shoes a long way from the mosque.

The mosque was closed and I stood at the glass doors looking in at the vast room like I did my first time there, getting some stares from a few families and tourists clustering around. Ammar spoke to some people and the doors opened, just for the film crew, Mamoon, and me.

There were at least fifty yards between the entrance and the mihrab indicating the direction of Mecca. Faisal's mihrab wasn't the traditional niche in the wall, but what looked like a giant Qur'an standing upright and open. The carpeted floor was light blue and wide enough that I imagined it as a lake.

One of the imams approached with curiosity and I greeted him with proper salams. I told him the story of how I had come here so long ago and studied with Qari Khurshid Ali Alvi, who had since moved to the United States. The imam asked the questions I didn't want to hear, whether my mom was Muslim and if I had been trying to bring her to Islam.

"She's a good person," I said. And I told him how she worked three jobs to raise me by herself, and how she sent me money when I was in Pakistan. She was the one who bought my Islamic books and rugs and everything, the one who drove me to the mosque and never discouraged me, even when everyone in my family and the principal and guidance counselor at DeSales High School all thought that I was nuts. None of that mattered, though. I knew it already, having had this conversation before.

"But there is much benefit to embracing Islam," he said. I couldn't betray my mom, not like I had last time around when the Tablighis told me that she'd burn in hell and I just nodded.

"Yes," I answered. "Insha'Allah." *Sure, there's benefit to embracing Islam. Just let me make my prayers and get out.*

* * *

FOURTEEN YEARS AGO, men at Faisal Mosque asked why I had come to Pakistan. To learn Islam, I answered, and they said that this wasn't the place; Islam in Pakistan had been too corrupted with non-Muslim sources and ideas and practices with no root in the Qur'an or Sunnah. In that Saudi-built mosque named after a Saudi king, they told me that if I wanted to learn Islam, I'd have to go straight to the source.

Go to Saudi.

Globalization moves in more than one direction. What I experienced in Pakistan was a franchise of Saudi globalization, Saudi Arabia like the Wal-Mart of Islam coming in and wiping out unique downtown Islams to make it all the same convenient price-cutting religion everywhere. At lectures in the madrassa, we only learned about Pakistan's contributions to Islam when it came to great kings of the past, Mughals who built giant mosques like palaces as signs of their power, and the modern dream of Qaid-e-Azam to carve a Muslim state out of postcolonial South Asia. Beyond a lecture demonizing the Ahmadiyyas, the native heresy founded by Mirza Ghulam Ahmad in the Indian Punjab, we never caught a glimpse of native religious life straying from the straight path laid down 3,500 miles away in the center of the Islamic universe, Saudi-occupied Mecca.

I acknowledged that reality in prayer, facing the direction of Mecca as I made my rakats on the blue carpet. Turning my head to the right, I saw Mamoon praying. Mamoon's family were Ahmadiyyas of the Lahore branch, which moved closer to orthodox views and denied that Mirza Ghulam Ahmad was a prophet. At that one Faisal Mosque lecture, they told me that Ahmad was an agent of foreign subversion. British scholars had trained him in the Qur'an and propped him up as a prophet to cause trouble among the Muslims: "The British are the masters of 'divide and conquer,'" my teacher said.

The Ahmadiyyas were the first Islamic missionaries to

America, and recognized as influences upon Noble Drew Ali and Master Fard, who could have been Ahmadi himself; the Qur'an that Fard gave Elijah Muhammad was a translation by the Ahmadi scholar Maulana Mohammad Ali. In Pakistan both branches of the movement fell to persecutions, sanctioned by the state in 1984 with General Zia Ul-Haq's Ordinance XX, which forbade Ahmadis of either branch from calling themselves Muslims, their religion Islam, or their temples mosques. Under penalty of law, they could not perform the call to prayer, pray in the manner of Muslims, quote the Qur'an or hadith, greet each other with "as-salamu alaikum," or recite the shahadah. If your identity card says "Ahmadi," you can't be buried in Muslim graveyards. And you can't make the pilgrimage to Mecca.

In the Islamic Republic of Pakistan, it was illegal for some people to say, "There is no god but Allah and Muhammad is his Messenger." Mamoon coming into Faisal Mosque and praying was a criminal act, and I prayed with him.

THE FILM CREW led me to a quiet place in the courtyard, far from the main building and clusters of tourists—though some still passed by and gawked at us, standing around with their hands on their hips and staring like they were involved with our business—and I gave a long interview. In front of the camera, hovering boom mic and big white reflector, I poured my heart out for a while and then they let me go. I walked the courtyard alone, holding in my farts so that I could make Asr prayer clean; while on these grounds, I wanted to do everything right by the standards of seventeen-year-old me as though that kid was watching from up in a minaret. After Asr I thought of praying my usual two rakats out of respect for the masjid, but remembered what they taught me here: it's bad practice to pray after Asr, because it's too close to the sunset, and you don't want to be like the old pagan sun-worshipers who prayed at sunsets.

Before saying goodbye to Faisal Mosque, I went to the souvenir shop and bought a gift for Sadaf's mother, a wall hanging replica of the golden Ka'ba door. She liked that kind of thing. In her living room, she had a huge photo of the Ka'ba door with pilgrims reaching up to hang on as though they were lost at sea and the Ka'ba would carry them to land. But that door would never open for them.

So this new replica Ka'ba door in my hands was a symbol of political power, the control of a Saudi king to literally open and close the gates of Islam at his whim. Faisal Mosque was also a device of power, not only Saudi's international influence but also the Pakistani state's reaffirmation of its own Islamic legitimacy. Constructed a generation after Pakistan's political divorce from India in 1947—the largest and bloodiest relocating of populations in history—Faisal Mosque's construction fulfilled the psychology of partition, a cutting away of South Asian Islam from its Indian-ness, a pull towards the Arab Middle East. On the other side of the border, India was purging its own culture of Islam, with a sixteenth-century mosque destroyed to reclaim the birthplace of Ram, Hindu nationalist Bharatiya Janata Party rioters telling Muslims *Pakistan ya Kabristan* ("To Pakistan or the graveyard"), and calls to genocide on Hindutva sites.

Between India and Pakistan, religion was only a flag for nation-states to wave at each other. Hindu revivalists claimed ownership of Islam's soul, arguing that the Arabs were savages and ignorant of God until taught and civilized by Vikramaditya, the Hindu king—as proven, they insisted, on a gold dish that once hung inside the Ka'ba, which was originally a temple to Shiva. The Black Stone was really Shiva's lingam, they argued, and the pre-Islamic Arabs believed the sacred well of Zamzam to be Ganges water. Meanwhile, Muslim scholars argued that even Hindu scriptures pointed to Islam, with Muhammad fulfilling the Puranas' description of Kalki Avatar, the final teacher of humankind.

As Islam was equated with patriotism, Faisal Mosque appeared on the five-thousand-rupee note and hosted the tomb of General Zia Ul-Haq, who had taken over the country in a coup and instituted the policy of "Islamization." In such a deeply Islamic but diverse place as Pakistan, that really meant military Sunnification. Zia implemented Shari'a law, cutting off hands, and when his Shari'a court declared stoning to be un-Islamic he overruled them. He banned alcohol and punished drinkers with lashes, banned fornication and adultery, and sentenced a thirteen-year-old blind girl to three years in prison for getting raped by two men.

Zia overturned the blind girl's conviction when the United States threatened to withdraw its military aid; but for the most part, Islamization enjoyed full American support, as a means to squash godless Communism in Pakistan and head off the Soviet expansion into Afghanistan. So the general overthrew Benazir's Socialist father Zulfikar Ali Bhutto, put him on trial and hung him, redistributed land to allies, brutally suppressed worker protests, and then used Mystery Islam to suck the blood of the poor: "It is not for the employers to provide food, clothing, and shelter. It is for God Almighty who is the provider of livelihood to his people. Any increase or decrease in your sustenance comes from him. Trust in God and he will bestow upon you an abundance of good things in life."

Times have changed. After 2001 Musharraf had to juggle the "Talibanization" of the Northwest with U.S. pressure to squash Islamists. Right there in Islamabad, Basim had shown us the Lal Masjid, which in the 1980s assisted the recruiting and organizing of mujahideen to fight the Soviets in Afghanistan; but General Zia and the Soviets were both gone, and the mosque now found itself at odds with America. The anniversary of Musharraf's bloody siege of the place was approaching, Basim warned; "shit could go down."

I passed by General Zia's tomb and knew that I never would

have become Muslim if I was raised in this country. As a rebellious American adolescent, I had chosen Islam because it was the religion of Malcolm X, a language of resistance against unjust power. But in Pakistan, Islam was the unjust power, or at least part of what kept the machine running. Pakistan's Islam was guilty of everything for which I had rebelled against Reagan-Falwell Christianity in America. *yes.*

From there it seemed logical to consider Islamic anarchism—though that was another crock, since the Prophet created order, not chaos. The Prophet was a head of state. For Muhammad to smash those idols in Mecca looked fairly cool and anarcho-punk, but it only expressed a regime change. Nothing anarchist about that. People reacted to me as an advocate of "antinomian" Islam, *the chains of law have been broken*, that kind of thing, but antinomianism felt like a cop-out: a way to sound deep and legitimate when you're confessing to religious laziness, or worse, religious cowardice, treating Islam as an art project because you can't handle the real thing. Enjoin good and forbid evil, the Prophet said.

Allah's Book seemed more agreeable than Muhammad's career to religious freedom, since it prohibited compulsion and instructed us to tell the kafrs "to you be your religion, and to me mine." Apologists threw those lines around all the time, even when mainstream opinion viewed apostasy from Islam as a punishable crime.

I understood that religious identity was a complicated matter and that apostasy could have meant different things at different times. In the Prophet's years, a chief would convert to Islam and his whole tribe followed; did that mean that everyone in the tribe had undergone a personal transformation? Conversion was an oath of allegiance, and apostasy was treason against the state. The connection was forever established by the first Sunni caliph, Abu Bakr, who declared a handful of tribes to be infidels because they refused to pay taxes, leading to the Ridda

Wars. That's fine for history, but what the seventh century ate isn't making me poop; death over a change in conscience couldn't work in the only historical setting that really mattered, the one in which I lived.

WHATEVER SPECIAL THING I had here the first time, before all the questions, wasn't coming back. In the culture of Faisal, I was still a scourge and criminal, which hurt because this place was my womb and I returned after so long, wanting to crawl back in . . . but I could only go so far, because I'd still pray with Ahmadis, Lahori or Qadiani, and all the Muslims who aren't Muslim enough for the biggest mosque in the world. If I had anything to apologize for, it wasn't to Faisal Mosque; but maybe Faisal owed *me* some words. In the sad end, no matter how bad I wanted to just check my brain and submit to the ruling version of Islam, I'd have to be a radical and stay away from mosques named after kings.

Radicals have value, at least; they can move the center. On a scale of 1 to 5, 3 is moderate, 1 and 5 the hardliners. But if a good radical takes it up to 9, then 5 becomes the new center. I already saw it working in the American Muslim community. For years women were neglected in mosques, denied entrance to the main prayer halls and relegated to poorly maintained balconies and basements. It was only after a handful of Muslim feminists raised "lunatic fringe" demands like mixed-gender prayers with men and women standing together and even woman imams giving sermons and leading men in prayer that major organizations such as ISNA and CAIR began to recognize the "moderate" concerns and deal with the issue of women in mosques.

I've taken part in the woman-led prayer movement, both as a writer and as a man who prays behind women, happy to be the extremist who makes moderate reform seem less threatening. Insha'Allah, what's extreme today will not be extreme tomorrow.

8.

Imran's roommate, absent during our stay, seemed like the religious one, at least judging from the Islamic decorations that filled his walls. Because his room also had big ceiling fans, I stayed in there while Noble Drew worked on a new song— "Mash'Allah," the Arabic for "as God has willed," though for a discreet pun they'd pronounce it as "martial law."

Thoughts of a compulsive masturbator in the City of Islam: it had been almost a week since arriving in Pakistan and the urge hadn't hit me at all. Maybe from the devastating heat, or poor sleep, or jet lag, or the lack of external stimuli since there wasn't anything to look at with the women all covered and locked away. But even with no sex in my brain, I still felt a heaviness in the balls and considered emptying them out. Part of me wanted to keep depriving and see how far I could go with it, falling back into my original mindset in this city. At one point I considered going into the roommate's bathroom to just pump it out, but the guy had a du'a taped onto his bathroom door: invocation after leaving the washroom: ghuranaka (i seek your forgiveness). How sad for him, but I couldn't disrespect my brother, so my pants stayed zipped. Searching through his DVDs, I found *Transformers* (the original 1986 cartoon movie) and popped it in for all the heavy religious darkness of a robot planet with gaping mouth lined with metal fangs, coasting through space on the hunt for worlds teeming with life to suck into itself, Unicron al-Mumit manifesting Allah's attribute as Divine Destroyer who sometimes must crush the innocent for no reason that we can ever see. The story was more New Testament than Qur'an, with the blood sacrifice of Optimus Prime for Hot Rod's error, and Hot Rod's ascent into *Rodimus* Prime, New Autobot Christ Victorious who defeats God's Wrath and saves all robots forever, building the new

Cybertron Jerusalem on Earth. That movie's deep if you watch
it in the right frame of mind.

9.

Faisal Mosque had me restless to see the real Islam of Pakistan,
the one that I had been sheltered from in my Saudi-sponsored
bubble the first time around. I wanted to see the places where
sanitary Sunnism mingled with the unclean.

No culture was ever a blank slate before the arrival of Islam,
nor could Islam always erase old traditions. In rural Bangladesh,
Muslim converts often continued their respect for Hindu deities
and the spirits who lived in trees and rivers. While invoking Allah,
shaman healers also called out to Krishna, Hari, Mahadeva,
Laksmana, Makali, and Sita. The Qur'an and Sunna spoke against
magic, but magic was Islam in Pakistan. Zaynab's grandmother
had memorized the entire Qur'an and taught at a mosque but also
did black magic: she'd wrap verses of the Qur'an in a deer skin
for you to wear around your neck and could control your mind
that way. She had made one for Zaynab's weak-willed father
containing a verse about men being dominant over women, and
it transformed him into an abusive asshole.

While our driver ran into a store for cigarettes, a pair of
snake charmers came up to the car and let out their snakes to
put on a show. It wasn't all that charming; they just had some
little sidewinders that one would push around with a stick
while the other played his flute. The things barely moved but
did threaten to bite a couple times. I had Ammar ask the guys
if I could touch a snake. One of them pointed to the charm
hanging from his neck and said something in Punjabi.

"Only he can touch the snakes," Ammar explained, "because
he believes in Ali."

"Tell him that I believe in Ali too," I asked. The charmer accepted my word but still took caution, holding the snake by its head so that I could touch it safely.

DRUGS DOMINATED BASIM'S flat, partially due to an extended visit by Malang Party. Things moved slow enough in Pakistan even with everyone sober, but the hash brought life to a halt. After the driver ate some of Zaynab's hash brownies, he was unfit to drive for the next two days. When Ammar tried calling him, his mom answered the phone and shrieked, "What have you done to my son?" She had called both the hospital and a Sufi *pir* to come exorcise him.

It seemed like a good time to get out of there, so I took a train without Noble Drew to Multan, the City of Saints. The film crew went with me.

The real Islam of Pakistan lived at the enshrined tombs of Sufi saints, which were sometimes only the Islamic redecorations of earlier sites held sacred to Zoroastrians, Hindus, Buddhists, or sun worshipers; the shrine of Lal Shahbaz Qalandar was built on the old Sivistan, "place of Siva." For the orthodox, this was all pollution. Islam's integrity was in its separateness, the religion of God distinct from the religions of humans.

Ibn Taymiyya condemned the reverence of shrines as not only compromising the Unity of God, but also the centrality of Mecca. Every Muslim had to visit the holy city at least once in his or her lifetime; but for perhaps the majority of Muslims throughout history, the journey has been either physically, financially, or politically impossible. God is forgiving, but who wants to miss out on holy land? So we make our own land holy and, in doing so, pull away from the center, bringing the religion back to us.

WHATEVER IDEOLOGIES DEFINED their claim to power, governments often found it useful to suppress folk religion. The authority vested in shrines not only threatened Saudi Arabia's

"Islamofascism," but also Turkey's Europe-styled secularism. Pakistan's rulers negotiated with its shrines. Zulfikar Ali Bhutto played up the saints' social messages as relating to his "Islamic Socialism"; his daughter Benazir followed a similar practice of using Sufis for Islamic credibility while marginalizing the Sunni scholars. To further his cause of Islamization, General Zia deemphasized mysticism, but repositioned the saints as ulema, learned men within the strictures of institutional Islam.

During Islamization the government's Auqaf department was empowered to take over any shrine if locals complained that its income was more than its expenses. *Auqaf* meant "pious endowments." The ordinance not only made the shrines a money machine for the state; it also turned the imams into government employees.

Ammar called some government people to ensure that the cameras would be okay, and then we headed for the first shrine: a round, smooth, white dome atop an octagon of red brick. On the way in, we passed tombs of the saint's disciples. A man showed up with shawls and sodas for each of us and pink flower petals to sprinkle on the saint.

This was the shrine of Baha-ud-din Zakariyya, a Sufi who contributed to Multan becoming a center of the Suhrawardiyya order. I poured the flower petals on the shrouded tomb, prayed for him, and headed back out. In the courtyard another brother was selling birdseed for the pigeons—the idea was that any blessing you earned for feeding the birds would go not only to you but also to the saint.

Then we went to the shrine of Shams, a smaller, white building with a modest green dome. Some people believed that this Shams was Shams-i-Tabriz, the friend of Rumi. But that Shams had shrines everywhere, and this Shams was more likely Pir Shams, a thirteenth-century Ismaili Shi'a. The men there gave me another shawl and Coke and told me the story of how it came to be so hot in Multan: Shams wanted to cook a fish, so he asked the sun to come closer. The sun complied but never returned to its former position.

Shams was Arabic for "sun," but the story had more layers: before Islam came, Multan was a center of sun worship. In another time, pilgrims came to Multan to circumambulate the sun god's temple, after which they ritually shaved their heads and beards. Multan was a minor Mecca long before people used "Mecca" as a generic term for any place that attracted lots of visitors. The sun god was gone, but pilgrims still came to Multan; the "City of Saints" attracted roughly one hundred thousand Muslim visitors every year.

Multan's sun god was originally an idol of solid gold with rubies in its eyes and a gold crown. The first Muslim to see it was none other than Muhammad ibn Qasim, the legendary Syrian general who first invaded South Asia for Islam. The story goes that he walked into the temple, discovered the idol, and drew his sword, thinking that it was a man. The Brahmans fell before him, pleading that the statue be spared and confessing that beneath it was a treasure placed by the king of Multan. Muhammad ibn Qasim ordered the idol to be removed, revealing the subterranean treasure room filled with gold and jars of gold dust. The general asked how Multan obtained its wealth, and the Brahmin Ten Percenters explained that it all came from offerings to the sun god.

The idol was destroyed in 976, restored in 1138, and still standing as recently as 1666, with pearls for eyes and dressed in red leather. The Mughal king Aurangzeb destroyed it for good, but Muslims would later have their own holy sites reclaimed by invaders: in 1818 the Sikhs took Multan and used Shams' shrine to house their scripture, the Granth.

The protocol was the same as at the Zakariyya shrine. I placed pink flower petals on the tomb and made a du'a for the buried Shams. Outside I poured more birdseed for the shrine's pigeons.

On our way to the car, I was stopped by an old man with white robes and white beard and dark skin, his cheeks so hard and tough they looked like he had been carved out of wood. He was smiling and then his hard face moved to speak.

"He is making a du'a," Ammar explained. The old man put up his hands in the regular way, and I followed along while a small circle of witnesses gathered around us. We finished the du'a and then he dropped some extra wisdom that Ammar couldn't quite translate—something about how first I'd reach the crossing of loss, and then the crossing of greatness, and then come to a lake. Ammar wasn't sure that he heard it right, but the man looked into my eyes like he could beam the meaning into me. I let him give it to me, whatever it was. Then onto the next shrine.

ON THE OLD FORT mound, near the spot where the sun god once accepted offerings, people now came for the Rukn-i-Alam, the "Pillar of the World," a white hemispherical dome atop two octagons of burnt bricks, more than one hundred feet high. Inside rested Zakariyya's grandson. Rukn-i-Alam was a national pride, extensively renovated by the government in the 1970s, and graced the backs of special five-rupee notes celebrating Pakistan's fiftieth anniversary. I didn't know enough about Zakariyya's grandson—who himself was known as Pillar of the World—to place much emotional investment in him, but I was a fan of the sun and could just thank Allah for it while I was there.

Sun worship was a true world religion, a simple idea that you could get across to people anywhere without having to tangle up their brains in foreign concepts. It's a natural tendency to love a creation so much you forget the Creator. Knowing what he's up against, Allah refers to the sun in the Qur'an as an example of his own power. "By the sun and its brightness," he swears in a sura called al-Shams.

The prime tourist attraction in Multan, Rukn-i-Alam had

a good crowd of people outside, and when they saw me with the film crew everyone swarmed around us. It was all love, especially when word spread that I was a) American and b) Muslim. I smiled, said countless *as-salamu alaikums*, and shook so many hands that I felt like I was campaigning for public office. Someone showed up with another shawl to put on me, third of the day, and more Coca-Cola. I walked with all my new friends in a circle around the shrine, tossed birdseed for the shrine pigeons while the crew filmed me and brothers took pictures on their phones, and told everyone that most Americans were better than our president.

Multan had more tombs, but I was dizzy and already covered in shrine shawls and feeling gross from all the Coke. The driver stopped at a mosque so I could join its Maghrib prayer, after which a few kids gave me the same treatment but quieter and with respect to the men still praying. The crew and I went to our two rooms at the Multan Ramada. Everyone hung out in one room, watching the day's footage, while I decompressed in the other. Before joining them, the boom mic operator gave me a pinch of opium and a bottle of Nestlé water from the minibar to wash it down.

In a hotel room in Pakistan, you could typically find a folded prayer rug in the closet and an arrow on your desk indicating the direction of Mecca. I took out the rug and chose a good place to lay it down. My prayers looked the same as Muslim prayers everywhere. I said the same words and took comfort knowing that if any other Muslims were praying out there in the world, we all faced the same point, the House in the holy city. But Multan was also a holy city, where sun gods morphed into Sufi saints and maybe back again.

Hazrat Babajan, the Sufi saint from Baluchistan who studied under a Hindu teacher and became one of the Perfect Masters of her time, made pilgrimage to Mecca and Medina, but it was in this holy city of Multan that she received God-realization from

Maula Shah. In turn, she passed it onto Meher Baba through a kiss on the forehead. Meher Baba, father of the phrase "Don't worry, be happy," defined God-realization as the soul learning that it is God. "Man can become God," he said, "and men who become God can become Perfect Masters," like the Perfect Master of my American Islam, "Allah who appeared in the person of Master Fard Muhammad." Fard was supposedly born in Mecca, but he was more likely South Asian, possibly naming his Lost Tribe of Shabazz after Lal Qalandar Shahbaz, and some even claimed his birthplace as Ehsanpur, right there in the Punjab.

On the surface, calling a man Allah was the worst violation of Islam; but if Fard came from the Punjab, his deification had roots in the Muslim world. Could something betray Islam and still be *Islamic*?

SPREAD OUT ON one of the beds, I turned on MTV Pakistan, which was more like the MTV I grew up on than the current American version: it had a request show, and the host brought out a guest, they had conversations about music, and they played videos. The commercial breaks featured goofy animated vignettes, like the MTV logo appearing on the back of a ricksha. I almost expected to see Fab 5 Freddy on there in a shalwar kameez.

I watched Fox News too, hearing a blonde woman ask a Muslim man what the Qur'an said about gay marriage and relating it all to Obama—the Democrats weren't going in a direction that would help traditional Muslims, she said, since Muslims shared common ground with conservative Christians and wouldn't be into such "crazy social trends." First Obama was a secret Muslim, and now Muslims were supposed to vote Republican? It wasn't the day for me to worry about those things. Too tired to get much out of the opium, I just felt at peace, and by the time it started to work, I was falling asleep anyway.

10.

During the long train ride to Lahore, Omar and I shared a compartment with a married couple and their two small children. The husband was a bit of a nerd in Western clothes; the wife dressed traditionally and wore the full veil. Omar and I made small talk with the husband while avoiding any direct glances at the wife. She pulled away the veil to use her cell phone, which came with all the awkwardness of a woman breast-feeding in front of me—overly deliberate to look everywhere else but at her—a face now holding the power of a boob.

A cricket landed on Omar's arm and he tried to gently guide it off, but the husband reached over and slapped the thing off him and then crushed it under his foot. It hadn't seemed that the man had it in him.

"There's a real anger in Pakistan," Omar told me later, "but you only see it come out here and there, in little moments like that." When you live in a military state that gives you no power, and you're working-class in a society run by unwritten caste rules and family names, sometimes you have to break something just to show yourself that you can. Men crush their wives, and the wives turn into mothers who dominate their sons even into adulthood, which pushes the sons to assert their masculinity outside the house by acting tough, getting into fights, and finding their own women to marry and push around, and it goes on forever, those women giving birth to little boys on Jail Road who throw rocks at a bloated dead dog.

11.

I pored through the Punjabi Sufi poets, searching for the jewel in each one. When Sultan Bahu (1629–1690) was young, his mother asked him to search for someone to be his spiritual master. He replied, "You are my spiritual master. I don't need to find any other." He bowed his head to her and she became his teacher. Sultan Bahu said that he was neither Sunni nor Shi'a but sick of both, and that both paradise and hell were irrelevant. Sultan Bahu did not fast for Ramadan and was terrified of the mosque, and he said that if you could find union with God through celibacy, then castrated bulls should be counted among the Sufis. Sultan Bahu never made wudhu with water, he was cleaned by the Holy Name; he mocked the ones who counted on zikr beads because they couldn't count the beads of their hearts; and he said that his body was the house of God, home to the real Ka'ba where he made thousands of prostrations. Baba Farid (1175–1205) said that your life was a single bird chased by fifty hunters and that only trust in God could save you from being trapped. Baba Farid said, "Those who were proud of their pomp and show with people praising them now lie in their graves like orphans." He told me to find a tank of clean water; I couldn't find anything in a muddy pond.

When dropping knowledge, the poets always addressed themselves. Waris Shah (1722–1798) said, "Waris Shah! What is the certainty of life? Man is but a goat in the hands of butchers." And Waris Shah said, "Waris Shah! Time once lost cannot be recalled even by a saint." I remembered the old man at the tomb of Shams, the one who delivered that cryptic line about crossing loss and greatness and a lake. He looked like he was old enough to have hung out with all these saints through the centuries as they came and went, absorbing their lessons and waiting for me to show up from the far side of the world.

Shah Husain (1538–1599), who pioneered kafi poetry as a
means of teaching Sufism, said that it was impossible to hear
the truth, falsehood was too deep in us, part of our blood and
bones . . . and Shah Husain made knowledge born:

> O proud man!
> Try to understand this life.
> What did you bring here?
> What will you take away with you?
> The whole world is mortal.
> Staying here in the world is but for a few days,
> So why are you proud of it?
> Says Husain, the humble faqir,
> Finally you will merge into the dust.

But everyone's favorite was Bulleh Shah (1680–1752), who
said that the pious exhausted themselves pointlessly with the
Vedas and Qur'an, wasted their lives away in mosques and
temples, and that pilgrims sold their hajj. Bulleh Shah laughed
at the memorizers of Qur'an and called them dogs. He said to
burn the prayer rug and crack the wudhu vessel.

Noble Drew went with me to his shrine in Kasur, another
long ride—what a cool thing to say, as though instead of a living
punk band it was Noble Drew Ali from 1925, in his turban and
sash, sitting next to me on a train. Along the way we spotted
gas stations with their own minimosques for weary travelers,
and cannabis growing wild by the road; but when Shahjehan
checked out the weed, he found that all the good stuff had been
taken. Ali played tapes of girl singers who sounded hyper and
psycho and sometimes like they were getting fucked right there
in the studio. Basim said that this interpretation would make
even more sense if I understood the lyrics.

Kasur was a small town with streets jammed more with people
and donkey carts than with cars, but going slow gave me time

to read the signs in store windows: BULLEH SHAH SODA WATER, BULLEH SHAH ELECTRONICS, I LOVE ALI PAWN SHOP. Walking across the dusty, dead land past cricket games and barefoot kids to the shrine, Basim told me about how Bulleh Shah said to just seek the alif, the first letter of the Arabic alphabet.

"Read the first alphabet and be free," he said. In classical readings, alif signified unity; just a single stroke, it looked like the number 1 in both Western numerals (which were Arabic in origin) and Arabic numbers (which were really Indian). In the Five Percenters' Supreme Alphabets, *A* was for Allah.

 The real soul of a shrine is almost never the body in the box, but the characters you find around it. In the alley before the shrine, an old man dressed in green stood playing an ektara, a one-stringed instrument made from a gourd. He held the ektara on his shoulder like a violin, plucked the string, and made a beat by tapping his thumb against the gourd while dancing in a slow circle and jingling the bells on his ankles.

"BULLEH!" he cried. We stood around him and heard the song.

"He is singing to Bulleh," Ammar whispered in my ear. "He is saying that he will dance for Bulleh like a prostitute."

We each gave him some rupees and went into the shrine lobby, where another white-bearded man called us over and told his story. He was 105 years old and a seventh-generation descendent of Bulleh Shah's servant. The shrine and surrounding land used to belong to his family, he said, until the government took it away. The walls were lined with small, framed paintings of Bulleh Shah for sale.

The shrine was located at the far end of a spacious marble courtyard. Inside, men read Qur'an over the tomb. I picked up a small booklet containing Ya Sin, the sura traditionally read for the deceased, and sat in front of Bulleh Shah. After the second verse, "By the Wise Qur'an," I didn't know what anything meant, apart from a few Arabic words and phrases that I recognized. But I kept reading, showing and proving my respect for the saint.

About halfway through the sura, I realized that if Bulleh Shah was alive, he'd slap me. My gesture of respect—reciting Arabic words without comprehending them—betrayed everything that he said. Bulleh Shah had no use for my reading Ya Sin or the whole Qur'an. What was Islam to him? Bulleh Shah loved Allah, but knew that names meant nothing; call the thing Allah, call it Krishna. Bulleh Shah's only religion was love, so I put down the Ya Sin and ditched the tomb for my living brothers outside.

This place did a number on the saint. Bulleh Shah had made it plain: "I am neither a Hindu nor a Muslim." When he was alive and mocking mullahs, "Islam" had no room for him. Pakistan's most revered saint, Ali Hujwiri, said, "Insult or ridicule of the friends of God is their nourishing food," and Bulleh Shah ate up hatred from the pious—but somehow, tradition absorbed the rebel into itself, and the man who said to tear down the mosques had become a mosque in his own right. Funny how that happens, like the U.S. government putting Malcolm X on a postage stamp.

12.

Lahore had shrines of its own, too many to visit or even name. Just walking through the old city, Shahjehan and I passed by nooks in the walls where oil offerings were burnt for coffins behind the grated windows. No one seemed to know which saints rested there, just local *pirs* with reputations for piety and probably lines of descent going back to the Prophet. The ratio of living citizens to dead saints in Lahore couldn't have been too high; even looking up at the buildings it seemed logical to imagine apartments occupied by shrines of dead holy men and their dead disciples and dead descendents. In the red-light area, Basim and I passed a storefront that looked like it might display TVs or furniture on sale, but instead it was just an empty room with a shrouded tomb and the same pink flower petals as all of them.

One Thursday night we went to Bibi Pak Daman, a shrine for the graves of six pious women. The popular story said that they were members of the Prophet's household, including Ali's daughter Ruqayya, who came from Karbala after the hypocrites butchered Muhammad's grandson Husayn. When the women arrived in Lahore, the local rulers feared they would be a political threat and ordered their arrest. Allah intervened when the soldiers came for them, causing the earth to open up and swallow the sisters. One soldier reached for Ruqayya's headscarf, just missing as it trailed her into the ground.

Another story said that the women were six sisters who came from Mecca after Husayn's murder, but some scholars argued that they were daughters of Syed Ahmad Tokhta, born in Lahore hundreds of years later. Their names were Bibi Haj, Bibi Taj, Bibi Nur, Bibi Hur, Bibi Gauhar, and Bibi Shahnaz, and none of them married. During the Afghan invasions, the six virgins prayed to be kept safe from rape. As in the other version, Allah came to the rescue by splitting open the earth to conceal them as the soldiers approached. For Shi'as who came to the shrine to mourn the Prophet's family, the stories completely merged, and Bibi Haj became equated with Ali's daughter.

Whoever rested in those graves, we went to check it out. Walking down the tiny street packed with vendors selling Shi'a banners, jewelry, books, zikr beads, and rusty blades on chains—zanjirs for whipping your bare back on Ashura—we heard the beating of drums alternating with a choir of men in song. They cried praises of the Prophet and his family, Ali and Husayn. The drums grew louder and scarier as we came closer—not scary like there was evil in the song, or scary like we feared for our safety, but scary like a mountain or the sun, scary like real power that makes you know that you're small.

A white horse stood in the street, garlanded and caressed by everyone who passed it. Imagining that this was the same white horse Zul-Jannah that Husayn rode in Karbala, they tried to comfort it from things it had seen. The horse's back was covered in flower petals like a tomb.

In Shi'a legend, Husayn's horse was originally owned by his grandfather. When Husayn was a small child, the horse lowered itself to let him ride, and Muhammad wept. People asked why this made him cry, and he answered that he knew what they didn't know: that the day would come when the horse again lowered itself for Husayn, because he would be too wounded to stay in the saddle.

I sprinkled flower petals on its back and continued towards the sounds of the drums—but they weren't drums. When we arrived at the shrine, it looked like an Islamic *Fight Club* with shirtless men drenched in sweat and some drenched in blood too, beating their chests and crying. Standing on the edge of the crowd, I started slapping my chest, then took my shirt off and really wailed on myself. My pale chest turned pink, and I thought I was tough, but other guys were drawing blood. I never got close enough to see the tombs or anything, but felt like I was at a funeral and going through the experience of survivors, grief for Husayn and what he endured. Then came the guilt because I couldn't have helped him, guilt that I was alive and comfortable even after saying the worst things against his family, when the pure and steadfast men were slaughtered in Karbala. Who am I to live when Husayn dies? Who am I to complain that my chest stings when they ripped out his heart? Then it was grief for the whole world because Husayn's death only summed up all the violence and oppression of every day everywhere, survivor's guilt for every injustice that I was spared from while monsters consumed the innocent—who am I to live when Malcolm dies? Who am I to vacation around the world when John Walker Lindh's in federal prison?

13.

Everything happened on Thursdays. One of Lahore's more famous shrines is the Shah Jamal, where they had weekly concerts with local rock star Pappu Sain and his dhol players. Shah Jamal, dead in 1671, was revered as a defender of Islam against the anti-Islam of Akbar's reign, but celebrations at his tomb drew upon elements beyond what most saw as legitimate Islam: pulsating music, ecstatic Sufism with Pappu Sain's dhol players, exaggerated Shi'a love for Ali, gratuitous drug use, and what Ibn Taymiyya denounced as "grave worship."

The Shah Jamal shrine consisted of various levels and walkways, feeling almost like a house party, crowded and full of dark places where you accidentally step on people and the only lights come from the smokers. A brother stopped me and introduced himself as Usamah, then asked if I smoked hash—"You smoke hash, let's see you smoke hash!" Holding a joint between his index and middle finger, another between his middle and ring finger, and one between his ring finger and pinkie, he made a fist for me to inhale through the gap created between his index finger and thumb. At Buffalo State College, they used to call that the "Gatling Gun."

The Shah Jamal shrine was said to be the center of Lahore's hash trade. Basim figured that whichever general oversaw this part of town also ran the drugs. The people didn't have much personal freedom, but since the government had little control, it almost evened out. Pakistan was like anarchy with uniforms.

Trying to get into the main area where the drums were

playing was like squeezing into the front at a punk show, and like most punk shows, it was a halal sausage fest of all men shoving into each other. As I squeezed past men, they'd ask my country and religion and then come to this American Muslim's aid. Before I knew it I was invited to step over everyone and take a seat right in front of the drummers, and then a sayyed invited me to a seat of honor beside him.

"George Bush is . . . mighty warrior," he said.

"George Bush is going to bomb Iran next," I told him.

"Insha'Allah, Iran will rise up against him." We shook hands on that.

I reunited with Basim outside the shrine, where a man was cooking bhang pancakes for ten rupees each—which came out to roughly fifteen cents. Bhang was the crushed leaf and flower of a female cannabis plant and so concentrated that ingesting it was like smoking a pound of weed. We had a couple.

"Let's go home," said Basim, "so we can fall asleep without getting robbed." During the walk we built on Punjabi Sufi poets, and I could see that Bulleh Shah had become a valid Islamic source for me. I used Bulleh Shah in my own way, seeing him as a Five Percenter who called the bloodsuckers on their lies. It works if you're enough into one or the other to see the similarities. If a Five Percenter taught *Allah* as "Arm Leg Leg Arm Head" to Bulleh Shah, he'd get it.

> Who is that Mystery God?
> There is no Mystery God. The son of man has searched for that Mystery God for trillions of years and was unable to find a Mystery God. So they have agreed that the only God is the son of man. So they lose no time searching for that which does not exist.

> —THE SUPREME WISDOM LESSONS OF
> MASTER FARD MUHAMMAD

My forehead is worn out doing the sujdah. Whoever has
achieved him has achieved him from within. Nobody has ever
found him from outside or elsewhere and nobody will ever
find him from anywhere except from within.

—BULLEH SHAH

Bulleh Shah already knew about the Ten Percenters, the
hypocritical mullahs and vain Qur'an memorizers. "The rooster
is better than the mullah," said Bulleh Shah, "for at least they
wake their friends who are asleep." It wasn't hard to picture
Bulleh Shah in Harlem building with the high scientists I knew
out there, a Poor Righteous Teacher in any time. Pappu Sain,
the star of the Shah Jamal musicians, had quoted Bulleh Shah as
saying, "Allah is a dervish," which has to be some Five Percenter
talk if I've ever heard it.

We were almost to the flat when a black-and-white kitten
started following us, meowing sadly. We slowed down to see if
she'd keep up, and her meows grew louder and more desperate,
almost a violent accusation. She went all the way up the stairs
and into the flat. Basim gave her some milk and named her
Nishai, which he said meant "intoxicated," or someone who
sought intoxicants. The thing was nuts, scrambling all over the
place and climbing on things and completely fearless, but she
had the same energy patterns as everyone else in the flat: after
flipping out for a minute, she'd collapse at a random spot and
sleep on her back with her long legs in the air.

The flat was filled and I took my spot in the corner. They
offered me pillows and seemed full of remorse but I told them
I was fine on floors, I loved a hard floor. While they continued
in their conversations, I slowly drifted out of consciousness.
When I came back to life around five in the morning, they
were still up and I was high. Lying flat on my back with my
arms spread out, I felt a tingle in my left arm, as though it was

falling asleep . . . and then it went numb south of the elbow and I thought I couldn't move it, so I flailed it like a dead thing attached to me. I remembered the malangs of Shah Jamal, the dirty, shirtless renouncers with ratty beards and dreads and bare chests covered in necklaces of prayer beads, throwing around their arms in Charlie Manson dances and whipping out their old ID cards to say look, I used to be someone and now I'm no one, I'm so lost in Allah that I've thrown away the whole world. Would that qualify them as Sufis? I didn't know how to measure it.

Whether the malangs were Sufi saints or just drugged-out bums didn't really matter. The lesson I took from them was that you're never disqualified from loving Allah, never. And I could see again that what I went through was nothing new, not even anything special in the history of Islam, not a clashing of East and West; it was always there. And that made me feel more Muslim than ever, because fuck it all, CNN, this is Islam too.

14.

On the Fourth of July I set out on a mission for the shrine of Shah Husain (1538–1599), near the famous Shalimar Gardens. All alone, no film crew or punk band or anyone, I walked up Canal Park Road and found a ricksha driver. He had never heard of Shah Husain but of course knew how to get to Shalimar, and we'd figure it out from there. It turned out that I had the name wrong: once my driver realized that I sought the shrine of *Madho Lal* Husain, he knew where to go.

Shah Husain was a Sufi saint who fell in love with a Hindu Brahmin boy named Madho Lal, and took his name to reflect their union. The two were now entombed together as one person, Madho Lal Husain. Shah Husain loved Madho Lal at a time when the Punjab was a battlefield between Abrahamic religions and Dharmic religions, when Sufi saints sought to reconcile the ruling class with the occupied, and poets spoke with an authority beyond sacred law. The late medieval Clash of Civilizations was about to produce offspring, a new hybrid faith drawing monotheism from one side and reincarnation from the other. The Punjab produced Guru Nanak, first Guru of the Sikhs, a born Hindu who made pilgrimage to Mecca and was recognized by all parties as a holy man. Shah Husain was born in the year that Nanak died. Sikhism was not yet Sikhism, but the seed had been planted and would be watered by both Hindu bhagats and Sufi saints whose poems became sacred in the Guru Granth Sahib. This was the Punjab in which Sufi and Hindu lovers could be enshrined together as one composite soul. Of course, their love is now acknowledged as simply "great friendship," nothing to cause alarm or discomfort.

Passing graves on the way to his, I flipped through my book of Shah Husain, knowing that somewhere in it I'd find a blessing. *I dance because the doubt has vanished*, he said. *I'm full of faults and without any quality.* It looked as though the cemetery had developed around the shrine, as though burial near a saint made the ground softer or less cold or cushioned a body against the torment of the grave. I opened the book again. *Let us plan our departure*, Madho Lal Husain told me, *as we are not meant to stay here.*

The precincts of the shrine housed two small buildings, each topped with a green onion dome. The larger, central shrine was decorated with plastic flowers. I went inside and found two coffins, both shrouded and covered with flower petals. I did not know which half of Madho Lal Husain rested in which coffin, but prayed for both of them.

In the smaller shrine I found what looked like a small aquarium with a baby-size, wooden coffin inside, completely covered in flower petals except for two carvings in the shape of hands.

Who was this? A baby saint? Had to be someone, so I recited al-Fatiha and walked out. Then the government servant who ran the shrine walked over to greet me.

"What is your country?"

"America."

"Are you Muslim?"

"Yes."

He smiled and led me back to the smaller shrine, where he took out a skeleton key and unlocked the aquarium. It seemed that the appropriate action was to place my hands on the little hand carvings.

"Holy Prophet," he said.

"What?"

"Holy Prophet, foot." Muhammad's footprints.

"Mash'Allah," I gasped, kissing them. He closed it up again and we walked outside. No reason to ask how the Prophet's footprints became little hand-shaped wood carvings at a shrine in Pakistan; the details don't matter. Shrines of the Qadam Mubarak—blessed footprint—were all over South Asia. Wherever the Prophet stepped, his foot left an imprint, even in stone, and pilgrims to Mecca would obtain stones bearing his mark and bring them back home. Sometimes the footprints became political props: Masum Khan Kabuli, an Afghan chief who led a revolt against Emperor Akbar, garnered support among the people by purchasing a set of Qadam Mubarak and building a shrine for them. Shrines for the Prophet's footprints could also be found across the Muslim world, in Istanbul and Cairo and Jerusalem, where the Dome of the Rock housed the imprint of his last step before his flight into heaven on the Buraq.

In South Asia, reverence for the Qadam Mubarak spoke to the subcontinent's pre-Islamic life, Buddhists and Hindus who venerated *buddhapadas* and *vishnupadas*. Buddhists would make rubbings of the Buddha's alleged footprints, transfer them to new stones, and distribute them throughout East Asia.

Hindus made pilgrimage to the Vishnupada Temple in Gaya, where they poured water on Vishnu's footprint on stone in a silver basin. Islam also figured into the spiritual lives of Hindus, who would traditionally take part in celebrations of Husayn and sprinkle rose water on the mourning Shi'as; and both Islam and Hinduism gave themselves to the Sikh scriptures. The religions of South Asia were so different and yet so interconnected, so much of one in the other that it was hard to see why they fought. But maybe I answered my own question.

Riding home, we passed another shrine—I could now recognize them as distinct from regular mosques—and asked the driver to stop. He waited outside while I walked around the gate. The shrine stood adjacent to a white mosque with blue trim, next to a quiet railroad track with an unmoving line of rusty freight cars.

First I took off my shoes, went into the shrine, and said al-Fatiha for whoever it was under the shroud and flower petals. Then I entered the mosque to make my two rakats and became the object of curiosity for a group of five boys, ages maybe nine to twelve, running up to shake my hand and say "As-salamu alaikum" and "How are you?" I told them I was fine, and then they said it back to me, "I am fine," asked my name, and laughed when I told them. I walked towards the mihrab, stopped abruptly, and looked at the floor, gestures to show my intention to pray—I even raised my hands to my ears to start—but they kept standing around me and giggling to each other.

"Namaz," I told them with my hands still at my ears. Then I said "Allahu Akbar," officially starting the prayer, and they lingered around but at least kept quiet. The qiblah wall had a picture of the Ka'ba in Mecca, which I'd find if I walked through that wall and kept going for about two thousand miles.

We couldn't say much to each other beyond greetings and introductions, but they liked when I took their pictures. On my way out, a shirtless malang called me over and signaled that I should join him behind the mosque. His upper body covered with long scars, he looked like hardcore wrestling hero Sabu.

"You drink chai?" he asked, and I accepted but asked him to wait while I got my driver, as he'd want some chai too. So I threw my shoes back on and ran out past the dead train track to my driver and told him to come for chai, but he only followed me as far as the servant outside the shrine gate. I waved him in, trying to communicate that he was welcome to chai, but he took a seat next to the gate servant and wouldn't move.

Behind the mosque, I found a handful of men sitting around, drinking chai, and smoking.

"As-salamu alaikum!" I called out to them.

"Wa alaikum as-salam!" shouted one of the men, standing to greet me in a white beard and red kufi and blue shalwar kameez. "What is your country?"

"America."

"I used to live in USA! Jackson, Queens."

"What brought you there?" I asked when we were close enough to shake hands.

"I'm an international bartender," he said, whipping out his wallet to show me his card. "I was trained for this degree; I've worked in the USA, the UK; I've worked in Pakistan but there's no money in it here; it's ridiculous and now I'm retired."

"General Zia?" I asked.

"General Zia made it hard." Pakistan used to have bars and discos, but General Zia closed them down. "You smoke hash? Please, you sit with us." We shared salams and hash. The imam of the mosque came over and the shrine keeper introduced us. The imam was younger. In his crisp white kurta, black vest, and shaped beard, he looked like a proper Muslim compared to everyone else; but even with the imam there, the shrine keeper went on about how you can't drink proper beer in Pakistan, no Budweiser or any of the good American beers. "USA the greatest country," he told me. "USA, you want wine, you drink wine; people see you, no problem." Everyone seemed to be fine with each other: the good imam, the zanjir-scarred malang, the shrine keeper/international bartender.

"Who is buried in the shrine?" I asked.

"He was Muhammad Sadiq. Ever since he was small child, he prayed to the god."

"Mash'Allah," I said.

"The Americans are coming," he said.

"The Americans?"

"I hope the Americans come and capture this fucking country; I am sick of these people. They cannot govern anything. Every time we get a new government, their sons come in, their uncles come in, and the poor cannot do anything. I pray to the god the Americans come and capture us; this country is finished. Only the Americans can change it. Not even India wants us anymore."

I couldn't say anything to that. "America is the best fucking country," he continued. "The UK looks like a village next to the USA. UK very prejudiced, USA only a little prejudiced, but not very prejudiced. USA is the greatest country except for the fucking shit blacks with their guns."

HAVING NOW FIGURED that I'm into shrines, the driver took me to another one. I didn't know who was buried there and would never find out; the only person I encountered was an old uncle who kept hugging me and touching my head while I tried to convey that I couldn't speak Punjabi or Urdu. His only word that I could make out was *American*. It was just another shrine, another box of dead person receiving flower petals, another handful of beggars outside hoping for rupees. None of these people were likely to ever reach Medina, resting place of the Prophet, but most local saints were sayyeds—descendents of Muhammad and Ali—so this seemed almost as good.

15.

Ammar, Basim, Zaynab, and I walked through Lahore's main market, and Allah kept throwing characters at us. First we were at the paint store getting paints for some art students to do up our walls—the plan was a portrait of Master Fard surrounded with Pakistani truck-art decoration with a verse of Waris Shah on one wall, and on the other a Buddha statue from Taxila—when an old world-renouncing Sufi malang stopped us outside, looked me in the eye, and started dropping malang knowledge. Zaynab translated for him, something about how the Devil was the only one who would be accountable. After dropping his science on us, he left to go back into the street and direct traffic.

Then a begging woman showed up to hassle Ammar and me. She had her son with her, who appeared developmentally disabled with a small misshapen head and wore a bowl around his neck. When they were gone, Ammar told me that the son's head had been deliberately shrunken; when he was a boy, someone made him wear metal caps that stunted the growth of his skull and retarded the brain inside. Because of the way that it shaped his face, they called these kids rats. Ammar said it was all for Dolay Shah, a Sufi saint buried in Gujurat.

Ammar believed the rumors, but later we learned that using metal caps to impede cranial growth was medically impossible; it'd impact the spinal cord and kill you. Microcephaly—small head syndrome—came from a recessive gene that manifested due to consistent marriage of first cousins. Regardless, there was some sinister shit going on with these kids: because it was considered bad luck to turn away a rat of Dolay Shah, they held prime value with the "Begging Mafia," which would pay hundreds of thousands of rupees to take one off the parents' hands. Most of the times you saw a rat of Dolay Shah on the street, the woman with him or her wasn't even the person's real mom, just an agent of the Begging Mafia.

We rented a van and headed for Gujurat, Noble Drew and the film crew and me. Gujurat was another town that didn't look like it had much besides the shrine. The Dolay Shah precincts had become a center of economic activity, surrounded by booths and tables peddling religious items. I bought what looked like voodoo dolls, little tin cutouts of men, body parts, and various animals. The idea was that if your foot was injured, you bought the tin foot and placed it at the shrine. Someone would then heal you, either Allah or the saint.

> I saw with pleasure and surprise one day,
> A peacock's feather in the Koran lay.
> —JOHANN WOLFGANG VON GOETHE

A peacock hung out in the courtyard, unbothered like it was supposed to be there, the mascot of the shrine. A sacred animal of this land since the Indus Valley civilization, the peacock was declared India's national bird in 1963. The peacock's cry warned of rain, and the spots on its tail represented the eyes of gods. Numerous Hindu deities used the peacock as a vehicle: Kartikeya, the god of war; Kama, god of love; Saraswati, goddess of wisdom and poetry and Brahma's consort; Lakshmi, goddess of wealth and luck and wife of Vishnu. The peacock at times represented divine force, cosmic unity, immortality, or the sun. The sacred bird persisted in South Asian Islam. The Mughal king Shahjehan constructed a gold peacock over his throne in Delhi, and at the Qalandar shrine, people still honored the saint's body with peacock feathers—an attribute of Krishna and the decoration of his crown.

The peacock theme also appeared in depictions of the Buraq, the winged creature that Muhammad rode through outer space. The Buraq was portrayed as a pegasus steed but possibly transgendered, with a woman's head and male peacock's tail. In Pakistan you'd see the Buraq on the backs of big trucks and little rickshaws and in framed paintings, sleepy eyes with long lashes, half smiling, like a Hindu god—but where did the image come from? The hadiths only described the Buraq as a white animal, smaller than a mule and bigger than a donkey. Nothing was said about it having a human head, which recalled ancient art and myth from the Middle East, the gates of Ashurbanipal II's palace at Nimrod guarded by statues of winged bulls with human heads and winged lions with human heads, Sargon II's palace at Khorsabad guarded by five-legged bulls wearing headdresses, Syrio-Phoenician flying sphinxes with human heads on lions' bodies with eagle wings, and Sumerian anthropomorphs holding up the sun disk for the sun god Shamash. The Prophet's steed as we have it today is the child of a mixed marriage, both Semitic and Indian.

I went inside to see the tomb, tensed up like I was preparing for a fight, wishing I could charge into the walls and push them over and send the whole thing crashing down on this body—but I couldn't judge Dolay Shah by what people did with his bones, Bulleh Shah taught me that. While men came in to give their devotions, touching their faces to the shroud and offering prayers with voodoo dolls, I did a lap around the tomb and looked at the walls decorated with shards of mirrors and a replica Ka'ba door just like the one I had bought at Faisal Mosque, encased in glass like it was the real thing. I couldn't stop staring at it, knowing what the door meant and what this place would have meant to the Saudis.

Dolay Shah might have been a real saint or a good Muslim with all of this magical shit only tacked on after he was dead, Allah knows best, so I gave my respect and walked out. Off to the side of the shrine, there were carpets for salat or reading namaz, whatever you wanted to call traditional Islamic prayer. It just so happened that to pray facing Mecca meant turning my back on Dolay Shah, which worked with how I felt about the place.

As I reached the sitting portion of prayer, reciting that there was no god but God and Muhammad was his messenger, the Hindu peacock walked in front of me. I don't pray to peacocks, so I lowered my gaze to the proper point of focus, the place where my forehead had touched the ground. I pointed my index finger, the silent declaration of tawhid.

Then I rejoined my friends. The film crew was interviewing people who pleaded that the rumors about metal caps were false, Allah made the kids this way and Allah made all kinds of kids all kinds of ways, you saw birth defects in America too. People with microcephaly have been banned from the shrine precincts by the government, but one remained, a thirty-four-year-old woman named Nadia sitting by the shrine entrance. One of the men brought us to her. I introduced myself and a man who appeared to be her caregiver coaxed her to shake my hand. With our language barrier, I couldn't get a full sense of where Nadia was mentally or how she felt about this attention. After a few minutes, she stood up and walked away from us.

Near the exit I saw a man talking to Shahjehan about how people at this shrine lived on a higher level of spirituality and in accordance with the Qur'an and the Sunna. Even people in America are embracing Islam, he told Shahj. That was all I could take. I put myself into the conversation and said that I was an American Muslim, that I was born Christian and came to Islam. Of course he smiled and said, "Mash'Allah."

"You know why I became Muslim?"

"Why," he asked, still smiling.

"Because Muslims don't pray to dead bodies. I was raised Catholic, and Catholics pray to their dead: Jesus, Mary, the saints, all kinds of bodies. But I'm a Muslim, we pray to God."

He was nervous but kept up the smile as a defense. I said

"as-salamu alaikum" and left him to choke on it. On our way out, I noticed a sign in Punjabi above our heads and Basim explained that it was put there by the government, condemning the traffic of children.

Outside I got into it with Basim and Shahj, railing on the superstition and these little bullshit tin voodoo dolls in my hand, where was any of this in the Qur'an? The Qur'an said to take refuge from magicians, the ones who blow into the knots and such. I'm the last one to pull out this kind of argument, but where in the Qur'an did they find a justification for voodoo and dead saints and Beggar Mafias? It's the Eighty-Five Percent like Master Fard said, I told Basim—the deaf, dumb, and blind, slaves to mental death and power, manipulated by the Ten Percent with these unseen mysteries. It was nothing for an American to buy handfuls of these voodoo tins, but eighty rupees or whatever meant a lot to people in Gujurat, and these guys were ripping them off and they knew it—Shahjehan even said that the guy who sold them to me was smirking, like *I can't believe you're really buying this shit*. We piled back into the van. I kept looking at my new voodoo dolls, clanging them together.

Our guide told us that shrines did not reflect true Islam, and I asked him, "Why not? We worship the ultimate dead body in Medina, the shrine of the Prophet."

"Have you ever been to Medina?" he asked. He insisted that it wasn't like that. The Saudis won't let people worship the Prophet's tomb; they have guards with sticks who hit you if you try. He looked at me like this was a serious answer. Those are our choices? Either people forget Islam and worship skeletons or we just beat the shit out of them? "Trust the experts," he said.

"Yes," I replied, "the experts. Because if you feed someone enough books, they assume heightened ethics. Because scholars of religion are not of this world, they live above politics, right?"

Our guide looked at me and then asked Shahj in Punjabi,

"Who is this guy? What does he know about Islam?"

In Pakistan being a convert earned me two reactions: first, that I was doing something heroic; second, that I couldn't possibly know my religion. Brothers would take time to explain the simplest things to me, prayer and wudhu and such, even after I explained that I had converted nearly fifteen years ago. Sometimes it was sweet—I knew they wanted to take care of me—and sometimes it just came off as arrogant and condescending, like I could never be a full adult Muslim in their eyes and my opinions could never be qualified.

My reaction to Dolay Shah embarrassed me; my problem wasn't with superstition or folk religion, but with abuse of the disabled. However, the place did show me the potential good in someone like Ibn Taymiyya, attacking what he saw as the corruption of Islam: the innovations of Sufis and Shi'as and the infiltration of non-Islamic traditions into Muslim practice. I at least accepted that village Islam wasn't always better than state Islam. Shari'a was just another construction, and I wanted to tear it down, but the Prophet had said to correct wrong when you saw it, whether by your hands or words or just in your heart, and I ran the risk of making Islam so open-ended and free to our desires that it stood for nothing at all.

We dropped off our hired guide, and before we were out of Gujurat, the guide's dad called Ammar and requested to speak to me. He asked if I'd come over for tea to discuss religion. I said that I'd love to, but we had a long drive back to Lahore.

"Those people with you," he pleaded, "are not competent to teach you Islam."

"Okay," I said.

"If I only have time to say this one thing to you, here on the phone, please remember this: just look to the Qur'an."

"Thank you," I told him, and meant it.

16.

Bhang was neither approved nor condemned by the Qur'an, though Indian Sufi traditions placed the spirit of Khidr—the immortal Green Man, mystical teacher of prophets—within the cannabis plant. But Khidr couldn't be found in the Qur'an either, at least not by name. Bhang was a sacred drug of this land since 1000 BC; because of its association with Shiva, world-renouncing sadhus used it to find union with him. When Muslims found bhang, bhang became Islamic.

Mamoon came over with a bag of bhang and one of his servants who knew how to make bhang lassi. The drink was popular at the festival of Holi, when Hindus set bonfires to imitate the burning of she-devil Holika. Mamoon's servant and Ramazan-bhai made a mixture of bhang, milk, sugar, and maybe butter and then strained the liquid into a big pot. It looked like the Shamrock Shake that I used to get at McDonald's on St. Patrick's Day.

Everyone took a big glass.

"*Aoudhu billahi mina shaytani rajeem, bismillahir Rahmanir Raheem*," I said. I seek refuge in Allah from the cursed Devil, in the Name of Allah, Most Gracious, Most Merciful. "*Rabbi zidni ilma.*" Lord, increase us in knowledge. We chugged Khidr's spirit, refilled our glasses, and went again, and then we hit up the shrines.

THE DATA DURBAR complex in the old city hosted Ali Hujwiri's shrine. During the ride there, my left arm started to tingle; by the time we arrived, I was tripping. I left my shoes somewhere under the black sky and drifted into the blinding, white fluorescent lights and white marble everything—white floors, white walls, white tomb of Hujwiri right in front of me, where men put their heads on the tomb and said prayers. The guards made them form single-file lines to keep it orderly. I still didn't know how I felt about shrines and saints. Were people praying for Hujwiri or *to* him? I couldn't hear what they were saying, but watched each man touch his head on the tomb three times.

I believed in *tawhid*, the Oneness of God, a Creator who doesn't beget children and takes no partners beside him, no intercessors, no helpers. Hujwiri's Sufism was theologically conservative; he believed that Allah might allow saints to perform supernatural feats, but only if they obeyed the law. Miracles did not come through the saints' power, he reminded us, but Allah alone. Hujwiri was called "a manifestation of the Light of Allah for the people" by Moinuddin Chisti, the most beloved saint of Chisti Sufism, who came to Lahore from Afghanistan near the end of the twelfth century and prayed at Hujwiri's shrine for permission to continue on his way. The permission was granted, and Chisti spread his order throughout India. Chisti's maqam, the spot where he prayed, had become a shrine of its own, adjacent to the tomb, with a red-carpeted area for us to give prayers. I decided to make my two rakats, rationalizing that even if I prayed facing Chisti's maqam, it wasn't superstitious devotion to him. Chisti was a Muslim and prayed like one, so to stand behind his maqam only meant that I was facing Mecca.

I stood, bent over, put my face to the red carpet . . . and when I rose from the floor, it felt like an amusement park ride blasting me fifty feet into the air. After the prayer I floated over to the tomb, walked around, and tried to understand what was happening: men touching the tomb, kissing the tomb, and weeping for what I didn't know, prayers and cool religion, voices and sounds that I couldn't interpret, my brain unequipped to deal with anything. Then I found myself in one of the lines through no action of my own, unknown forces just putting me in a spot and directing me. There were only three or four men ahead of me, my turn coming up fast, and I still wasn't sure what I'd do, and then I was on deck, and the last man did his thing and then left me with Hujwiri, nothing between us, so I stepped up to him—*Hujwiri, I know you advocated sober, Shari'a-compliant Sufism, none of the ecstatic heretical stuff, and you belonged to the Junaydi school and Junayd was the one who signed al-Hallaj's death warrant, so you don't fuck around at all . . . you probably wouldn't be cool with my showing up at your shrine while tripping balls, sorry. It is what it is.*

I touched my head to the stone, and it spoke.

Qul huwa'Allahu Ahad, it said, a verse from the Qur'an. *Say he is God, the One.* I didn't see the words or hear them, they were just *there*, coming up from the saint's body and through the walls to reach me. People called Hujwiri *Data Ganj Bakhsh*, "The Giver who Bestows Treasure," and this ayat was his treasure for me. I cupped my hands as though to make du'a like everyone else, but all I could say was "God bless you" in English and then I went along on my way, my inner fundamentalist satisfied, God bless Ibn Taymiyya too. I was drifting through the people like Spike Lee's trademark shot with the actor sitting on a dolly, in my own world in my head.

The camera crew had never followed me into the main shrine, but I found them easy enough, just going to the big commotion outside and pushing through to the center of it. This time I caught a bad feeling but was in no shape to process what was happening—I just heard Omar say, "We should probably stop filming now," and next thing I knew, a guard with a stick was leading us to a door in the corner. *Okay*, I thought, *we're getting thrown out of the shrine.* I was fine with it, having already had a genuine Islamic experience whether it came from Allah or Hujwiri or Khidr or just the bhang, but we weren't going out the way we came in. *Okay, we're going downstairs, I don't remember any stairs.* Maybe it was time to worry; intellectually, I understood that a guard with a stick leading you into a door could end up being a bad thing, but Nihang Sikhs called bhang the *sukkha prasad*, "peace giver," and now I knew why. The bhang shut off my ability to panic and I just drifted along with the situation in absolute tranquility, a pure Sufi idiot completely helpless in Allah's care. *It will work itself out, insha'Allah.* I looked behind me to make sure that I wasn't going down the stairs alone. At the bottom was a parking lot, and I started to walk away from the building until the guard directed me to another door, this one taking us through a poorly lit hallway into the office of the shrine manager. We all sat down.

"Are we getting arrested?" I asked Omar. He just put a parental hand on my shoulder and said that everything would be fine. I reflected on what jail in Pakistan was like. In WWE, the Great Khali wrestled in what was billed as a "Punjabi Prison Match" with the ring encased by bamboo cages, but Basim had told me that a real Punjabi Prison Match would just be a man in khaki pants shoving a stick up your ass. Thinking about Basim, I noticed that neither he nor his girlfriend were in the room. They were probably looking for us upstairs. It was a good time to be full of drugs and religion: *If God wills me to get fucked with a stick, nothing in the created universe could pull the stick out of my rectum, and if he wills that I don't get fucked, nothing will ever penetrate me, all praise is due.*

I wouldn't have been able to put together a sentence in English, but now everyone spoke in Punjabi. The shrine manager was just a regular guy in off-white shalwar kameez and moustache, but he looked so gangster behind his big desk with guards standing around holding their sodomy sticks, ready to give it to us. He ended a long statement in Punjabi with "thirty-thousand rupee fee." *Okay, we're getting shaken down, that's cool. Omar will just pay him off, and we'll get out of this basement, back to the world with anal cherries intact.* Omar said something about us coming back tomorrow with the money—*he doesn't have the money but at least he's smooth*—and stood up, and I stood up too, but then something was said and Omar sat back down and I sat back down. *Mash'Allah*, I thought. *Whatever Allah wants.* And we had Ammar negotiating for us with the guy in Punjabi, he could handle it. They went back and forth for a few minutes, Ammar doing his thing, and I nodded my head as though I comprehended their exchanges. Everything seemed fine. *We'll be out of here in five minutes, God willing.* Then Ammar turned to me and said, "Mike, I'm so high right now, I'm flying, I have no idea what I just said to this person."

I was flying too and couldn't tell if he had said it loud enough for anyone else in the room to hear. I just put my arm around him and smiled.

Shahjehan, Ammar, and I grew progressively higher as the night went on. At times Ammar would just start whistling or singing softly, and I had to put a hand on his shoulder to pull his mind back into the basement and our present condition. My consciousness checked in and out. Someone, I don't know who, probably Omar, whispered that we had been offered water forty-five minutes ago and it hadn't come yet—*we've been here forty-five minutes?* Ammar declared himself a Communist to the manager and said that he supported the revolution, and I was powerless to do anything but sit there and wait for Allah to save the day. I blacked out for a while, snapped back, and now the manager was showing us video on his phone of money boxes being opened to reveal armfuls of rupees. Someone explained to me that the manager was showing us how much money the shrine made; at his previous position running seventeen shrines in Lahore, his office produced 10 million rupees per annum, but now at Data Durbar he made the government 170 million rupees. I couldn't work out the math in my head, but it was at least multiples of millions of U.S. dollars. The guy beamed a subdued but proud gangster smile.

The water came, and also sweets, a good sign that we weren't getting raped or shaken down or thrown in prison unless this was regular procedure for that kind of thing, you never know how absurd manners can get. If everything had been settled, I just wanted to get out of there and couldn't understand why we had to stick around. Then Omar asked if I wanted to interview the manager.

What?

He wanted to be in the film. He came around from behind the desk and someone told me to sit next to Shahjehan. I'd ask questions and Shahjehan would translate them into Punjabi and then translate the manager's answers back to me. I tried to remember what this place was about and just said "Hujwiri," and the guy said something, answering it like a legitimate question, and then I said "Chisti," and he said something about Chisti, a pretty shitty interview, but everyone seemed okay with it because then we were posing for photos with him. Next thing I knew, we were back upstairs but still not leaving; a guard was walking us around the place, giving us the tour. He led us to a big golden door that was supposed to be special, why, I didn't know, and I wasn't sure what to do but Ammar kissed it, and so I kissed it too.

The street was right there, so I walked out. Shahjehan told me that I had to come back, our shoes were at the other entrance, and I told him nevermind, we'd buy shoes tomorrow. But they brought me back in, and I slipped my sneakers on, and then we had to track down Basim and Zaynab. We passed a round table covered with small bowls for lighting devotional fires; there was nothing in the Sunna about that but people did it anyway. I put my fingers in one of the bowls and touched the oil to my head like a quasi-Catholic Sufi Hindu. It made sense at the time.

Upon spotting our car, I crawled into the backseat and waited for everyone to figure out their plans. Hearing someone mention money for a ricksha, I said I had money and pulled thousands of rupees and my passport out of my pocket. Someone got into the car with me and said it was a bad time to flash that stuff around. Outside the car there was a mob of people standing around, which was normal for us but now felt ominous, and I couldn't handle it. At one point Zaynab was sitting on Basim's lap next to me, but with our audience someone figured out that it wasn't smart, and then they were gone. People crammed into the backseat, and after another blackout I was walking down the hall in Omar's hotel, thinking, *All I have to do is get through the door, and then I can fall down.* Then we were in his room and I was lying on his floor, people around me worrying though I promised that I was okay.

I woke up at noon and was still clumsy. We told Basim the story and he said that government agents who ran shrines were Ten Percenters. I couldn't believe that the shrine manager would actually show us video of money collections and brag about how much the place earned. It seemed like the kind of thing I'd hallucinate, but everyone confirmed that it had really happened. Shahjehan added that corruption was so deep in Pakistan that no one tried to hide it; they don't even pretend but just show it off and laugh.

Omar told me that our saving grace was Ammar, the nineteen-year-old Marxist production manager who was stoned out of his mind but still had the sense to call his uncle, who happened to be a major figure in the PPP, and passed the phone to the shrine manager. Even sitting next to the kid, I had no idea that this had taken place. While our heads were all up on the Mothership, Ammar's uncle and the manager talked it out, and with that connection it didn't matter if Ammar was singing or waving a hammer and sickle flag, everything was fine. Allah provides.

That's the truth: before drinking the bhang, I asked the Lord to increase my knowledge, and Allah gave it to me. On the ground level of the shrine, the Oneness of God jumped out at me from the corpse of a saint; but in the basement, Allah pulled back the veil and revealed the shrine's secret face, a government official counting lakhs of rupees. The lesson might have been that shrines aren't real *or* bullshit, but they're both, depending on what you want from them.

17.

America needs to understand Islam, because this is the one religion that erases from its society the race problem.
—MALCOLM X, *letter from Mecca (1964)*

The white man is still God in Pakistan.
—MICHAEL KNIGHT, *email from Lahore (2008)*

It was at least a week before I could go back to Data Durbar, paranoid that I'd be remembered by the wrong guy and sent back downstairs, but I wanted to see it sober.

I went during the day and found a line of people outside the complex turning into a royal rumble over something, I couldn't see what. Walking up the ramp and peering over the ledge, I saw a man shoveling yellow rice out of a big steel drum, scooping it out for the people with their open plastic grocery bags or scarves or bare hands. They pushed and fought, women and men, young and old all mashed together, anxious to get their rice before it ran out. Maybe this was where Data Durbar put its millions of dollars, Allah knew best.

I took off my shoes and handed them to the man at the front entrance. He asked my country and without asking the usual follow-up of whether I was Muslim, he said simply, "One peace!" I shook his hand and went inside. The believers still packed around Hujwiri's shrine, but people were also hanging out throughout the precincts, the cool floors of shaded areas occupied by friends and families sitting around. Data Durbar wasn't just a holy ground but also a nice place for human beings to escape the noise and heat of the city.

Turned out that the complex was also home to a large mosque that I hadn't even seen the first time, with perfectly smooth minarets that looked like giant spikes. Hujwiri had built a mosque here long ago, but this was a sleek new one with modern Turkish design. Inside there was no need for carpets—the cool marble was more refreshing—and tall fans stood among worshipers at scattered points as though they were in prayer too. The walls were decorated with almost Christmasy ornaments, tinsel streamers of various colors. Birds hopped in and out of the open doors.

I sat against the back wall, rubbed my feet on the marble, and read Hujwiri's *Kashf al-Mahjub*. Hujwiri told the story of a dervish who always wore blue, which in his culture was the color of mourning. When asked why, the dervish explained that the Prophet had left behind three things, and each of them had been lost.

The Prophet left us his poverty, but poverty was used by dervishes to enrich themselves.

He left his knowledge, which Muslims taught but failed to live out.

And he left his sword, which has been misused by kings for their own power.

The dervish wore blue, he said, to mourn these three losses.

I flipped through the pages. Hujwiri quoted al-Razi, who said to avoid three classes of people: 1) heedless savants out for worldly gain, 2) hypocritical Qur'an readers who bent the Qur'an to their own desires, and 3) ignorant pretenders to Sufism. I always found regret in Hujwiri, who saw Islam and Sufism as already compromised and corrupted by the dirty affairs of this world, and he lived what, a thousand years ago? Back then he said that most Sufis were imposters in Sufi costumes, that Sufism was once a reality without a name and has since become a name without a reality, and that was a quote from someone even earlier than him.

Islam is finished, he'd say today, Islam is done. We used to have the Prophet and Ali, and now it's a bunch of self-serving dickheads. Of course it'd go downhill, where else could it go?

I was interrupted by a man asking my country. His wife was with him, holding their baby.

"American," I said.

"Are you Muslim?"

"Yes." He smiled and asked my good name, I said Mikail Muhammad. Then some nearby men started shouting at his wife for being in the main section of the mosque, the men's area, though she was perfectly covered and hadn't said a word. The couple went outside and gestured for me to follow them. Just beyond the door, he asked if he could take my picture. I said yes, and then his wife handed me their baby.

After smiling and posing and returning the child to them, I went back inside and dwelled on that strange moment. An American Muslim was something rare and special, and I could see why with the world in its present condition. But it was more than that, more than the brotherhood and love found by Malcolm X in Mecca: Pakistan was a white supremacist country.

It was so obvious that I had to say it and keep saying it in confrontational ways, and none of my friends in Lahore liked to hear it, but they couldn't say that I was wrong. Walking down Jail Road, on the street I saw brown people and black people; looking up at the Coca-Cola billboards, I saw white people. At least in the United States, there was a chance of seeing the Original Man in a Burger King ad. Passing a billboard for "skin whitening facials," at first I only smirked at the possible innuendo but then realized what it actually meant.

Smiling at me from political posters, I saw white people. Nawaz Sharif looked Russian or something. Benazir Bhutto was white and had a status in Pakistan that appeared somewhere between JFK and the Virgin Mary, but her face wouldn't be posted everywhere if she was a *dark* dead woman. Before leaving the states, I read an article suggesting that many in Pakistan held a favorable view of Barack Obama, hoping that his election could mean good things for the whole world, and now I understood why: he was fighting their fight, since a man of Obama's complexion couldn't lead the Pakistan Muslim League Q or N or the Pakistan People's Party or any of it.

Driving around town with Mamoon, I asked him if Lahore had any hip-hop, and he complained about Pakistani rappers "acting like monkeys."

"You're the drummer for a band called Noble Drew," I told him. "Do you know what that means? It means that you don't call people monkeys."

"I don't mean 'monkey' as anything racial," he said. "That's just, you know, when a person tries to act like something that he's not, it's like he's an animal." Except that Mamoon and his cousin and all the rich kids in Lahore had lived like white kids in America and maintained American white stoner culture in their parents' gated palaces, and I never heard "monkey" about any of that.

I met an emcee during one of our Thursday trips to Shah Jamal. Dehydrated, I had left the shrine and headed down the street for a Pepsi, and the rapper offered to buy it for me. He was just a teenager but called himself the rap king of Lahore.

"I love 2Pac," he told me, "because 2Pac hated the police." It's as good a reason in Pakistan as anywhere. "I battle online," he said. "I battle with the American niggers, and I beat them."

The next day in the flat, I told the band that I had met the rap king of Lahore and Mamoon asked if he was wearing a flat-brimmed hat.

"What do you mean?" I asked.

"To protect his lips."

"Huh?"

"You know that joke, why do black people wear flat-brimmed hats?"

"No."

"Why do black people wear flat-brimmed hats?"

"I don't know, why?"

"So the birds don't shit on their lips."

"I don't get it." I did, but wanted him to say.

"Because, you know, black people have big lips."

I left the flat and walked down Jail Road. One billboard had a guy looking like Tom Cruise in big designer douchebag sunglasses with an expression like he was getting blown by some unseen girl while another white girl handed him a Shezan juice box. Went to McDonald's and got their McArabia (a gyro with two chicken patties inside) and looked at the family on the placemat, a pale South Asian couple and their pale daughter all smiling over french fries, and I looked at the poster for some cell phone promotion with a fat white man carrying his loaded McDonald's tray with his new phone pinned between his cheek and shoulder. He was actually something of a celebrity in Lahore, the singer for a popular band. His brother was a music promoter who had shown up at the flat to meet with Noble Drew.

Basim and Shahjehan weren't sure what to do with Mamoon. They had named their band Noble Drew, painted Master Fard's face on their wall, and now their drummer had revealed himself to be a racist. I didn't want to push the issue with them, because they had already lost all of their friends and collaborators and even a guitar amp over my Wikipedia page. Basim said that he hoped to reeducate Mamoon, looking for a way to "teach the meaning of civilization," as Master Fard put it.

Eating this terrible McArabia, I remembered Master Fard's Supreme Wisdom, just a few lines from one lesson:

My uncle cannot speak his own language.

He does not know that he is my uncle.

He likes the devil because the devil gives him nothing.

Why does he like the devil?

Because the devil put fear in him when he was a little boy.

Why does he fear now, since he is a big man?

Because the devil taught him to eat the wrong food.

Does that have anything to do with the above question?

Yes, sir! That makes him other than his own self.

What is his own self?

His own self is a righteous Muslim.

When Pakistan was a little boy, the British Empire put the fear in him. Now that he's a grown nation, he still fears and loves the devil, and the devil has him eating the wrong food—the kind of realization that dawns on you in McDonald's. Fast food in Lahore caters to the upper class: a foot-long sandwich at Subway costs four hundred rupees, the daily wage for our driver and much more expensive than the superior Pakistani food you can get on the street.

The billboards, movies, and music videos all speak to the fantasy life of the Westernized upper class, which seems embarrassed by the rest of Pakistan. Clothing stores at the Fortress mall sell fashions that no woman could wear in public, only rich girls behind closed doors when they dance to American music and do coke and hook up at secret mansion parties. "Radical Islam" or "Islamism" or the best one, "Islamofascism," almost appear logical as a knee-jerk reaction to all of this, and extreme patriotism has risen from the confusion of kids who buy up culture from a country that they assume will someday bomb them.

That's why everyone loves white Muslims—only 1 percent of the world's Muslim population—and not just any Bosnian Albanian Chechen but the especially rare white convert, the one who really comes from the other side. Here's a blue-eyed

American who buys up *your* culture, who wants what *you* have, coming from the land of blue jeans and John Cena and going back with a bag full of religious trinkets.

At Omar's hotel room we'd always have his television on, since there wasn't one at the flat, and happened upon that Bollywood douchebag Shahrukh Khan, who endorsed Fair and Handsome creams.

"Denzel couldn't be a movie star here," I said to H—, Basim's journalist friend.

H—thought about it and countered, "He could be a villain."

It's a hard truth for American Muslims of all colors inspired by Malcolm's journey to Mecca, where he became convinced that Islam was the magical answer to racism. But Muslims loved white people, even white people who yelled about what bad Muslims they all were. On Peace TV (Pakistan's religious channel), we found a white man with bushy beard and English accent lecturing the audience of brown men about how his wife never takes off her veil, even when she's driving. And they ate it up.

18.

Shahjehan and his girlfriend took me to the Wazir Khan Mosque, to which Shahj felt a bond because it was built in the reign of his namesake, the Mughal king Shahjehan. On the way we walked through the hectic old city, dodging rickshaws and passing a few tombs of unknown saints. Spotting an Islamic bookshop, I paused to see if they had a Ya Sin I could buy. The man dug up a pamphlet-sized copy, and when I asked how much, he just asked my country.

"American."

"Muslim?"

"Yes." He smiled and waved as though shooing away my money. Before I could thank him, the owner of the shop next door took my sweaty hand in his and smelled it.

"Even when Muslims sweat," he told me, "they smell good."

WAZIR KHAN MOSQUE was red brick with multicolored glaze, purples and yellows faded but still jumping out at me. We saw the minarets first, the actual mosque still hidden behind the drab buildings.

The masjid was also a shrine, hosting tombs in the courtyard. There was one above ground and another in a basement. We went down the winding stairs and could have stayed there all day in the dark on that cool marble floor, propped up against the wall watching men come in and sprinkle flower petals on the tomb and give it prayers. The tomb belonged to Miran Badshah, who was known by various other names and came to Lahore from Persia in the thirteenth century. He was enshrined at that spot some four centuries before the construction of the mosque. They called him Sabz Pir, "Green Saint," because the vine that used to grow from his tomb was believed to cure diseases.

Wazir Khan was an open mosque, with an inner prayer area dug into the wall. There were already men around but they weren't praying or anything, just enjoying the shade and quiet. They left us alone and we left them alone, making our separate prayers and then lying on our backs to look up at the ceiling. The calligraphy above me formed words in a circle—sacred Arabic *lams* like arrows pointing into the center—*there is no god but God*. Lyrics popped into my head: "Throw up your He Allah Now Divine Saviors." It was from Gang Starr's "Moment of Truth," with Guru spelling out "hands" in the Five Percenters' Supreme Alphabets. I knew what it was and why he did it, but Lahore was millions of miles from where that could mean anything, and all the American stuff seemed just as far from me in time, a year for every mile.

I sat up and looked around the big empty space, noting the green kufis left lying everywhere so that a man could put one on and add to the reward for his prayer, since hats were Sunna. The courtyard was silent until a distant hammer hit metal. The echo startled pigeons out of their hiding places, sending them jumping into the air like fragments from an explosion, flying in clusters around the minarets like the tawaf of pilgrims around the Ka'ba.

Shahjehan was sitting with his girlfriend, the two of them whispering to each other. I remembered that she was a girl. She wasn't wearing hijab, but none of the tired men took any issue with her. I had my own girl on the other side of the world, and she had a mom, and the mom auntie had asked me to pray for her while I was in Pakistan. I stood up and made my niyya, my intention. But during the prayer for Auntie I feared that Sadaf would feel left out of our sweet religious bond, so I added her late, and finally prayed for all three of us. And then I just sat there, staring out at the empty courtyard with my back to Mecca. Shahj asked if I was ready to leave. We took a different way out, this time stumbling across a children's playground with a little girl on a swing going way too high, the chains almost completely parallel to the ground, and every time she went up I was sure she'd lose her grip and break her head on the concrete—but less than a hundred feet away stood a green-domed structure that looked like it might have another saint buried inside, so perhaps he'd look out for her.

19.

H— introduced me to a woman named Z— who ran a small bookstore and would "discreetly" deal in subversive materials off-shelf, such as an academic book on lesbians in Islamic societies.

"She's interested in your novel," he said. The Muslim punk rock novel, *The Taqwacores*. "She might be able to distribute it here—not on the shelves, of course, but if you'd be interested . . ."

Basim and Shahjehan came with me to her store, the film crew too. Omar thought it was important for the story of Muslim punk rock and/or my own journey, seeing how my book would fly in Pakistan.

She seemed like a cool person, and we were friends until the cameras turned on.

"Michael, you're leaving, you are able to just bring the book here and then be gone. What's going to happen to all these kids who try to act out as your characters have? How are you going to feel if you inspire kids to speak like that and something happens?"

What the fuck was her problem? She expressed an interest in the novel, she wanted to meet me and have a conversation but came out swinging. "People here aren't interested in religion," she said. "They just leave it alone. What do you think your book has to give them? I don't think you write about religion, though. You write about identity."

Then she took it to a ridiculous level: "Are you going to just invade Iraq and then leave?"

I tried to tell her that people did care about religion, because some of us still claimed a stake in the religions that devastated us. "Religion's not the problem," she snapped. "Culture's the problem. There's a difference between religion and culture."

"No, there's really not," I told her.

"Can the camera be off for a minute?" she asked with a nod towards the crew.

"Sure," I said, and they walked out with their equipment to get food.

Then everything flipped.

"I'm sorry if that was harsh," she said with a genuine smile.

Just like that, we were friends again. Her hostility was all performance. She would have been out of her mind to be filmed as the gateway for my blasphemies to enter Pakistan. We talked some more and Basim and Shahjehan tried to tell her that my work had done them some good. She was less aggressive than during our shoot but still had her reservations, which were all legit—*I* wasn't even sure if I wanted the novel to be read in Pakistan. People who could afford to buy the book, read it in English, and even comprehend some of the Western subcultural references weren't exactly "the people." And how would the punk element, everything said in the worst way possible, translate to life in Pakistan? *The Taqwacores* reads like a literary equivalent of that artist who soaked a painting of Jesus in his own urine.

> The easiest way to get a reputation is to go outside the fold, shout around for a few years as a violent atheist or a dangerous radical, and then crawl back into the shelter.
>
> —F. SCOTT FITZGERALD

"You could recant," H— suggested. "You wrote what you felt at that particular time, and your feelings have changed, and you can just apologize." *Recant* sounded so medieval, like I was hanging from a dungeon wall with Galileo or somebody. And it became impossible when I opened *The Taqwacores* and saw the part where a girl's wearing a button that reads, NEVER APOLOGIZE FOR YOUR ART.

At times, I did want to take it all back. Sometimes I looked at my novel or the Wikipedia page and was mortified. Once you say something, you never stop saying it, and whatever I said I'd be saying for the rest of my life. Even worse were the Muslims who had never heard of me and wrapped me up in all their ummah love, which only made me feel like I was stealing something from them.

Even if I recanted a specific quote or buried the book and pretended that the blog never existed, I still wouldn't be acceptable in their eyes. I could say it in pious language or academic language and still look only half Muslim to them, just a convert who didn't know anything. Or one of those spiritual slackers who couldn't handle the full duties of a Muslim, so he just followed whatever parts he wanted and threw away the rest—which could have been right.

I've been through some things, I've grown, and might say it differently if I had to say it today, but it'd be wrong to forget why I felt as I did. That's why old people look like hypocrites to young people. I could still hold my mean books as a mirror to my religion and my brothers and my sisters and say, *This is what you can do to people, how about you let up?* And maybe they'd let up, or not.

WHENEVER I CAME close to disowning my work, I'd hear something that would make me want to say it all over again. There are Muslims who deserve it, and they deserve it for doing more damage to our religion than I ever could. They're wearing PhDs and speaking from the pulpits, and those lectures end up as tapes or pamphlets—*What Is the Status of Women in Islam?*—or excerpted for the online-fatwa sites. I'm talking about respected faces in our community, the turds sliding out of their mouths so smooth you'd think, "Wow, of course! A man can only beat his wife *lightly* and as a *last resort*, and only if it *helps the marriage!* I'm sorry for ever being confused about it." That line of thought is worse than anything I've said; sometimes I throw a tantrum on paper and swear, but at least I won't use flowery religious language to make violence seem benevolent. So when those crooks wipe their own fecal matter off the Prophet, I'll apologize for mine.

* * *

WHEN *THE TAQWACORES* was released in a separate UK edition, the publisher, Telegram Books, insisted that I allow them to censor the manuscript, removing anything deemed offensive or challenging to Muslims. Following the Danish cartoon controversy, cuts of outright blasphemies should have been expected; but the publisher also wanted to delete any obscene word that appeared in the same sentence as Allah, the Qur'an, or the Prophet, regardless of whether it was in direct reference. Even a character being described as "anal" in his adherence to the Sunna had to go, since the editor thought that this associated the Prophet with anal sex.

Besides words, they went for ideas. With the help of an anonymous "consultant," my editor suggested the deletion of "problematic" sections dealing with facts of history, such as the Qur'an being collected and put into book form after the Prophet's death, or the story of the necklace, in which Ayesha speaks to the Prophet in a defiant manner, or her age when she married him—though these are accepted by the Muslim community and included in pious literature. Islam itself has been tagged as offensive to Muslims.

Because the uncensored U.S. edition was also available in the UK, and each instance of censorship would be noted with an asterisk, I agreed to the cuts for their theatrical value; the whole book would become a performance, censorship as spectacle. The mutilated text served to demonstrate how ridiculous our discourse on religion has become—that non-Muslim editors are telling a Muslim author how he can properly relate to his religion and how Muslims will interpret his work.

The novel's burqa-wearing feminist character, Rabeya, self-publishes a zine called *Ayesha's Hymen*. My UK publisher insisted that its title be cut. If these changes were motivated by a fear of violence from offended Muslims, then the publisher has supported an image of violence as a Muslim's natural response, while also justifying the threat of violence as a means to govern speech. The bookseller has joined the book burners, leaving Rabeya as voiceless as she would be under the Taliban.

If the publisher's intention was to show respect for Islam, it was only a certain kind of Islam—the monolithic Islam of uncompromised orthodoxy, the Muslim community as defined by its most conservative members, in which all Muslims are assumed to believe and practice in one uniform fashion. As Pakistan showed me, this is an Islam that does not exist. The publisher was okay with my Muslim characters listening to the Sex Pistols, drinking beer, and having sex—in short, conforming to secular Western culture—as long as they never questioned the truth claims of their faith. It took a religious novel and stripped away the religion. Instead of engaging Islam with any honesty or imagination, daring to express doubts and unpopular beliefs, these characters were reduced to the children of immigrants who broke some rules on their way to assimilation.

The censorship of my novel in the UK expressed the publisher's view that my own experience of Islam is not legitimate and that Islam is most accurately represented by so-called fundamentalists. In the name of tolerance and respect for cultural differences, the publisher denied that Islam itself could be diverse.

One reviewer wrote that this novel asked, "How do you define a 'true' Muslim? On what grounds? And does anyone have the right to judge?" The answer is yes, someone has claimed the right: the non-Muslim editor reading a manuscript with black marker in hand, running thick lines over *my* Islam.

After all of this, they had the sack to declare, "*The Taqwacores* is to literature what the Sex Pistols were to music."

I am a Muslim and a writer. All praise is due to Allah and they can fuck off.

20.

Noble Drew set up a rooftop show at one of the restaurants in the old city overlooking Badshahi Mosque, but the owners got cold feet and bailed out. They found another restaurant with basically the same view of the mosque and fort, and I went with them to scope it out. Looking over the ledge, we saw Badshahi's three onion domes and vast courtyard on one side and on the other, tiers of flat roofs with all kinds of flags— Garvey-style PPP flags, tattered green and white PML-N flags, solid black Shi'a flags with Hands of Fatima on the ends of the flagpoles.

In a matter of days, I was leaving Pakistan again, and probably for the last time, so any remaining lessons had to be learned quick. Hollywood narrative told me that if a trip abroad truly served its purpose, I needed to be born again.

A man who constantly remade himself can't be captured on a T-shirt.

—*People* magazine on MALCOLM X, 1992

There were all kinds of ways to be born again. Eldridge Cleaver, cofounder of the Black Panther Party, fled the United States for exile in Algeria and the Soviet Union, but came home as a Mormon Republican. Anytime I felt that American culture had some good things to give the world, I'd get scared of pulling a Cleaver and look for someone to set me straight—*Ammar, tell me about Che, right this second, I'm begging you . . .*

As Omar filmed Noble Drew preparing for the rooftop show, I made solitary ricksha trips around town. I went to Data Durbar again and found a smaller shrine just a block or two down the street. After making my du'a for the anonymous saint, some men called me over and offered a Coke and biscuit. The man in the center of the group, who did most of the talking, was a grandson of the saint—a sayyed, he told me, with assurances that the shrine was still privately owned and the government had no hand in it. After the Coke and biscuit I took my leave and checked out the merchants around Data Durbar, picking up some ridiculously oversized zikr beads and five wallet-size laminated cards of saints. The first was of Husayn on his white horse, baby Ali-Asghar in arms, Ali-Asghar already a martyr with a tulip in his hand, halos on both father and son. I also picked up one that was supposed to picture Shahbaz Lal Qalandar in ecstasy at his shrine, but it was an image of Jesus cut and pasted into the scene. I had a portrait of Waris Shah, which might have been Baba Farid, but I couldn't tell, and two kind of goofy ones that I loved anyway for being so earnest. One had a saint in a chair in green and gold robe and big white turban, and standing at his side was some dude in a brown European suit and tie, probably his son or disciple, and that guy had a green turban with huge triangle flap off the side, and next to them on a table was an open book and long ornamental sword. On the other side of that card was a photo of a man in white robe and blue turban, superimposed on a photo of a shrine, and I didn't know what any of it meant. The fifth card had what looked like a black-and-white photo with airbrushed color of a grandpa-looking guy in big Coke-bottle glasses, thick moustache, and green turban, a falcon sitting on his shoulder. It could have been an eagle; I only guessed falcon because *Qalandar* meant falcon. He looked more like a sweet old codger than a spiritually powerful friend of Allah—but then I remembered Yoda in *The Empire Strikes Back*. Who would have expected him to lift an X-Wing out of the swamp with just his brain?

The cards reminded me of Catholic saint candles bearing the image of Mary or Lazarus, or the Mary scapula that my grandfather wore for the whole second half of his life. I had forgotten that it was still in my wallet, now in Lahore with Husayn and Lal Shahbaz Qalandar and the falcon man. On one side was the Holy Virgin, and on the other a heart with a sword going through it and blood dripping and a crown of fire—wow, religion's awesome—and around it the words, IMMACULATE HEART OF MARY PRAY FOR US NOW AND AT THE HOUR OF OUR DEATH. Discovering Islam as a sophomore at St. Francis DeSales High School in Geneva, New York, I saw tawhid as the antidote to Catholic saint worship. When our lacrosse team prayed to the school's Mary statue before games, I was the one standing while everyone around me knelt. They asked for Mary to help us in the game, and I'd repeat the shahadah to myself: there was no god but God. Just reading the Qur'an, it never occurred to me that Ali's ghost protected snake charmers.

MY OTHER GRANDFATHER was a Pentecostal preacher, but I had never met him, and I never stepped foot inside a Pentecostal church until Pakistan. I had spotted the church near the venue of the first Noble Drew gig and wanted to check it out before leaving the country. Omar brought the crew. It was bright inside, the door open and the sun shining in, and I could see the Islam in this church—shoes left outside, everyone sitting on the floor, men and women on opposite sides of the room, the women covering their hair in dupattas. The songs were beautiful and in Punjabi, so I didn't have to worry about what they said—the only word I could make out was "Hallelujah"—but then they'd turn off that joy like a switch and go into hyper-hellfire prayer mode, everyone closing their eyes and opening up their hands to receive Christ when he'd come smashing down through the roof.

Christianity came to South Asia during British rule, with the first Anglican bishop of Lahore appointed in 1877, and Catholicism brought by Irish members of the army. When India won its independence and then began killing itself, no one knew where Christians stood—not even the Christians themselves, who occupied a no-man's land while India worked out its bloody history. As Hindus and Sikhs fled what was to become Pakistan, the Christians stayed. In the half century since, Christian life in Pakistan has been a mixed bag: there are no official laws against a Muslim converting to Christianity, but sometimes the streets have their own courts. Pakistan's blasphemy laws, intended to protect against "anti-Islamic activities," prevent the free expression of Christian views. A Christian's testimony does not carry the same weight in court as that of a Muslim, but a Christian can participate in government, occupying any position except head of state.

IN THE COLONIAL period, Christianity had appealed mainly to low castes and Untouchables, who hoped for a better place in God's kingdom than what they were given as Hindus. In its earliest beginnings in America, Pentecostalism did the same for women, since anyone could have a direct experience of God. With this church divided by gender, it was easy to notice that there were twice as many women as men. Women also got up on stage and sang alongside men, and all I felt was embarrassed for my Muslim brothers, the ones who say that a woman's voice in the mosque can make them forget God.

Ammar came by and whispered that everyone had assumed that I was Christian, and wanted me to *testify*. I told him that I couldn't, but to please thank them. After the service, Pastor Selim introduced himself to me and told Ammar a story for him to translate.

"There was a sick man," Ammar told me while Pastor Selim looked on. "He was so very sick, and he was Muslim, and he prayed to Allah, 'please make me better.' But nothing happened. Then, finally, he said, 'O Allah, if you are the father of Christ, if you are the God of Christ, please help me.' And then God cured him, and he accepted Christ." Pastor Selim had a look on his face as though this story alone would have me drop to my knees and accept the Baptism of Holy Ghost and Fire. I thanked him for welcoming me into his church. Despite the beauty of their songs, I knew that I was a Muslim. Religion is like an art gallery. One painting will speak to you more than another, and there's no need to explain or defend your taste.

21.

The next show, the rooftop show in the red-light district, went better because we made it free and just ran up and down the street getting guys to come up, guys in dusty shalwar kameezes and guys carrying cricket paddles and whoever. There were even some girls. This time the band knew what to do, initiating the audience with punked-out Bollywood covers (including four performances of "Cholli Kapeeche Kya Hey") and then busting out their own songs with Punjabi choruses that everyone could get. Shahjehan called on the audience to stand up and they did, and all the working-class guys got into it, dancing and jumping around and even joining me in what may have been Pakistan's first mosh pit. At the end I got on the microphone, screamed GEORGE BUSH *BHENCHODE!* (sisterfucker) and then they all mobbed me with hugs and kisses on my head. Complete success.

After everything died down and the equipment was packed up, we crammed into a ricksha, Basim and Shahj and me, and sorry, religion, but I fell in love with being alive in this world of flimsy *duniya* mischief, despite knowing what the Punjabi poet-saints all said about our time running out—yes, Waris Shah said, *Waris Shah! What is the certainty of life? Man is but a goat in the hands of butchers.* But that made me love the *duniya* more. You could only enjoy food or money or time by using it up and then having none. I watched ragged dogs on the street and packs of young men with their arms around each other and truck drivers and our ricksha driver with his eyes on everything, and it must have been such a long day for him, now driving us at 2 AM. I hoped that Allah had smiled on him too in some way, and I hoped it as a prayer.

22.

In my last two days there were nine or so blasts throughout Pakistan, including five on one night in Karachi and the inevitable suicide bombing at Lal Masjid in Islamabad, just as Basim predicted. Life went on. Our final night in Pakistan, everyone came over to Omar's hotel room to laugh and tell stories and deal with the fact of us missing each other. Early in the morning I slipped out with Shahjehan to make a secret Fajr prayer and du'a in the dim hallway. Shahjehan prayed that I make it home safe, and I prayed that he takes care of himself and knows that he's not alone. I also prayed that Shahj and Basim come back to the States.

"The way things are going," I told him, "either you come to America, or America's coming to you."

"We're *so* Muslim," he said when we hugged. An hour or so later we piled into cars, Shahjehan and I in Mamoon's, and headed for the airport. Time would slow down and speed up like in a movie: waiting around the hotel was awful and dragged on, just prolonging the sad goodbye, but then in the car Mamoon blasted the Kominas album and everything raced by as I looked out the back window at all the same sights for the last time, rickshas, donkey carts, psychedelic trucks, mosques, billboards, Pakistan rolling up for me like a carpet to be stashed away, or a flag. In front of the airport, we all hugged a bunch of times for the camera and then had our real goodbye. Basim taught me a final bit of Punjabi, *sab ki choot:* "fuck everyone."

The henna-bearded guard walking me through the metal detector noticed the big tasbih around my neck and asked if I was Muslim. When I said yes, he gave a warm smile and said "Welcome," even though I was leaving. I shook his hand, knowing that it wouldn't be like that on the other side of this flight.

It felt like I was still in Pakistan even flying over Russia and Europe and the Atlantic Ocean, saying *shukria* when the attendants poured me chai, and it would feel like Pakistan until I finally said *khuda hafiz* and walked up the long white corridor and parted ways with all the Pakistani passengers to go through Canadian customs and reenter the Western world. The flight took thirteen hours, but traveling over time zones, it worked out that I'd leave Lahore at 8 AM and be in Toronto at 2 PM, sitting on Laury's couch thinking, *fuck, this morning I was in Pakistan.*

Skimming through the "Western" portion of PIA's music selection, I listened to Lupe Fiasco and then Eddie Vedder's "Society," its lines about greed and selfishness making me think of the Prophet all alone trying to call us to something better. The tears came without warning, and I couldn't believe them, but they were real, streaming down my face cold and through the beard down my neck.

It didn't seem that anyone would catch me crying, maybe just a flight attendant going up and down the aisles, and I didn't make a sound. I was bawling for the Prophet. I loved him, and after everything I've said I couldn't explain why or how, just that I could see him standing up against all the terrible injustice in this song and giving what he could to the world that he knew would only stay mean, knowing that even his good works would be flipped upside down and turned against him, that we'd forget his words and misuse his sword and ruin everything. After realizing that I had shed sincere tears for the Prophet, I started to feel good about it, like I was something special to cry for him, and then the tears stopped. There's no moment so rare and special that your nafs, your ego, can't step in and poison it. Then I played the song again, imagined Vedder's voice being the Prophet's voice and the Prophet saying those things—*society, I hope you're not lonely without me*—waited for the feelings to come back, and cried again. I looked at the passengers around me, Muslim families with little Muslim babies, and I wiped the tears all over my face as a shield from my own fire, the fire whose fuel is me and my words. I remembered the way that I treated the Prophet, and it came out harder, and I was at least ready to say sorry to him, *I'm sorry, I'm sorry, I'm sorry, all I can ever say to defend myself is that I hurt so bad over everything.* And then I distrusted myself for clinging to my offense, still rationalizing and excusing. Maybe it was right and reasonable or maybe it was only for the nafs, my vanity and arrogance that I couldn't let go, but then I thought of all this and cried more. The tears were a comfort. I didn't deserve to have religious experiences, but sometimes they happened, and I just felt like the World's Champion of Lucky Assholes.

The feelings and the moment faded. Over our fourteen-hour flight, I thought of all kinds of things, missed everyone back in Lahore, missed Sadaf in New York, and fell asleep for a while.

23.

Pakistan was a real pilgrimage for me, a Mecca for what the young republic meant in my life. Considering the lessons that a Muslim might learn in Mecca and whether I had learned any of them in Lahore, I thought of two American Muslims who became pilgrims. One was a student; the other, his teacher.

The student was Malcolm X, who traveled to Mecca after a

heartbreaking split from his teacher and the Nation. Suddenly friendless and out of his religion, hajj seemed like a good idea. Putting on the ihram, the simple white cloths worn by male pilgrims, Malcolm merged into the sea of humans around the Ka'ba—Arab Muslims, African Muslims, Turkish Muslims, Indian Muslims, even pale European blue-eyed devil Muslims, their tribes and nations and races gone. He prayed, ate, and slept side by side with his new brothers of all colors and backgrounds, reclaiming the lost part of himself signified in the X. Hajj, he would say, was the first time in his life that he ever felt like a "complete human being."

For all of the meaning placed on Malcolm's hajj by scholars, biographers, poets, and filmmakers, claimed by secular black nationalists and pious immigrant Sunnis and white converts, there's another American pilgrimage that gets no attention, though it says just as much as the experience of Malcolm: the journey of his teacher, Elijah Muhammad.

Elijah went to Mecca in 1959, years before his student, at a time when Sunni opponents began to attack his Islamic credentials. The first criticisms came from former members like Hamaas Abdul Khaalis, who would claim to have only joined the Nation with the secret aim of bringing it to orthodox Islam. Then Palestinian Jamil Diab, who was credited with bringing some orthodoxy to the movement's practices, quit to start his own rival mosque in Chicago. Elijah Muhammad's Nation of Islam, he announced in a public statement, was "totally lacking in the requisites which constitutes any Muslim group." The Nation was "not now, nor has it ever been" truly Muslim, and was in fact guilty of corrupting the "very cornerstone of Islam, universal brotherhood of man, black as well as white . . . into hatred." While asserting himself as a legitimate Muslim, Elijah was not overly troubled by the divide between his teachings and Sunni doctrine nor by the charge that his Islamic liberation theology was less valid:

My brothers in the East were never subjected to conditions of slavery and systematic brainwashing by the slavemasters for as long a period of time as my people here were subjected. I cannot, therefore, blame them if they differ with me in certain interpretations of the Message of Islam. In fact, I do not even expect them to understand some of the things I say unto my people here.

Antigua-born Talib Ahmad Dawud, founder of the Muslim Brotherhood, Inc., tore into Elijah at the embassies of Muslim nations, calling Elijah's Muslims "phonies" who could claim "no connection whatsoever" to the religion of Islam. Not only had the Nation of Islam strayed in doctrine from legitimate Islam, charged Dawud, but the Nation had even refused to "adhere to the proper Muslim prayer rituals." In the 1950s, Elijah Muhammad had published a manual to instruct his Muslims in elements of traditional Islamic salat, including ablutions, the call to prayer, and proper times for the five daily prayers. Nation members, however, were advised to worship in English; the Arabic, they were told, would be integrated into the community's rituals "some day in the near future."

Dawud bolstered his own image as an authentic and recognized Muslim leader by claiming, fresh after his pilgrimage to Mecca, that Elijah Muhammad would not be allowed in the holy city. Elijah called his bluff, embarking on a tour of the Muslim world that would include a pilgrimage to the Ka'ba in Mecca. He arrived first in Turkey, where he prayed at the Islamic Center of Istanbul, then city-hopped from Damascus to Beirut to Jerusalem before reaching Cairo. He visited Al-Azhar University, which had denounced Noble Drew Ali a few decades before, and had tea with the imam of its tenth-century mosque. After meeting with Gamel Nasser, Elijah claimed that Nasser, insisting that Americans would never embrace Islam, suggested that Elijah instead devote his resources to teaching Islam in

French West Africa. Elijah disagreed, as God had told him to resurrect his own people from mental death. Elijah would also claim that Nasser had offered him a seventy-five-room palace in Cairo, even promising, "If you don't like it, we will build you another one." Elijah again refused and continued on his travels. Dawud made his own declaration, equally suspect, that Elijah had been asked to leave by Egyptian authorities for falsely "posing as a Muslim."

Elijah Muhammad next went to Ethiopia and the Sudan, where he found inequality and ethnic tensions among people that he would have identified as all black. Already disillusioned, he continued on the pilgrim's journey, putting on ihram and heading for Saudi Arabia. He reached Mecca on Christmas Eve.

In terms of racism, the Middle East lagged a century behind America. Bahrain had only abolished its slave trade in 1937; Kuwait in 1947; Qatar, 1952. Elijah's pilgrimage was still years before the legal end of slavery in Yemen (1962), the United Arab Emirates (1963), Oman (1970), and even Saudi Arabia itself—which would *officially* abolish slavery in 1962, but still possessed a slave population of three hundred thousand a year later and executed its captured runaways.

In July 1965, less than six months after Malcolm's assassination, a United Nations report revealed that King Ibn Sa'ud still possessed hundreds of slaves. Saudi Arabia would be considered a principal importer of African slaves as late as the mid-1970s. Even pilgrimage to Mecca became a device in the slave trade, as African pilgrims were duped by would-be "escorts" who immediately sold them into slavery upon arrival in Arabia. Some Arab pilgrims would also bring slaves, often small children, to use as human currency along their journey.

During his hajj, Malcolm fell into a new Islam with the same blind faith that he had given to Elijah. Since he lived just a year after his hajj, Mecca became the neatly presented and cinema-friendly conclusion to his lifelong thread of transformations:

he finally found the Truth and then Allah took him home. But if he lived longer, I think he would have called out the Arabs.

yes

BACK TO THE TEACHER: led by an appointed guide, Elijah fulfilled the rituals of pilgrimage. He prayed in Arabic, walked barefoot around the Ka'ba, and kissed the Black Stone. The trip gave him everything he needed to prove himself as a genuine Muslim; he had been welcomed in the holy city, fully supported and assisted by the Ka'ba's custodians, walked in the footsteps of the Prophet, praying as he prayed. Elijah was, as far as the authorities considered him, a Muslim and a leader of Muslims in America.

Following a stop in Medina, Elijah left Saudi Arabia for a four-day stint in Lahore—Shahjehan's dad had actually attended his lecture at a local university—and then returned home with a broken heart. Though he had passed all tests and scored a boon for his legitimacy, Elijah lost interest in trying to prove himself to mainstream Muslims. His son Warith Deen believed that Elijah was disappointed with the trip, having expected Mecca to be a utopia with "streets of gold." But the moral authority of correct belief had been shot to hell, and Elijah realized that he owed the Sunnis nothing—no apology, no conformity, no submission to "true" Islam if true Muslims were still enslaving, mutilating, and castrating black people. As the Messenger of Allah, who had appeared to him in the person of Master Fard, Elijah claimed his right to teach Islam as best suited his own people. Why not teach American Muslims to fast in December instead of the lunar month of Ramadan? And pray in English too, who cares?

your say / he never spoke of this or publicly

Even as a grafted white devil with six ounces of brain, I understood. Elijah Muhammad and I had both gone through stints as naïve converts, expecting to see a difference like day and night between the West on our backs and the East that we faced in prayer. American converts travel abroad in search of the Islam that we read about in books. Considering how Elijah might have felt in the Sudan, I looked back to myself in Pakistan at seventeen, walking past marble mansions and palatial Saudi-built mosques and watching the children of Afghan refugees eat newspaper. Elijah Muhammad and I had chosen Islam in part because we held it to be everything that America was not, but in the Muslim world we found the same injustices magnified. And like Elijah, I did not speak Arabic, nor did I have any training as an Islamic scholar, but somehow the question of who was authorized to speak on Islam no longer seemed to matter.

Both Malcolm X and Elijah Muhammad came back from Mecca with their eyes open. Malcolm's pilgrimage had repeated the truth of the Prophet's farewell hajj, which universalized local and tribal rituals for Muslims who would someday come from every corner of the world, uniting all human beings as children of Adam and creations of the same Allah. For Malcolm, Mecca promised the friendship of a larger global community, the ummah, with the promise of international solidarity in the struggle for human rights and independence, but Elijah's pilgrimage showed that his American Muslims would have to pull themselves up without anyone's support.

Malcolm's Mecca story has since been mythologized, becoming the dominant and defining parable for American Islam, but the pilgrimage of his teacher has been ignored. People talk about the "ten thousand roads to Mecca" but never mention Elijah's road, where he witnessed the gaps between a religion's promise and its reality.

The lessons from my time in Lahore spoke more to the truth of Elijah. I felt some transcendent Malcolm-style Islamic brotherhood in Pakistan, if I chose not to overthink the love at Rukn-i-Alam, but couldn't run home as Malcolm had and declare Islam the solution to all American prejudice. I loved Pakistan, but knew that I couldn't wander through that country as a woman or receive the same affection if I was black or find the same respect if my friends were from lower classes. American history reads as ugly as history anywhere—the communal violence of India's partition only reminds me of the American South's legacy of lynchings—but it shamed me that a so-called Islamic Republic wasn't better, that Muslims weren't saving the world.

Starting to feel okay with my American-ness, I hoped that American Muslims had something to offer the rest of the ummah: Islam as the answer to white supremacy, or the developing feminist theology of Progressive Muslim scholars. But in the same breath, I gave up. There's no ummah. American Islam will just have to speak to its own experience, Islam as understood by Americans, praise Allah and *sab ki choot.*

> The orthodox Muslims will have to bow to the choice of Allah. Allah will bring about a new Islam . . . We are seeing this change now and entering into it. The devils oppose this change, and the orthodox join them in opposing us because of their desire to carry on the old way of Islam.
>
> —Elijah Muhammad

After landing in Toronto I spent a week at Laury's house, and she told me about the Noor Cultural Centre, where women gave sermons to mixed-gender congregations and even performed the call to prayer. They didn't go as far as having woman imams, and called themselves a "Cultural Centre" instead of a "mosque" to stay out of trouble. Laury was preparing her own presermon lecture while I was there, and she told me about all the cool Muslims that populated the Noor scene, Muslims who marched in gay pride parades. The place was falling into its own controversy, though, with a debate over performance of gay marriage. Everyone at Noor supported gay marriage on the secular political level, but remained unsure of how to approach the issue in terms of Islamic law. Laury and other scholars worked to find a solution in which the marriages could be supported within an Islamic call for human rights and social justice, but the issue still hadn't been resolved.

I understood why it mattered but didn't want to play those games. We needed reformers like Laury who could work within the tradition, engaging conservatives with proper displays of piety and legal knowledge; but if the old mosque was burning down, someone also had to say that we're not waiting for anyone to save the building, we'd rather jump out the windows.

Christians have gone through it too. A Catholic scholar named Mary Daly had hoped to undo what she called the "antifeminism" of Christianity, two thousand years of gynophobic theologians: St. Paul, who wrote to the Corinthians that men shouldn't cover their heads in church, because their heads were the glory of God—but women should cover their heads, because their heads were only the glory of man; Tertullian, who called women "the devil's gateway"; St. Augustine, who said that women were not made in the image of God and who believed, along with Saints John Chrysostom and Ambrose, that women must veil at all times; Thomas Aquinas, who viewed women as misbegotten males. By the time that Daly received an invitation to be the first woman preacher at Harvard Memorial Church, the tradition's "crushing weight" had become too much to bear: the only solution was a retreat for new land. She delivered a sermon about the Exodus, invited women and men to join her in an exodus from patriarchy, and then literally walked out of the church.

She couldn't have done that at Faisal Mosque, of course; for women to stage a walk-out first requires that they can walk in.

The Five Percent stuff about "Arm Leg Leg Arm Head" and "I Self Lord Am Master" gave me some tools to build with, and I had met a queer Five Percenter at a drag show in D.C., but the culture was also overrun with hypergendered homophobes.

Give me a Nation-styled heresy to speak on gender issues, with a Mothership powered by female orgasms and piloted by a transgendered drag king Elijah Muhammad in purple suit with a pink triangle on his fez. Give me a poetic genius riot grrl who received a book from Khidr with the new wisdom for our age, I'd follow her. At least until we can have a place like the Noor in every city.

"They need to call that place by its right name," I told Laury. The Noor was a mosque, no apologies.

LAURY'S FIANCÉ HAD an old junker blue van that he was willing to give me, which led to another lesson learned: driving an unregistered vehicle across the U.S.-Canadian border with a passport stamped by Pakistan turned out to be incompatible with the current historical moment. After four hours of sitting in the waiting room as vacationing families and couples and lonely massage parlor guys came and went, with occasional officers stopping by to search my wallet and bag ("You were gone for a month, but there aren't any clothes in here! What were you wearing?"), confiscate my phone, and offer me a Coke, investigators from the FBI Joint Terrorism Task Force arrived and led me to the back for a two-hour interrogation.

There were three men sitting around me: an officer who had earlier brought me the Coke and the two agents—Messina, the nice guy who seemed to know the most, sitting in the middle directly facing me, and Fallon, also a nice guy but a little tougher. First they asked me to walk them through the trip, how I got my tickets and who I flew with and why Toronto, did I stop anywhere on the way or was it a direct flight, did I ever pay anyone to stamp or not stamp my passport. I told them about the birth of punk rock in Pakistan, my starting the first mosh pit, and they asked how I was received. While the words came out, I realized that this story had to sound ridiculous. But everyone loved me, I said. I didn't mention calling George W. Bush a sisterfucker.

They asked where I went besides Lahore. Islamabad, Kasur, Gujurat, Multan, I told them. They asked if it had been my first trip to Pakistan, so I told them about my time in Faisal Mosque a decade and a half ago.

"How about madrassas?" asked Messina, saying *madrassas* like he expected to catch me off guard with his use of terms, like the word had some special devastating weight that would just knock me down.

"It was a school inside a mosque," I told him. "If you want to call that a madrassa, I suppose it is."

They asked me what the rhetoric was like at Faisal in the 1990s, and I told them the truth: the program brought in a full range of scholars, some cool like my old imam Dr. Shafiq, and others insane like Rushdie the Palestinian who told us that Hitler was prophesied in the Qur'an as a punishment for the Jewish people.

They asked about my books. I told them about the novels, the memoir, the Five Percenters, my road book. They asked why I had so many names in my past: I told them that I was born Michael Roland Unger, my mom remarried when I was ten and changed my name to Michael William Schutt, and then she divorced the man and took her maiden name back, which meant that my name was still Schutt but my mom was Knight and my father was Unger, so then I took her last name and her father's name and the Prophet's name, becoming Michael Edward Muhammad Knight.

"And what's your business in Syria?" asked Messina.

They had looked through my text messages.

"My friends have family there," I explained, "and they said I'd have a place to stay, so I'm taking them up on it." Messina told me to be careful out there, lots of guys thought they could just backpack around, and no one knows what happened to them. I refrained from adding that I had bought tickets to Damascus because I was considering ziyarat to Iraq, to celebrate the birthday of the Mahdi.

"What about letters?" asked Fallon.

"Letters?"

"Did you ever write letters to prisoners?"

"Yeah, when I was researching the Five Percenters—there are a lot of Five Percenters in prison—I wrote letters and visited inmates."

"What about John Walker Lindh?"

"John Walker Lindh?" The American Taliban. I had forgotten that one.

"You wrote him a letter, and it was sent back to you."

At this moment I realized that somewhere, in a filing cabinet in Buffalo or a basement in Washington or a database that these guys could look up, the FBI had a folder with my name on it. Maybe it was dumb not to know that already, but you're never ready to hear agents reciting your life back to you.

"I wrote to him a few years ago," I replied. "I thought that his story was similar to mine in a lot of ways. I was just lucky enough to get out of that mentality, and he wasn't." I added that they didn't return the letter, just my self-addressed stamped envelope with a note saying that I couldn't send stamps to federal inmates.

"Michael," asked Messina, "would you say that you were *recruited*?"

We went on for a while and it became almost fun to answer their questions, until I remembered that these guys weren't graduate students emailing me about how Muslim punk rock "reformulates notions of space and subjectivity, redefining community, identity and territoriality" or some reporter writing "Slam Dancing for Allah" for *Newsweek*. Messina asked me if I knew anything about explosives, had I seen any explosives while in Pakistan, and he asked me why I had a full beard in my Pakistan pictures but came to the border clean-shaven. I just said that there was no reason to shave in Pakistan, and it helped me at the mosques. Whenever I opened my mouth, they jotted things down on their yellow legal notepads. Remembering Master Fard's eight-hundred-page FBI file, I wondered if this would end up looking like the memos I used to skim through: "Subject stated that he initiated the first mosh pit in Pakistan."

Messina asked if I'd have a cup of coffee with an agent sometime in the near future. Coffee destroys your prostate, but I said sure.

They let me go—Messina even said "as-salamu alaikum" with a wink—but I still couldn't take the van across the border without proper paperwork, so I drove it all the way back to Laury's house, and she bought me a Greyhound ticket for the next day.

When the bus stopped at the Peace Bridge, everyone was instructed to take their belongings and go through customs. They decided to hold me again and took my cell phone. I sat in the same waiting room as last time, long enough for it to feel like my daily routine and natural state of existence, this waiting room and this same seat and vacationers coming in and then leaving. The bus left me behind but another one came every hour, so I might have been fine once they decided to let me go. Looking out the window, I saw at the far side of the parking lot the street to America under a big green highway sign reading DOWNTOWN BUFFALO with those red, white, and blue interstate icons for the 90 and 190. I doubted that it'd help to tell the officers that a quasi-Sufi community, the Moorish Orthodox Church, had named me Mikail El, Sultan of the Interstate 90, and that the road out there fell under my spiritual jurisdiction.

An officer whose name tag said Banas came to the counter with my phone in his hand.

"From your text messages, I see that you're going to Syria."

"Yes, sir."

"What's in Syria?"

"My friends have family there who said they'd put me up. I had a conversation about it with Mr. Messina."

"Oh, okay."

He walked away, still holding my phone. Three hours later, an agent came in and put me on the next bus without a single question. He never even said a word to me, just "okay" to Banas, and then he went back home. The bus took me under the big green sign saying DOWNTOWN BUFFALO. I have never been so happy to be in such a hole of a town.

24.

It was more of the same in America. *The New Yorker* came out with a cover cartoon of the Obamas in the Oval Office, Barack dressed in a white turban and flowing jalab, fist-bumping Michelle who looked like a 1960s Black Panther Angela Davis in huge afro and ammo belts and machine gun, with a bin Laden portrait on the wall and burning American flag in the fireplace. As commentators debated whether the cartoon satirized the Secret Muslim hysteria or fed into it, one of McCain's surrogates announced that America was "at war with the Muslims," and that the Muslims wanted to kill us if we didn't kneel to them. He was an old man from a different time, back when Popeye downed spinach before beating up dirty Japs and you could talk like that. I didn't know which one I was to him, the "Muslims" or the "us."

In that political climate, Obama walked a tightrope between selling his Christianity to the 12 percent of Americans who still believed he was a Muslim and alienating millions of American Muslim voters. Keith Ellison, the nation's first Muslim congressman, was asked to cancel his appearance on Obama's behalf, and two women in hijab were prohibited from standing behind

Obama at a rally in Detroit—a city home to the largest Arab population outside the Middle East. Obama did appoint a national coordinator for Muslim Affairs, but his denials of Islam wouldn't even come with a "Not that there's anything wrong with that."

A WEEK AFTER coming home, I saw the new Batman movie, whipping out a notepad and scribbling thoughts in the dark:

post-9/11 PTSD

I felt it in the first shot, the camera zooming in on a building from the POV of Mohamed Ata in a cockpit.

The plot: Gotham City, the fictitious New York, has been overrun by a villain who betrays all the motives and methods of conventional crooks. The Joker is killing cops, assassinating officials, blowing up hospitals, freezing the city with videotaped threats, and declares himself the new ruler of Gotham, but he's not in it for money or power, they say that he just "wants to see the world burn." The good guys explicitly refer to the Joker as a terrorist, in case you failed to catch that he's Osama bin Laden.

On the public surface, the Joker's opposition is Harvey Dent, the idealistic new district attorney who wields the power of law and structure. Compulsive coin-tosser Dent believes in a dualistic universe of Good and Evil, with good guys and bad guys clearly defined by the way that they fight. The Joker burns off half his face and murders the love of his life, turning Dent into the monstrous Two-Face who now sets out to kill everyone he blames for his loss—both the criminals and heroes—to make things "fair."

Batman continues the good fight underground, in ways that the public could never understand. The Joker is only defeated when Wayne Enterprises CEO Lucian Fox—played by Morgan Freeman, whose voice of moral authority has, various times in his career, allowed him to play God and the president of the United States, as well as Malcolm X nearly two decades before Denzel—agrees to temporarily suspend his ethics and spy on Gotham's citizens through their cell phones. Batman gives him the promise that it's just this one time, after which the computers will be destroyed. Lucian Fox is rewarded for his faith in the outlaw, while Batman shoots Dent and realizes that Gotham cannot know what became of their beloved district attorney. Batman takes the blame for Dent's violence and becomes the sacrificial scapegoat hero who is never thanked, only despised and hunted by the city that he saved.

Knowing that the Joker is bin Laden, my question would be whether George W. Bush saw himself as Harvey Dent—the earnest public servant transformed by the monsters that he fights—*You thought we could be decent men in an indecent world?*—or Batman, our vigilante who does the wrong things for the right reasons and carries that burden because no one else can.

The film's moment of truth emerges with the Joker's "social experiment" in which two barges filled with evacuees are both rigged with bombs and the passengers of each are given a remote-control detonator to blow up the other. Whichever set of passengers decides to push the button first will be spared, but if neither have done so by the stroke of midnight, both will be destroyed. One barge is occupied by inmates from the local prison, the other filled with apparently upstanding citizens. The Joker plays off their class prejudices, with the good citizens arguing that they shouldn't sacrifice themselves for criminals.

According to the Joker, people are only as honorable as their situations allow them to be; if you threaten their security, all ethics and values go out the window. Batman counters that the people of Gotham are good, and he's right; the people on both barges reject the Joker's ultimatum, refusing to destroy the other. But Bush and bin Laden had a similar conversation with

America, and we failed the test: the reelection of Bush during his war in Iraq was owed to Americans saying, *Yes, to save ourselves we will blow up the innocent.* Bin Laden wins.

25.

I took one of my souvenirs from Pakistan, a gaudy little replica Ka'ba purchased outside Bibi Pak Daman, and set it on the kitchen table. It was a black box with plastic gold Arabic calligraphy running along the sides on top and a glued-on golden door that looked ready to fall off, and appeared to be roughly an appropriate size for my vintage *Star Wars* figures (from the original 1977–1983 Kenner line, stored in a Tupperware container). So I brought them all out, witnessed their shahadahs and assembled them as pilgrims around the Ka'ba, imagining Islam as each of them lived it. Yoda was an eccentric Sufi malang out in his swamp hut, a green master like Khidr drinking green bhang lassi and levitating shit. Darth Vader and the Emperor stood at the other side of the spectrum, total Saudi hardliners twisting Jedi religion to serve their own power—closer to the current state of the holy city. Between them stood Obi-Wan Kenobi, a Sufi hermit who still appeared Shari'a-compliant.

Then my phone rang, Sadaf pulling me back into grown-man world. She told me that while I was overseas, her family started to move forward with our wedding plans, and we'd have to act fast to have any say in how it went down.

"Are we getting married in accordance with the Shari'a?" she asked, though the answer was already yes, and we both knew that it meant some problems. Islamic law came from a time in which weddings were purely business transactions, an exchange of financial support for sexual access. This means that today, Islamic law has no concept of marital rape. As a Muslim, I'd call this our most hurtful shame in the modern world, even more so than political violence, because it has yet to be disowned by the mainstream "moderate" Islam. All those moderates came out after 9/11 to condemn political terrorism as the work of a lunatic fringe, but domestic terrorism between husband and wife remains protected.

It was still insane to me that we could even have a conversation about possible excuses for sexual violence. Our intellectual heritage had some raging misogynists, like Ibn Sina who made marriage equal to sexual slavery; a man feeds and provides for his wife, with his due compensation being ownership of the vagina. "He must own her," said Ibn Sina, "but not she him." But even if Shari'a allowed it, did rape fall into anyone's notions of imitating the Prophet? Could these scholars imagine the Prophet forcing himself on his wives? Did the wives ever give reason to believe that he had? No sooner do I put these words down than I hear the scholars' knee-jerk reaction: *Of course not, because Allah SWT gave the Prophet PBUH wives of such exceptional virtue that they would never refuse him . . .*

All I have to say: the only man who would defend rape is the man capable of doing it. Remember that when you ask a scholar about it to his face.

TRADITIONALLY, MY ANSWER to those questions would be, fuck Shari'a; I had no stake in Islamic law. Shari'a couldn't impact my life in America and meant nothing in my own religion; Shari'a wasn't a stone tablet coming to the Prophet from heaven, but a system devised long after his death to meet the administrative needs of a growing empire. I didn't owe it a thing.

That all changed with Sadaf, since we had to negotiate with Shari'a at least as a social reality, the way that things were done in her family and community. "Fuck Shari'a" wouldn't work in adult life; we needed a way that it could make sense for us—to marry in the tradition without accepting its worst parts. The progressive scholars have made moves in this area, arguing that since marriage was a business agreement over which the parties negotiated, a bride could name her own terms. Sadaf could include her right to consent as a demand in the contract—not because she needed it in writing from me, but it'd help us make our own statement about what Islam stands for, or *should* stand for. Something like that would even turn a wedding into activism.

I HAD DECIDED not to celebrate the Mahdi's birthday in Iraq, which meant that I wouldn't have the title of *Karbala'i*; but a girl crying so hard that she can't breathe, begging you not to kill yourself, takes the religious virtue out of visiting holy skeletons. At least I had my plane ticket to Damascus, which still had Sadaf scared and sad. Don't do anything stupid, she told me; Guantanamo Bay's just an endless pit of nightmares.

SYRIA'S EMBASSY WASN'T a far walk from the Islamic Center of Washington, D.C., so I headed over to pray and take a nap on the soft carpet. It reminded me of all the mosques and shrines in Pakistan that were places of relief as much as worship. A group of white school kids and their teacher came in with the imam, the girls in big hijabs that covered their hair and entire torsos but still wearing capri pants and even shorts, and the teacher seemed like a dumb white guy with good intentions. I almost stuck around to perform a prayer just to show that people who looked like us could be Muslim too, but stepped out to the mosque bookstore. It had the usual apologia: volumes defending the status of women, proving the truth of Islam with modern science, or introducing the non-Muslim reader to basic Islamic concepts. I picked up *Fortress of the*

Muslim, a pocket-size collection of du'as for every occasion. It had invocations against the oppression of rulers, invocations for visiting the sick, and what to say when you walk out of a mosque or sneeze or eat, but I bought it for the invocations of travelers. The book was printed in Saudi Arabia.

Then I found *Three Essays on Tawhid* by Shaykh Muhammad ibn 'Abd al-Wahhab, pioneer of the puritanical, "fundamentalist" Islam that now bears his name. The essays' translator, Isma'il Raji al-Faruqi, was the teacher of my old imam back at the Islamic Center of Rochester, Muhammed Shafiq.

Born in 1703 to a jurist father, al-Wahhab studied Hanbali law in Mecca and Medina and set out to purge Muslims of their deviated practices, the shrine worship and superstition of folk Islam that had overrun Qur'anic Islam. To prevent Muslims from worshiping human beings instead of God, he called for the destruction of holy sites, even the Prophet's shrine in Medina and Husayn's shrine in Karbala. His teachings were used by tribal leader Muhammad ibn Sa'ud to build the religio-political construction now called the Kingdom of Saudi Arabia, more on that later.

I spent most of my time in that bookstore looking through the second volume of *Riyad Us-Saliheen,* a collection of hadiths, trying to decide if I should buy it. One hadith said that every Friday had a small window of time in which whatever a Muslim prayed for would be granted, but the Prophet put his fingers together to show that the moment was very short. Sometimes I liked that stuff. There was another hadith about a du'a that the Prophet used to make in times of distress, which I saw as important mainly to know that the Prophet could feel things like distress; it kept him human for me.

There were cool hadiths to remind me of death in the good way, the ones that could slap me in the face when I loved the world too much. Abu Musa narrated the Prophet saying, "If anyone died and the mourner gets up and says: 'Alas! For the mountain among men. Alas! For the chief . . . ' and such like, Allah will send two angels to beat on the dead man's breast and ask, 'Were you like that?'" Johnny Cash also said that God would cut you down, Allahu Akbar.

Then I came to the hadith that made me put the book back on its shelf, narrated by Jarir, who heard the Prophet say, "When the slave runs away from his master, his prayer will not be accepted." I wanted to know about the original compiler of the book, who for some reason saw that hadith as important enough out of thousands to put into a short volume, and about the commentator for this modern edition:

> The institution of slavery does not exist in the modern world, but if it exists anywhere or a situation arises in which it reemerges, the principle stated in this hadith will be applicable. The hadith also made it clear that if someone has expressed his commitment to serve somebody, he should not back out. It also urges us to show gratefulness to one's benefactors and to reciprocate the good one receives.

This couldn't have come from American Muslims; we were too close to that history, and the whole page betrayed Islam's special meaning in America. What would Malcolm say to that page? Turning to the front of the book, I learned that it was a "gift presented by the Custodian of the Two Holy Mosques, King Fahd ibn Abdul-Aziz Al-Saud." But it wasn't just a problem with the Wahhabs; classical Shi'a texts quoted Ali as warning against marriage with black people, since they were a "distorted creation."

In the same store, I found *Bilal ibn Rabah: A Leading Companion of the Prophet Muhammad*, by Muhammad Abdul-Rauf and printed in Maryland in 1977. Bilal was an Ethiopian slave who rose in the early Muslim community to become the first muezzin, delivering the call to prayer from the roof of the

Ka'ba. I remembered reading the exact same book with the same orange, white, and black cover years ago at the Islamic Center of Rochester. When I went up to the counter with *Bilal ibn Rabah*, *Fortress of the Muslim*, and *Three Essays on Tawhid*, the desi uncle gave me a fourth book for free: *Understanding Islam and the Muslims*, which also contained three pamphlets as bookmarks: *Islam at a Glance* and two tracts showing off praise for Islam from non-Muslims: *What They Say About the Qur'an* and *What They Say About Muhammad (PBUH)*.

No reason to get annoyed. Sadaf and I found that same sweetness while browsing Islamic bookstores in Brooklyn, brothers welcoming us in and giving me free handbooks on how to pray, assuming that this Muslim girl was trying to convert a Christian boy for a good Shari'a marriage. They just wanted to do their part. When people acted like that and I got a cool vibe out of them, sometimes I wanted to come back a week later and stage a conversion just to give them good feelings.

Sitting in the shade of a tree in front of an embassy, didn't know which one, I let those pamphlets teach me basic things like the Five Pillars. *Understanding Islam* was printed by the Saudi embassy and provided sweet one-paragraph missionary answers to questions like "What do Muslims think about Jesus?" and "How do Muslims treat the elderly?" It seemed mostly harmless.

26.

I imagined Islamic history as a series of concentric circles, like the ripples caused when you toss a stone into a pond. My American Islam with its Western liberalism and black supremacist heterodoxies would have been on the outermost circle; Pakistan was further inward, and Syria was even closer to the center circle. I realized that this was most likely a naïve and overly simplistic way of looking at things, but at first glance it worked. Islam came to Syria just three years after the Prophet's death, with Umar's conquest of Damascus in 635.

As the Islamic territory expanded after Muhammad's death, Mecca and Medina remained the goals of pilgrims, but were too far down the desert Peninsula to function as political capitals. Syria, on the other hand, was in the neighborhood of Egypt, Greece, and Persia, leading to the rise of Damascus as Islam's imperial center. The shifts in political power led to civil wars that became holy wars, and the religion has been wounded ever since.

Modern Syria was mostly Sunni, but ruled by the Alawis, an offshoot of the Shi'as. The Sunni-Shi'a thing is usually explained as a difference in beliefs over the succession of the Prophet: Sunnis wanted to elect a caliph, and the Shi'as believed in hereditary rule. That was the way I first understood it, but now wished that our schism had been that meaningful.

Abu Bakr was elected and sworn in as caliph by a handful of Muslims, while Ali—who would have been the rival candidate—was busy washing Muhammad's body for the funeral. Wary of Ali's position as Muhammad's nearest male relative, Abu Bakr quoted Muhammad as saying that prophets left no inheritance, then robbed Ali and Fatima of the Prophet's property and forced them to live on alms while granting property to the widows, who included Abu Bakr's daughter Ayesha.

Abu Bakr designated Umar as his own successor, rather than risk Ali winning an election. When it came time to determine Umar's successor, Umar appointed a group of six men—including Ali—to elect the new leader from among themselves. 'Uthman won and became caliph, but aggravated old Arab tribal beefs that would split the community. Ali was a

Hashimite, and 'Uthman was an Umayyad. 'Uthman filled his administration with Umayyads, with the aim of centralizing the new Islamic state.

Since a caliph's right to rule was based on his defense and preservation of Islam, centralization of government also depended on religious unity. Both the religion and empire, however, had spread so fast that they escaped 'Uthman's control. The Qur'an, taught primarily through oral tradition, had developed into variant readings. 'Uthman decided to pull in the reins and issue a "standard" edition of the Qur'an, sending copies to major cities with orders to destroy all other versions. The move disenfranchised reciters and teachers of the Qur'an who had been teaching the text as they knew it. Following the precedent set by Abu Bakr in the Ridda Wars, 'Uthman declared that anyone who opposed his Qur'an was an apostate. Muslims came from throughout the empire to Medina to protest outside 'Uthman's home, and the protests climaxed with 'Uthman's murder.

Many Umayyads fled Medina for fear that rage against 'Uthman's administration would lead to a clan war, and the remaining leaders in Medina elected Ali the new caliph. The election was opposed by 'Uthman's cousin Mu'awiyya, the governor of Syria, who claimed that the Umayyads had been underrepresented in the election. Ali ignored Mu'awiyya's demands that 'Uthman's killers be punished, and set about purging the government posts of Umayyads appointed by 'Uthman.

Ayesha raised an army against Ali, but was defeated and taken captive. A year later, Mu'awiyya led a Syrian revolt and won. Mu'awiyya declared himself the new caliph and moved power to his own base in Damascus. Ali was brained with a poison-tipped sword by a member of the Kharijites, a third party in the dispute.

Before Mu'awiyya's death, he proclaimed the next caliph to be his son Yazid, who would negotiate with Ali's son Hasan for allegiance and then slaughter Hasan's brother Husayn. With the ascent of Yazid, the ummah now had a royal family.

Islam, traumatized by the wars, was broken, and the division brought by political and tribal rivalries would grow into religious differences. The winners and losers understood their world and religion with two separate histories, two sets of authorities, two canons of text. The winners, the Sunnis, viewed themselves as the legitimate heirs to the Prophet and his companions. For the losing party of Ali, the Shi'as, Husayn's slaughter at Karbala was only a continuation of what Abu Bakr had started: the robbery and degradation of Muhammad's family.

Shi'ism became the official Islam of Persia with the ascent of Shah Isma'il, first ruler of the Safavid dynasty. Coming to power at a time when devotion to Ali was already popular among the people, Shah Isma'il used Shi'a identification to build his state and rally support against his Sunni rival, the Ottoman Empire. In the process, he widened the religious divide between Sunni and Shi'a: he commanded the public cursing of Abu Bakr, Umar, and 'Uthman (as early Umayyad caliphs had cursed Ali), supported ritual expressions of grief for Husayn, and instructed his state-appointed scholars to make frequent mentions of Ali and Husayn in sermons. By encouraging pilgrimage to Shi'a shrines within Persian territory, Isma'il made his kingdom the center of its own religious universe, and less dependent on the Ottomans who controlled Mecca.

Isma'il even instituted a change in the call to prayer, inserting an additional line declaring Ali to be the friend of God. Prior to his decree, the practice was marginal among Shi'a Muslims, with scholars questioning its validity. In declaring the change to be compulsory, Isma'il established the adhan as a pledge of allegiance to Shi'a Islam—and by extension, to himself against Sunni empires. I liked to say *Ashadu anna Aliyyun wali'Allah*—it felt good, especially after building with the Ali-loving malangs in Pakistan—but did it matter where that came from? It's a hard question when you turn on the news and see the battlefield still burning. The Ottomans and Safavids are both off the map, but the land that once lay between them, conquered and reconquered and occupied Iraq, still hosted their war with Sunni and Shi'a death squads and men and women strapped with dynamite.

It ate me up that I had backed out of pilgrimage to Karbala, that I'd face this history from Syria and not Iraq, but Husayn rested in both countries. While his mutilated body remained at Karbala where the shit went down, his head was carried to Damascus and presented to Yazid. The head was once Yazid's trophy, but now sits in a shrine in the Umayyad Mosque, and no one knows where Yazid is buried, he's just lost in the dirt.

27.

Sitting on the plane, waiting to take off, I read a du'a from *Fortress of the Muslim* for the traveler starting a journey. In English it said:

> Allah is the Most Great. Allah is the Most Great. Allah is the Most Great. Glory is to him who has provided this for us though we could never have had it by our efforts. Surely, unto our Lord we are returning. O Allah, we ask you on this our journey for goodness and piety, and for works that are pleasing to you, O Allah, lighten this journey for us and make its distance easy for us. O Allah, you are our companion on the road and the One in whose care we leave our family. O Allah, I seek refuge in you from this journey's hardships, and from the wicked sights in store and from finding our family and property in misfortune upon returning.

Not everything from the Saudis was bad. I also read a du'a for Sadaf: *I leave you in the care of Allah, as nothing is lost that is in his care.*

28.

The first leg of the journey went from D.C. to Frankfurt. *Fortress of the Muslim* instructed the traveler to say "Allahu Akbar" when going up a hill and "Subhanahu Allah" when going down the other side. I applied that to the ascent and descent of the plane, but on the way down it was hard not to get distracted with Germany outside my window getting closer, cities and autobahns and patchwork farmland and the fact of being somewhere and wanting to jump out and see it. Arriving early in the morning with a twelve-hour layover, I'd have ample time for my German ziyarat mission: to see the mosque where Muhammad Ali had once prayed. I got out of the airport, found a taxi, gave the driver the Nuur Moschee address, and then plunged into Europe, another dumb American with a backpack, how corny.

Nuur Moschee was an Ahmadiyya mosque, which had me thinking that Muhammad Ali might have been keyed into the secret Nation-Ahmadi history, with Master Fard allegedly an Ahmadi; either that or the Greatest was simply above sectarian pettiness. The front of the mosque—they called it a mosque and so do I, this wasn't Pakistan—was white with a modest, unpainted dome and narrow, green-pointed spikes rising up on each side, meant to look like minarets. I entered through the side door and called out "salam alaikum" the desi way. An uncle came out to greet me wearing baggy white pants and no shirt, looking like he lived there. He led me towards the small, eight-sided prayer room with plain, white walls and a light–blue wooden mihrab bearing the same shahadah that all Muslims said everywhere. Some plastic chairs placed throughout the room gave evidence of four or five men too old to bend over for prayer. In a masjid this small, that would make a significant portion of the congregation.

It looked like the mosque of a poor community, decorated only with a few green and white party streamers tacked onto the walls, nothing to leave me in awe of the ones who paid for them. But this was the kind of mosque where it'd mean something to see the heavyweight champion of the world in a humble prayer. I felt around the little room for a spot to recognize as the maqam where Muhammad Ali prayed and did my rakats. It would have been a good time to read the Qur'an, but they only had German translations.

Reading the Arabic shahadah on the mihrab, I knew that I found some real peace from mosques, but was it only religion or something else? I thought about it in terms of Pakistan's native heresy, the Ahmadiyyas. The movement was about a century old, so now people are born into it with Ahmadi parents and grandparents and great-grandparents and traditions, but just a few generations ago it was a religion of converts, with every Ahmadi having made the conscious decision to follow Mirza Ghulam Ahmad. Was it for his magnetic charisma or logical arguments? Did/could anyone convert just for belief, or were there social factors—economics or tribal dynamics or colonial-era politics? When I first picked up the *Autobiography of Malcolm X*, I found more than a new way to serve God. My teen rage found expression as something political, an anger at American history and America's actions in the world, and this fatherless boy also found his male hero. There could have been yearnings for spiritual fulfillment and personal growth, but from where I stood politically (Public Enemy lyrics) and socially (misfit at a Catholic high school), I couldn't have answered them with Christianity. Or even Hinduism or Buddhism, alternative religions of my mother's generation, no longer threatening to white Americans. Only Islam could really burn my life down and rebuild it. "Religion" came later.

Last thought on leaving Nuur Moschee: how did Muhammad Ali fit in that little room? Because I imagined him as a giant, like the thirty-foot-tall prophets from Noah's time. I gave salams to the uncle and walked down the street too tired to think straight but too tired to stop walking, eventually drifting into a supermarket and going up and down aisles without a working brain. My eyes scanned the items, but I wasn't really looking at anything. I lurked around long enough for employees to assume that I was unwell, bought some chocolate cracker things and a toothbrush and walked out, finally taking a rest on the grass across from a Holiday Inn. Physical reality—streets, trees, cars—turned out to be pretty much the same as where I had come from, almost like I could just walk home if I wanted.

From Frankfurt I flew to Vienna, and Austrian Airlines felt so Austrian with its Mozart in the speakers and the green and red and blue scheme, green seats and flight staff in red outfits, even red stockings, and powder blue scarves. These were my people, roughly three centuries removed—how can I swim those nine thousand miles? But my people were also the Ottomans who sieged this city.

29.

Flying to Damascus, I remembered wise words from Pakistan: *Just stick to the Qur'an.* I still had the miniature Qur'an from Sadaf's mom in my hand, clutching it tight during turbulence. But the Qur'an was also a political document, and I couldn't separate it from the caliphs who gave it to us. The Sunni narrative of the Qur'an's compilation holds that two years after the Prophet's death, a battle at Yamama resulted in the deaths of numerous Qur'an memorizers. Fearing that more casualties would cause large parts of the text to be lost, Umar suggested to Abu Bakr that the Qur'an be compiled as a written manuscript. Abu Bakr initially shunned the idea as religious innovation: "How dare I do something which Allah's Apostle did not do?" Umar replied, "By Allah, it is something beneficial." So they went to the Prophet's scribe, Zayd ibn Thabit, who raised the same objection but also agreed that it was for the best. Umar and Zayd sat outside the Medina mosque to hear Muslims' recitations, collecting every verse that could be vouched for by at least two people. The verses were transcribed on sheets that remained in the custody of Abu Bakr and Umar. After Umar's death, the sheets were passed to his daughter Hafsa. She handed them over to the new caliph, 'Uthman, who would use them for the first Qur'an to appear in book form.

Problem is, the story contradicts several narratives and cannot be found in the earliest sources. By all appearances, it seems to have been constructed to exclude Ali—who, according to other accounts, had compiled the Qur'an himself—and make the first three Sunni caliphs central to the preservation of Allah's Book.

The Sunni version of the text's history suffered from rumors that parts of the Qur'an had been changed or removed before Abu Bakr's collection. It was said that Umar had remembered multiple verses that couldn't be accepted because he found no witnesses for them, and Ayesha had written a verse on skin which was then eaten by a domestic animal and lost forever. These accounts, which had originally served to prove the urgency of Abu Bakr and Umar's project, would later cast doubt upon 'Uthman's codex, becoming ammunition for Shi'a attacks. Though the Shi'a Imams accepted the 'Uthmanic

Qur'an, Sunnis would in turn accuse Shi'as of universally holding the Qur'an to be an incomplete and altered text.

BELIEF IN THE incorruptibility of the Qur'an has nearly become a third component of the shahadah. *I bear witness that there is no god but God, Muhammad is the Messenger of God, and 'Uthman's Qur'an is right and exact.* To suggest otherwise amounts to apostasy, but it wasn't always like that; the early Muslims engaged in debate over the Qur'an that would be inconceivable today. Imam Malik, founder of the Maliki school of Islamic law, held the view that no less than seventy verses were missing from the ninth sura in 'Uthman's Qur'an. The collections of Ibn 'Abbas, Ubayy, and Abu Musa contained two entire suras that 'Uthman omitted. Ibn Mas'ud's Qur'an was missing the suras al-Fatiha, al-Falaq, and an-Nas, while including words or whole phrases gone from the official version, and there were claims of numerous verses deleted or changed by Sunnis because they mentioned Ali.

My Qur'an was a token of the Prophet's experience. Not the miracle itself, just a souvenir of the miracle. The words had once been the center of a power struggle, and what we had now was a text handed down from the winners. That was how it always worked. Early Christians fought each other, and their fights were only settled by born-again Emperor Constantine, who gathered all the bishops together for a conference because he feared instability in his kingdom.

I released the Qur'an onto my fold-out tray. It was the Qur'an of caliphs, the Qur'an of power, the only Qur'an that could last this long. If there was ever a Qur'an of poor people, or slaves, or women, or mukhannathun, we've lost it.

30.

For early Christians, the schisms that required imperial intervention dealt with the true nature of Jesus, whether he was God or man or man-God and how to properly understand the contradictions. Jesus was the proof of God on earth, the appearance of God among men.

The Muslim conquest of Damascus marked Islam's meeting the world; and as Muslims encountered the same heritage of Greek philosophy that moved Christian debate on Jesus, they entered into similar discussion of their own Christ—not Muhammad, just a man born and dead, but Islam's real Christ, God's Word, the Qur'an. Was the text created or eternal? If God's Word was created, did this mean that a part of God was temporary and limited? If the book was eternal, would this make it an idol beside God? In both religions, the debate was won by those who argued against createdness. Christ was an eternal part of the Trinity, and the Qur'an existed before time itself. The Word, whether manifested as a virgin-born son or a book, was everlasting like God, case closed, monotheism reconciled.

With the Book inseparable from the Author, it became impossible to question the Qur'an's compilation as earlier Muslims had. I took my miniature Qur'an out of its box and flipped the pages with my thumb, squinting at the unreadable print. I thought of Sadaf and the verse that she wore around her neck and her mom reading the Qur'an not just for knowledge or guidance, but as a ritual act in its own right. And I thought of the verses found on the walls of mosques and homes, verses that I said in prayer. My script for dealing with Allah.

No one who said, "Just look to the Qur'an" could really live that out. Scholars would say that while standing in front of bookshelves lined with hadith collections and histories and commentaries; they weren't coming to God's Word empty-handed.

What do you do when a verse confuses you? Scriptures lead to more questions than answers; did the universe *emanate* from Allah, or did he actively *create* it? Do I find the answer in Ibn Sina or al-Ghazali's response to Ibn Sina? We let the great scholars become Allah's co-authors and implant themselves into the Qur'an, along with all the other books we've ever read and our life experiences and whatever, whoever it was that taught us how to understand books. The Qur'an has a history, and *you* have a history, and these paths brought you together and that's what makes the Qur'an what it is when it sits in front of you on the little wooden stand. It's not about arguing whether the Qur'an is the word of Allah; the question doesn't mean anything. And it's not that the Qur'an is unable to stand alone as the source material for Islam; the Qur'an can't even stand alone as the Qur'an. There are millions of Qur'ans, billions of Qur'ans. To pretend like I had the right one seemed kind of, I don't know, dickish.

> Songs are there for people, to be used by people, in any way they want to use them. It makes me happy to see the amount of different interpretations you can get from one song and one set of words.
>
> —PJ HARVEY

The tradition allowed me to hope for an Allah as cool about his own songs, his suras, as PJ Harvey. The father of my Sufi literary criticism, Ibn 'Arabi, said that all possible meanings drawn from the Qur'an were Allah's intention. Rather than a singular message to be accepted and followed by everyone in the same way, the Qur'an contains infinite meanings but only gives you what you are ready to see. The book becomes a mirror of our own intentions and limitations: whether you want to be a good person or an asshole, the Qur'an will give it to you. Laury used Ibn 'Arabi to deal with one of the toughest verses, 4:34, which allowed men to beat their wives.

The idea of infinite meanings also meant that someone could dig deep into the words and pull out something bizarre—as one scholar called Ibn 'Arabi's reading of sura Nuh, "At best, reckless, and at worst, flagrantly heretical." I read Ibn 'Arabi's Nuh commentary on the flight to Damascus, the city where he wrote it. Every chapter in his *Bezels of Wisdom* was centered on a prophet, and the Nuh (Noah) chapter built on the sura named for him. Ibn 'Arabi saw the flood as an allegory but sided *against* Noah: the pagans wouldn't submit to Noah's black-and-white religion because they had something better, an elevated awareness of God, and chose instead to drown in the sea of divine knowledge. For Ibn Taymiyya, Ibn 'Arabi only proved the mischief and danger of Sufism—the man was lost in his own ego, twisting his religion so far that he said the exact opposite of the book's clear meaning. The Qur'an said that truth stands free from error; but it also said that wherever you turned, there was God's Face. To Ibn 'Arabi, there couldn't be clear meaning in a world that manifested each of God's Attributes, with all things in creation just signs and signifiers of the Creator and thus Allah gives you an infinity of mixed signals every second. How can Allah be the Abaser and Exalter and the Judge and Protecting Friend all at once?

If the Face was everywhere, how could you comprehend it?

Muhammad's miracle was to pass through the complexities and paradoxes to receive the full Face, but the rest of us were left to our own devices. The ordinary believer, wrote Ibn 'Arabi, "believes only in a deity he has created in himself, since a deity of 'beliefs' is a construction. They see only themselves and their own constructions within themselves." When talk of God agrees with believers' imaginations of him, "they recognize him and affirm him, whereas if presented in any other form, they deny him, flee from him, and treat him improperly, while at the same time imagining that they were acting toward him fittingly." Ibn 'Arabi was allegedly killed by an angry mob after telling a merchant, "The God that you worship is under my feet." My dream dinner guests would be Ibn 'Arabi and Master Fard; they might have some things to share with each other.

What was the day's Mathematics? I arrived in Syria on August 7, and 7 in Supreme Mathematics represented God. When Ibn 'Arabi obtained the meanings of Allah's Names, he realized them all as one Essence, "the object of my contemplation, and this Essence was my very own being." Mystical Sufism and the antimystical Fardiyya weren't a perfect fit, but you could stretch them, take something from one and a little from the other and make them work. I thought about Elijah Muhammad's deification of Fard in the Ibn 'Arabi way: for Elijah to call his teacher "Allah *who appeared in the person of* Master Fard Muhammad" could mean that Fard was Ibn 'Arabi's *insan al-kamil*, the Perfect Man who has mastered human potential and successfully manifested all of the Names.

Ibn 'Arabi had an encounter with the divine at Mecca, when a youth led him into the Ka'ba and then proclaimed, "I am the seventh of what surrounds the universe," which Ibn 'Arabi understood as the seventh Name of Allah's Divine Essence, al-Mutakallim ("He who speaks"). You could actually reconcile that with the Qur'an, as 19:17 says that the Spirit came down to Mary in the form of a "perfect man" (though some translators tried to make *Ruh* mean "angel" instead of "Spirit" to avoid theological awkwardness). Mathematically, 19 was Knowledge Born, and "Born" meant "manifest"; for Allah's Knowledge to become Born meant that he took it from the unseen to the seen, which coincided with the 17: Knowledge God, knowledge *of* God. Unsure of where that stuff would take me, I put Supreme Mathematics and the *Bezels* away and looked out the window at the brown land coming.

31.

"Ibn 'Arabi," I told the taxi driver, and he didn't know what I meant, but then I said "*Muhaiyadeen* Ibn 'Arabi" and he got it, taking me to a green-domed mosque at the foot of the sacred mountain Qasiyun. This version of the shrine, with mausoleum and built-on masjid, was constructed in 1517 by Sultan Selim I after he took Damascus from the Mamluks—part of the military expansion that would eventually bring Mecca and Medina under Ottoman rule. Later sultans maintained the shrine, revering Ibn 'Arabi for his prediction of Ottoman success.

The mausoleum was visible through windows on the mosque stairwell. Face against the glass, I said a du'a for him and for me and also for Laury and went upstairs to the red-carpeted prayer room, where I found the entrance to the mausoleum—with an engraving by a nineteenth-century Ottoman pasha:

> The greatest shaykh, may his secret be sanctified, said, "Every age is dignified by someone unique on account of whom it is exalted. It is I who shall be, for the rest of time, that unique someone."

Damn. It's one thing to believe in what you're doing, but the greatest shaykh, may his secret be sanctified, approached Lil' Wayne levels of arrogance. If he was around today, Ibn 'Arabi might be grimacing at the camera with Allah's Name swinging in platinum from his neck, dropping wisdom from a mouth full of diamonds between sips from a white Styrofoam cup: "Your personal nature seeks its paradise. There is nothing that pertains to a station which God reveals to you that does not greet you with honor, reverence, and exaltation. Cash Money, Young Money, Ibn 'Areezy F-Baby."

The mausoleum was locked, so I joined my brothers for

Maghrib prayer, the whole time thinking about Ibn 'Arabi and
these normal Muslims praying near his body like they did at
Bulleh Shah's tomb, maybe not even aware what a renegade
heretic he was in his time (enough for Ibn Taymiyya to declare
the greatest shaykh, may his secret be sanctified, an apostate).

Ibn Taymiyya condemned Shi'as and Sufis who relied on
esoteric knowledge instead of study grounded in the Qur'an and
Sunna. Ibn 'Arabi drove that car off the cliff, claiming that the
true author of his *Bezels of Wisdom* was the Prophet himself.
Muhammad had come to him in a vision, he said, holding the
book in his hand, telling Ibn 'Arabi to "take it and bring it
to men that they might benefit from it." Ibn 'Arabi accepted
the book, "carried out the wish, made pure my intention, and
devoted my purpose to the publishing of this book just as the
Apostle had laid down, without any addition or subtraction."

"Allahu Akbar," said our imam, and I brought my head up
from the red carpet.

In another vision, Ibn 'Arabi saw a Ka'ba built from alternating gold and silver bricks. The construction of the Ka'ba appeared to be complete, until Ibn 'Arabi turned to the Yemeni
and Syrian corners, finding between them space in two rows
for two missing bricks: a silver brick below, gold above. Ibn
'Arabi felt himself pulled to the Ka'ba, his own body filling that
space as the missing silver and gold. The Ka'ba's last silver brick
represented Ibn 'Arabi's outer form, in line with the law and
teachings brought by Muhammad; the gold was his inner form,
the reflection of Allah. Completing the Ka'ba, Ibn 'Arabi became
the ultimate fulfiller of Islam, the Seal of Muhammadan Saints.

I couldn't tell if Ibn 'Arabi was a Five or Ten Percenter. If his
claim to sainthood subverted the orthodox powers, you could
call him a Poor Righteous Teacher, counted among the Five;
but if he used these visions to sell his knowledge and make
mental slaves of others, then he belonged in the Ten Percent, the
bloodsuckers of the poor, no better than the rigid conservatives.

For Ibn Taymiyya, sainthood was bullshit, merely a way for people to claim prophethood without using the word. I could see where Ibn 'Arabi was coming from and felt thankful for imagination finding its way into Islam, but I could also see why Muslims like Ibn Taymiyya feared creativity. If you get creative, you get strange, and Ibn 'Arabi was walking a fine line on dangerous ground. Entertaining ideas like that, there were too many chances for the Devil to whisper in his ear. You'd have to be a real saint not to get corrupted.

Allahu Akbar. I sat up, silently mouthed the shahadah and stuck up my index finger like I was supposed to do, prayed for the Prophet's family—bless the descendents of Muhammad like you blessed the descendents of Abraham—and greeted the angels after the imam, then went back into my own thoughts. I was in Syria, I made it.

32.

"He who claims to know that God is his Creator without being perplexed," said Ibn 'Arabi, "this is the evidence of his ignorance." Ibn 'Arabi was okay with paradox and confusion, because if Allah was manifesting all of his Attributes at once in the same created universe, who could comprehend it? Ibn 'Arabi said that creation was God's way of revealing himself, that the Attributes would "shine through" the world and therefore God was in everything and only God's existence was real.

Ibn 'Arabi's Islam was bigger than Islam, and he stood against the rational philosophers and theologians who tried to squeeze Allah into definitions. The cool thing about Ibn 'Arabi was that if you really got into his ideas, you might leave the man behind, no *greatest shaykh* or seal of nothing.

Ibn Taymiyya believed that when the Qur'an described

God's hands and feet, it meant that God actually had hands and feet, even if they existed beyond our comprehension. For Ibn Taymiyya, the worst offense was anything that compromised the proper separation between Creator and creation, and Ibn 'Arabi's idea that God existed in everything seemed to suggest that everything was God.

Ibn Taymiyya was also buried in Damascus, and I wanted to pay respect at his grave, though he would have denounced me as a qabriyyun for it. Even if he seemed to be all kinds of unlikeable and his reading of Islam was regarded as the foundation for Wahhabism, I needed an inner Ibn Taymiyya voice to keep my inner Ibn 'Arabi in check. My personal Islam was an octagon in which the two of them swung on each other and went for gogoplata chokes.

Funny thing about Ibn Taymiyya: the man was actually a Sufi and studied with a shaykh. Rejecting the pursuit of advanced esoteric knowledge or higher stations of union with God, he at least saw the good in Sufism as an exercise in ego destruction. After his death in 1328, they buried him in the Sufi cemetery near his mother and brother. The funeral was attended by two hundred thousand men and fifteen thousand women, who fought to collect relics from the procession. Though Ibn Taymiyya had denounced worship even of the Prophet's tomb, his own grave would become the subject of miraculous tales and receive visits from Syrian faithful in hope of blessings. It was like a reversal of Bulleh Shah, the heretic whose shrine became semiorthodox; another reminder that once you're dead, it doesn't belong to you anymore.

My first full day in Damascus, I found a taxi and said "Moos-tash-fa francais" to the driver. French hospital. In the early twentieth century, the French colonists destroyed the Sufi cemetery to build a hospital. The only tombs that survived were those of Ibn Taymiyya and Ibn Kathir, another scholar loved by the Wahhabs. There were two stories explaining their preservation. One said that Syrian workers had refused to destroy Ibn Taymiyya's tomb, and the other claimed that Ibn Sa'ud intervened—another irony, since Ibn Sa'ud destroyed all kinds of tombs and historic sites in the name of religious purity. Dropped off at the Saint Louis hospital, I could only walk around asking random janitors and nuns if they knew anything: *Maqbarat Ibn Taymiyya? Shaykh ul-Islam?* Supposedly the grave was in a courtyard near the maternity ward, so I snooped around but saw no evidence of the shaykh. Every corner was occupied by a tree or dumpster.

The grave must have been destroyed, I thought; the modern semisecular Syrian state had no need for him or his fruit. Bashar and the ruling elite were all Alawis, who were considered out of bounds for their excessive Ali love. The Alawis began with a Shi'a who had declared himself representative of the Eleventh Imam, but retained elements of ancient Syrian religion and even borrowed from Christianity after the Crusades, celebrating Christmas, the Epiphany, and Pentecost and upholding a strange trinity in which Ali was the Meaning and Essence, Muhammad was the Exoteric Name, and Salman al-Farsi the Gate to Ali's Esoteric Essence. Ibn Taymiyya had denounced the Alawis for allegedly worshiping Ali as God and drinking wine as Ali's transubstantiated essence, as well as believing in reincarnation, and not even the mainstream Shi'as accepted them.

Syria had another Shi'a offshoot that became its own religion: the Druze, who followed al-Hakim the sixth Fatimid caliph in Egypt from a thousand years ago. Al-Hakim was a maniac who altered the adhan, banned chess and grape eating, ordered Jews and Christians to wear one red shoe and one black shoe with black belts and black turbans, forced everyone in Cairo to work at night and sleep during the day, and plotted to steal the bodies of Muhammad, Abu Bakr, and Umar, and bring them to Egypt. At age twenty-five in 1021, he rode a donkey into the Muqattam hills and was never seen again. Someone found his donkey covered in blood, but the man was gone like Master Fard. Ibn Taymiyya dismissed the Druze as non-Muslims, which in that setting would have legitimized violence against them as apostates.

The French partitioned colonial Syria and briefly assigned the Druze and Alawi their own states, but in modern Syria, everyone seemed to get along. The worst thing for Syria's pluralism (and Alawi rulers) would be the Sunni majority getting into Ibn Taymiyya, so Bashar must have razed the tomb to prevent shrine-hating Wahhabs from having their own shrine and rallying point in Damascus. Or the French Christian hospital just wanted to put a bench where the grave was and Wahhabs today couldn't appeal to Bashar about it.

I remembered a similar adventure in America, when I drove to Chicago in search of Elijah Muhammad's grave, wandering across a vast cemetery with no hope and no help from the office (due to an agreement with the "Moozlems," they told me) until a car pulled up to me and the window rolled down and there was Elijah Muhammad's grandson behind the wheel. I lingered around the Saint Louis maternity ward for a while, waiting to see if the guy mopping the floor would turn out to be a descendent of Ibn Taymiyya with keys to a secret room in the basement, but he wasn't.

My Saudi-printed *Fortress of the Muslim* contained an invocation to be made at graves. If I couldn't find Ibn Taymiyya's remains, maybe I'd go to the old Citadel where he was imprisoned and read it there. But the bones must have been in this ground somewhere, so I could just pick a spot and read and let it count as the grave. I whipped out the book: "Peace be upon you, people of this abode, from among the believers and those who are Muslims, and we, by the Will of Allah, shall be joining you. May Allah have mercy on the first of us and the last of us. I ask Allah to grant us and you strength." Amin.

Walking nowhere in particular with a can of Mirinda soda, drinking through a straw, I noticed a bunch of girls and realized that equating all Arab Islam with Saudi Islam was a mistake. Syria seemed relatively chill about girls, okay with their existence in a way that I wouldn't expect from the Wahhabs. They dressed all kinds of ways in Damascus, some in sleeveless tops and designer jeans and some in hijabs but still wearing club clothes just as glittery and tight. I had nothing for them, just missing an American Muslim girl who didn't dress like that—neither hijab nor club gear—and I was an American Muslim boy with no Dolce & Gabbana button-ups like all the slick sunglasses-and-gelled-hair boys, I could never be cool in Damascus.

Then, on my right, in the distance toward the hills, a green dome stood out among the colorless buildings. Ibn 'Arabi.

Taking taxis around town, I never had any sense of where things were and couldn't have known that Ibn 'Arabi was this close to Ibn Taymiyya's demolished grave. It felt like the right thing to turn and walk uphill back to the mausoleum.

Looking again in the window on the stairwell, this time I saw light coming in from the other side: the door was open! I went upstairs and made wudhu in the central fountain. Above me, the courtyard's tent roof left the sky partially open, allowing a view of the minaret towering outside. Young men with religious beards sat in a corner reading Qur'an, and in another corner a man with Down's syndrome twirled his zikr beads, and old men sat in chairs just chilling, and another group of men were having tea and olives. I said salam and headed for the bones.

The tomb was encased in what looked like a greenhouse under glass chandeliers and ceiling fans. I walked around to the other side and picked up a big Qur'an with light-blue pages and dark-blue margins. The bookmark was at the start of ar-Rahman, an early Meccan sura that never specifically mentioned Allah, referring only to "your Lord" and "ar-Rahman."

A married couple came in and touched the glass around the tomb. I watched them make their salat and du'as and wondered how I looked when I did that stuff. Why did I come to these things? Was it for a real belief in their spiritual power? Did I believe in holy places? Did I believe in relics? In 1305 Ibn Taymiyya tried to remove a Muhammad footprint from Damascus and was chased away by angry crowds who called him an apostate. I wouldn't have been a prick like him, but I could at least see where he was coming from.

If Ibn 'Arabi was right and all of creation manifested Allah's Attributes, then all of creation was holy and illuminated with the Presence. But you can't put your attention on the entire universe at once, so holy sites were just highlighters, points of focus. For Ibn Taymiyya, however, they corrupted the purity of tawhid. If he was right, then pure tawhid was kind of lame, too abstract to have any emotional pull or produce symbols.

I stayed in that room a long time and tranced out on the sounds of the ceiling fans. When I left, I took a different door and found myself on a busy market street. It was closer to noon but not as hot as when I came in.

33.

Learning that Saint Louis wasn't the only French-built hospital in Damascus, I went to the university hospital and asked a doctor, who led me to an office where we could see the tomb from the window. He told me how to get there and I ran behind the building, pushing through the ungroomed trees and past some noisy construction work.

There was no mausoleum with ceiling fans or glass chandeliers or green dome or anything, just the tomb in a little iron cage and weeds growing from cracks in the stone. Ibn Taymiyya's headstone was broken up and left in chunks before the fragment still standing, with no one who cared enough to fix it or even get some shears and clean up the vegetation. Rusty crossbars formed an X over the tomb. Outside the cage was another tomb, probably Ibn Kathir's, but I couldn't tell.

Yes, Ibn Taymiyya was harsh and mean and the great traveler Ibn Batutta believed him to be mentally ill, and he made takfir on just about everyone. But I tried to see him and Ibn 'Arabi in the worlds that made them. Ibn 'Arabi was born in 1165 in Muslim Spain, at a time when Muslims were the rising superpower. The world that made Ibn 'Arabi was an ummah at the height of its cultural power, Islam energized by its encounters with neoplatonism, Persian mysticism, and Hindu cosmologies. He was chased out of Cairo but found royal patronage at Damascus, where he completed his *Meccan Revelations* and the *Bezels of Wisdom*. Though his religion was strange, he kept a good relationship with the Ottoman sultan.

Ibn Taymiyya was born about twenty years after Ibn 'Arabi's death, in what is now Turkey, and came to Damascus with his family—his father would give sermons at the Umayyad Mosque—as a refugee of the Mongol invasions. The Mongols under Timurlane claimed a nominal Muslim identity, but Islam didn't appear to mean much when they slaughtered other Muslims. Perhaps worse than the Mongols' hypocrisy was that of the scholars, who offered no resistance against them, no call to jihad. The Islam of the scholars was weak, Ibn Taymiyya observed, because they had abandoned the Qur'an and Sunna for local superstitions, pagan practices, alien philosophies, and their own innovations. Everything was fucked, and Ibn Taymiyya found the answer in a restoration of Islam to its former clarity, an Islam of singular purpose with knowledge of right and the mandate to correct wrong. The world needed to make sense again. So yeah, God talked about his feet because he really had feet, no time to dick around with riddles while the cities are burning. The anger and desperation of Ibn Taymiyya looked much like the pain that inspires revivalists today: the idea that when people had their religion right, things were better—Muslims had dignity in the world and food on the table—and the current state of degradation serves only as a sign of how far the believers have fallen in God's view.

Ibn Taymiyya went on trial to face accusations of anthropomorphism in both Cairo and Damascus, and was imprisoned in Damascus for his attacks on pilgrimage to graves. His last legal battle was over fatwas he had made on divorce oaths, which led to a five-month bid. He was willing to stand and suffer for his religion, I had to give him that much.

It was hard to see, but Ibn Taymiyya and Ibn 'Arabi actually came from the same place, if you go back far enough. They both started with belief in Allah's absolute unity; it just led them to different conclusions. For Ibn Taymiyya, tawhid called us to respect the separation, because Allah was beyond this created world and all that it contained; for Ibn 'Arabi, tawhid meant that nothing could really exist *but* Allah, that the Oneness of God meant a oneness of creation within God. The two Muslims occupied far sides of the universe from each other, but it was all Islam.

There was another thing that I took from Ibn Taymiyya, which I couldn't have gotten from Ibn 'Arabi. The open-ended readings of Ibn 'Arabi gave me the Qur'an, but Ibn Taymiyya's idol-smashing gave me the Prophet. Ibn 'Arabi said some mystical spookiness that elevated Muhammad to an eternal semi-Christ, but I needed just the opposite: a Muslim to remind me that there's no god but Allah, and messengers die. Ibn Taymiyya never said "shit on him," but he wouldn't make Muhammad into more than a human being.

I hoped that if I could explain my rebellions to Ibn Taymiyya—that I didn't want a Superman or a Christ, I wanted Allah alone—there was a small sliver of a chance that he could

at least see my good intention and count me as ignorant instead
of a willful deviant. Ibn Taymiyya did say that the mistake of
allowing an apostate to live was better than the mistake of
killing a Muslim. I felt sorry for my brother in his neglected
ugly tomb behind a hospital, but this humbling place matched
Islam as he lived it. No hero worship, no Infallible Imams,
no miracles at blessed shrines, nothing to worship but God,
no sources but the Qur'an and Sunna, and no sacred place to
visit but the House in Mecca. It looked as though Allah had
rewarded both Ibn Taymiyya and Ibn 'Arabi with the graves
that they wanted.

34.

Ibn Taymiyya hated Shi'as and even defended Yazid the tyrant
Husayn-killer as fulfilling hadiths that would promise him
paradise, but I still wanted to see the city's numerous Shi'a
shrines. Awakened by the adhan for Fajr, I prayed and hit the
streets, finding a driver and telling him "Sayyeda Zaynab."

Ali's daughter now rested in a silver shrine, the walls around
it covered in shards of mirrors that made the whole big room
glitter. People were mobbing the shrine to caress it and then
rub the blessings on their faces. Outside, the golden dome and
blue tiles made it look Persian to me, while the courtyard was
filled with ziyarat groups gathering around their guides who
cried while telling the story. Zaynab was at Karbala for all of
it, then forced to march to Damascus in chains and unveiled, in
the same procession as the head of her brother. I didn't know
what the guides were saying, but I knew enough of Zaynab
and her brave words to Yazid while Husayn's blood was on his
hands and the flesh of martyrs fell from his mouth: *O Yazid! Do
you think that we have become humble and despicable owing*

to the martyrdom of our people and our own captivity? As you have blocked all the paths for us, and we have been made captives and are being taken from one place to another, do you think that Allah has taken away his blessings from us? Do you think that by killing the godly persons you have become great and respectable and the Almighty looks at you with special grace and kindness?

They cried and I cried. It was said to be in this city, while locked away in Yazid's palace, that Zaynab started the practice of lamentations and matam for her brother. The establishment of matam may have been influenced by Christian self-mortification, but Syria had seven thousand years of culture before there were Christians: layers of history piled on by Aramaeans, Assyrians, Babylonians, Persians, the empires of Cyrus and Alexander. Not too far from Damascus, at the sanctuary of Aphrodite in Byblos, mourners of Adonis once lamented his killing by a wild boar. They offered sacrifices to Adonis, shaved their heads, and cried for him while beating their chests.

Back on the street, I found a shop selling religious pictures and trinkets and bought a strip of pictures that made Islam look exciting and dramatic but also kind of insane: Husayn holding up his dead baby Ali-e-Asghar with a long arrow in the baby's neck, blood streaming down Husayn's arms, birds flying around them with flowers in their beaks, sharing the grief, except Husayn looks completely at peace, he's only offering this dead baby to Allah; a pious portrait of Husayn's father Ali and Fatima (her face turned away) holding baby Husayn, with the modern Ka'ba and its door glowing, since Ali was born inside it; another image of Ali in his green turban, bloody wound on his forehead, and he's got his own sword and staff and flowing cape and he's shirtless and completely jacked, looking like a roided-up Persian warrior from *300*.

35.

Was this okay in the "Islamic" sense? In the tradition of Abraham and Moses, Muhammad put an end to idolatry in Mecca, and images were supposed to be forbidden.

In its formative centuries, Christianity also followed Judaism's rejection of images. Important figures in the early church, such as Origen, Tertullian, and Clement of Alexandria, condemned sacred art for two reasons: first, as a knee-jerk reaction to idolatry; second, because human beings were incapable of doing justice to God or even Christ with visual depiction. Pope Gregory I softened the church's view of images; nearly a thousand years before translation and the printing press would make the Bible more accessible, he considered sacred art to be the "Bible of the laity."

The acceptance of statues into Christian practice took place as converts were making the religion less Jewish in character and more Greek and Roman. Likewise, as Islam spread beyond the Arab world, it encountered cultures that did not hold the same taboos regarding images. It is in these cultures, such as Iran and Turkey, that we find paintings of the Prophet, often with his head surrounded by golden flame (the equivalent of a halo). His face is usually veiled, but sometimes they show it, and he looks more or less like an ordinary man. Sometimes calligraphers would manipulate the shapes of words and letters to form an image of the Prophet's face, just vague enough to avoid being called a picture.

I have a picture of Muhammad as a black man. It comes from the Nuwaubians, once known as the Nubian Islamic Hebrews, an American sect that originated in Brooklyn in the 1960s. I love my Nuwaubian Muhammad, but am glad that the practice of painting the Prophet never became fully accepted. Because visual depictions of the Prophet are so rare, I have no conditioned image of him. Asked to close my eyes and picture Jesus, I see not a Middle Eastern man but a pale-skinned Florentine Italian, the Christ of my grandfather's church. Asked to picture Moses, I might see Charlton Heston playing the role. Imagining Muhammad, I draw a blank. I can't tell you the shape of his nose, the length of his beard, or his complexion or height or weight. Even in my dream, when I was embraced by the Prophet, Ali, Hasan, and Husayn, none of them had faces.

36.

The store also sold Ayatollah Khomeini pictures, so I bought a framed photo of him holding a tray of drinks; no big black turban, just a modest kufi, and it almost didn't look like him.

I found my taxi again and asked the driver to show me Sayyeda Sakina, the daughter of Husayn who was only four years old at Karbala. Her family found her at her father's headless body, having fallen asleep on his chest like she used to do. Yazid's army marched her to Karbala, where she was shown the head and died in prison. South Asian art depicted her in chains and jasmine garlands. Her real name was Fatima, but we now called her Sakina, which literally means "peace" or "tranquility." There was some older, deeper stuff to the title, but I hadn't worked that out.

Her shrine was almost identical to Zaynab's, but contained a smaller, child-size tomb behind the gilded grille. I touched the grille and then rubbed the blessings on my face. My driver came inside and noted all the women crying in black abayas. *Irani*, he said. They came to Damascus in busloads to wail at the shrines. Zaynab and Sakina were like female Husayns for their suffering, which basically made them female Christs. The stories were too much, the tears pushing out of me in little spasms.

Back in the car, the driver suggested another shrine.

"Maryam," he said, forming a cross with his fingers.

"Maryam umm Isa?" I asked. Mary, mother of Jesus?

He nodded. She had a shrine too, just outside of Damascus at Sayednaya in a sand-colored convent on top of a hill. He brought me there, and I couldn't know the story until I did research later, but I walked up the steps and joined the Syrian Muslim pilgrims and European Christian pilgrims, everyone revering her together under the big crosses and Christian icons. The focus of the shrine was a painting of Mary allegedly made by St. Luke. Besides the images filling the walls, it looked like a Muslim shrine, even with the cut-out tin feet and hands that I saw at the Dolay Shah shrine in Gujurat and prayer strings tied onto gates by the faithful as reminders to God—they were just white instead of green.

I stood in the dark little room where a guy dipped bits of cotton in oil and gave them to visitors who crossed themselves and took the relics home. If I knew the ayats regarding Mary— she's mentioned more in the Qur'an than the New Testament—I would have said them. Instead, I just softly recited the short sura al-Ikhlas about how no one begets God and God doesn't beget, and then hoped that the Christians couldn't hear me since I meant no disrespect.

One of the walls showed Mary visiting the Roman emperor Justinian. The man slaughtered pagans, burned and drowned Manichaeans, and prohibited Jews from praying in Hebrew, but the Virgin still thought Justinian worthy to see her in a vision in 547—first as a gazelle, then an icon—as she told him to build this shrine. The shrine was really just another monument to a king like everything turned out to be, but still had a good feeling to it, and I liked honoring Mary with both Muslims and Christians.

It was also cool that for all this pilgrimage to saints and Ahlul-Bayt people, the first prophet that I made ziyarat to was Mary. If you look at the description of her in the Qur'an, she qualifies. Mary has a direct encounter with Allah, who tells her to preach Islam, and endows her with a miracle (giving birth as a virgin); what more do you want? If Allah gave her that and we still won't call her a prophet, then yeah, Islam is anti-woman, discussion over.

37.

Islam was an Abrahamic religion, claiming a common heritage with Judaism and Christianity, and I always knew it, but I hadn't felt it until Syria. In South Asia, chugging Shiva's bhang and visiting peacocks at shrines to Sufi poets, Islam felt more Hindu. Syrian Islam was so Biblical that I could take a taxi to Mount Qasiyun and tell the driver, "Qabil wa Habil."

Cain and Abel.

In the hills surrounding Damascus was the Cave of Blood, site of the first murder in human history. The belief that it happened in Damascus came from Jewish tradition; but for the Greeks, Qasiyun was where Hermes killed Askos the Giant.

The driver took me up steep streets, and sometimes I doubted that we'd make it. The streets were barely wide enough for one car, so trucks coming downhill gave us tough choices, to back up and let them through or try to squeeze past beyond belief.

"Your name?" he asked me.

"Michael," I said.

"Michael?" He added something that ended with "television, Michael Jackson!" I smiled. Then he said, "Michael Knight!" as in the David Hasselhoff *Knight Rider* hero, and I laughed. He took me as far as the car could go, and then I'd have to hike up the alleys, following the signs for *Abrain* (Forty) on buildings until finding the long line of cement steps leading up to the mosque.

The steps, I had heard, were a recent addition by the government as part of a nationwide celebration of Syrian heritage. The climb was probably a lot harder before. Running up the steep zig-zag-zigs, I got all sweaty and dizzy and felt ready to start tripping on Allah.

A young man with scant facial hair was sitting at the entrance. After I greeted him and explained that I was an American Muslim, he led me through a room ornamented with calligraphy banners and hanging Zulfikar swords to the cave, which had been built into a small mosque with two mihrabs. The mihrab to the right of the doorway, he told me, was the maqam where Abraham had prayed. The one to the left was the maqam of Khidr.

I first prayed at Abraham's maqam. This mountain was where he watched the stars setting and realized the Oneness of God, the moment of enlightenment that would start the paths to Judaism, Christianity, and Islam. Then I went over to Khidr's maqam and prayed where he prayed.

Muslims disagreed about Khidr's nature, debating whether he was a prophet or saint or perhaps something not human, maybe an angel or creature of which only Allah has knowledge. Khidr the Green Man has been spotted numerous times through the centuries; there were shrines to him in Palestine, Turkey, Kuwait, and South Asia. Qom, Iran, became a center of pilgrimage and Shi'a theological activity after a shaykh there witnessed Khidr appearing with the Mahdi. Khidr reminded me of Master Fard, a mystery man with no known origin or fate.

Secular scholars suggest that Khidr was a pre-Islamic figure, linked with St. George, who himself was a merging of the historical St. George with pre-Christian gods—possibly Tarhun the Hittite weather god, or Sabazios, a Thraco-Phrygian vegetation/fertility god. Devotees of Sabazios used to carve images of his hands to be placed on stands and procession poles, like the Fatima hands that I bought in Pakistan.

St. George killed a dragon that had guarded a spring, pond, or lake—like Baal-Hadad, who had killed a serpent at the Tree of Life. His feast day, April 23, connected him to Baal-Hadad-Zeus cults of northern Syria. In Eastern Europe, St. George processions included a "Green George" character who was dunked in water to bring rain for the next summer.

A shrine to Khidr the Green Man was often honored as a St. George shrine and vice versa. Some equated Khidr, immortal guardian of the fountain of life, with Utnapishtim, a character from the Epic of Gilgamesh who resides at the "mouth of the waters" and had been given eternal life. Even Ibn Taymiyya, who accused everyone of blending pagan myths and legends with their Islam, believed in Khidr enough to consider whether he was still alive. He arrived at the conclusion that Khidr was a mortal man and had died, but many considered Khidr immortal and believed that he and the prophet Ilyas made hajj to Mecca every year. It was even said that if you mentioned his name, you should greet him with peace, since he may be in the room with you. When we talked on the phone at night, Sadaf maintained a rule against discussion of Khidr or jinns, because then she couldn't sleep.

Islamic scholars, confronted with the popularity of Khidr in local folk religion, absorbed him into Islam by linking him to an unnamed figure in the Qur'an, a mystical teacher of Moses described in the eighteenth sura. God sends Moses a servant "on whom We had bestowed Mercy from Ourselves and whom We had taught knowledge from Our own Presence." They meet at the junction of two seas. Moses asks Khidr to accept him as a student, but Khidr tells the prophet that they are holders of two different kinds of knowledge. Moses pleads with Khidr, who finally accepts him on the condition that Moses does not ask questions or challenge him.

In their travels together, Khidr does some strange things to confuse the prophet; first he destroys a boat that the two had used, causing Moses to forget his promise and open his mouth.

Moses apologizes to his teacher, and they keep going. Khidr then kills a child and Moses again complains, but again takes it back. Finally, Khidr and Moses come to a town that refuses to host them, and Khidr decides to repair an outer wall that had been damaged. Moses asks Khidr why he'd do that, violating his oath for the third time, and Khidr finally breaks it down for him. Khidr knows what Moses doesn't know; first, that the boat he destroyed was owned by poor fishermen, who would have lost it when the king began confiscating boats for military use. Khidr had only concealed the boat for the fisherman, who could retrieve and repair it later. The murdered child was innocent, but if he lived he would have caused much suffering. Khidr knew that God would replace him with one better. Finally, Khidr repaired the wall at the village of rude people because it was where two orphans had hidden their treasure.

Tired of Moses, Khidr then parts ways with the half-original prophet, leaving him to decipher the meaning of their encounter on his own.

Abraham and Khidr in this cave represented the same battle I internalized with Ibn Taymiyya and Ibn 'Arabi, the *zahir* (apparent) and *batin* (hidden). Abraham himself had no book or even a developed religion, just a primordial proto-Islam, but he was also the distant ancestor of Moses, who brought the Law and killed his people when they failed to uphold it. Khidr did all the wrong things, but with a special knowledge that went above the standard definitions. His path wasn't straight, but it still took him to the right place.

My prayer at Khidr's maqam reached the sitting position and I looked up at the mihrab and realized that even if I was praying to a solo monotheistic Abraham's God, I did so in honor of an idol. Khidr was a god. Syrian folklore attributed thunder alternately to Khidr and St. George (and sometimes Ali) riding a horse across the heavens. The idea that Khidr could have been Utnapishtim further confused the issue, since Utnapishtim was also the original Noah: The council of gods were going to wipe out mankind in a flood, but one of them warned Utnapishtim to build a huge boat and load up his animals.

After I finished my prayers, the cave keeper brought me to a closed-off room that I just thought was the women's section of the mosque, but it revealed an opening in the cave that had been painted black and red.

"They say that this is the spot," he told me, "where Qabil killed Habil. You see the cave—" He pointed to the hole in the cave wall, and I tried to see how deep it went. "When Qabil killed Habil," he continued, "the mountain was very . . . *shock*. You see, its mouth open here." He pointed out the cave's tongue and teeth. "And water came from here," he added, pointing to the cave roof, "but it stopped." The cave's tears.

"Mash'Allah," I coughed out.

"Jibril stopped the mountain," he said, evidenced by the angel's handprint in the cave ceiling. Jibril was the angel Gabriel. He put his hand on it to show me, and then I touched it myself, fitting my fingers into the grooves. "This is what they say," the cave keeper told me, "but Allah knows best."

Then he took me to the upstairs mosque—first a large, bare room with just two shrouded coffins and a flight of stairs. "My family," he said. His family has been maintaining the shrine for two hundred years. I said al-Fatiha over the coffins and went up the stairs to an airless, lightless prayer hall with just two high windows, one with a rattling fan. One man was lying on the floor, lounging against a pile of carpets. Others were making prayers.

Along the qiblah wall I saw exactly forty painted mihrabs. The Mountain of the Forty was the meeting place for the forty Abdals, a subclass within the secret hierarchy of saints who administered the universe. At the top of the hierarchy was the hidden Qutb, so advanced in his knowledge and union with God that these saints revolved around him like planets orbiting the sun. The word *abdal* meant "substitute" and there were hadiths alluding to them: the Prophet had said that at any given time in history, there were forty Muslims sanctified like Abraham, and when one died, he was replaced by another. "Through them," Muhammad explained, "people receive rain and are given help." According to another story, the cave and mosque had been the abode of forty prophets who had gone into hiding with just one piece of bread. Each one offered the bread to another, who in turn refused it and asked his brothers to eat before him, and the prophets kept passing that one piece of bread between them until all forty died of hunger.

Whether for saints or prophets—or maybe the hidden council of scientists who trained Master Fard Muhammad for his mission—I picked a random maqam and prayed, still unsure whether it crossed my Islamic boundaries. With the rattling fan and the sense of what this place might have been and this mihrab like a faceless idol in front of me but *la ilaha illa Allah* plus the dizziness of running up a holy mountain hungry and thirsty, I felt myself thrown down into each prostration. After the prayer I just sat buzzing on the place, cupped my hands, and recited short suras over and over, unable to stop until I noticed the man to my right inching closer to me and starting another set of rakats. I looked around and watched the other men in prayer and figured out what they were doing; the ritual of this mosque was to go down the line, praying at each maqam. So I stood up, walked over to the far end, and started.

Some African brothers in blinding white robes came in and broke into group zikr of holy phrases, Holy Names, shahadahs, and verses from the Qur'an. Sometimes it'd get loud and fast and my own prayers lost all the words, my Arabic verses getting broken up in theirs. At points I couldn't even think at all or keep track of where I was in the prayer, and I'd do added parts of repentance for any error. After finishing the two rakats at each maqam, eighty total, I sat and stared up and down the long line of mihrabs, contemplating a meeting of Abdals in capes and tights like the Justice League, each with special powers.

The Abdals were pretty cool on gender issues. Ibn 'Arabi told the story of a master who, when asked the number of true Abdals, replied, "Forty," and was then asked why he did not say "Forty *men*." The master replied, "Because there are women among them as well." Men and women together in this dark little room, praying side by side? The saints needed an education in proper fiqh.

Why was it always forty? Forty Abdals, forty prophets, forty days in the desert, forty days of the flood. The Prophet was first visited by an angel when he was forty years old and said that whoever memorized forty hadiths would be resurrected among the scholars and judges. Forty was the numerical value of the letter *mim* in his name. Al-Ghazali wrote his *Ihya 'Ulum ad-Din* in forty chapters. The number was all over Islam, but I knew that it didn't start there. St. Augustine was into it, the Jews were into it, and probably someone before them too.

It was also in my American systems. In the Five Percenters' Supreme Mathematics, 4 represented Culture, but some said that you could interpret 4 as Freedom in numbers of 40 or higher; so 40 would be Culture Cipher or Freedom Cipher. Master Fard's longest lesson runs forty questions, ending with, "What will be your reward in regards to the destruction of the Devil?" The answer: "Peace and happiness."

Islamic tradition claimed that Allah spoke to the mountain. When the Crusaders took Damascus in 1148, a shaykh took his companions up to the cave and recited "Behold, we sent it down on the Night of Power" twelve thousand times. Allah then played the role of a Semitic storm god and brought the rain upon Damascus, flooding the streets and drowning the Christians' horses.

I gave my salams and walked out of the mosque, leaving behind the Abdals, the prophets, Gabriel, Cain, Abel, Abraham,

Khidr, Hermes, Askos the Giant, and whoever else might have
been attached to that cave in the ten thousand years that people
have lived in the city below.

38.

From the weirdo cave I headed for the city's Sunni center, the
Umayyad Mosque, where the Prophet had supposedly said that
people would still be worshiping for forty years after the end of
the world. It's a sketchy hadith, since there was no Umayyad
Mosque in the Prophet's lifetime, but I guess that wouldn't stop a
prophet from speaking on the future. Remains of an old temple
were still standing outside; in the Aramaean era, this was where
people worshiped Baal-Hadad the thunder god. Then came the
Romans, who built a temple to Jupiter. In the fourth century
after Christ, Emperor Theodosius I built a shrine to John the
Baptist within the precincts of the old temple. In 705 Caliph
al-Walid purchased the basilica and allowed it to function as
both a mosque and church, until deciding to tear it down and
rebuild it as a "mosque the equal of which was never designed
by anyone before me or anyone after me." Umayyad Mosque
was built with stones from throughout the site's history, even
including a chunk from the Baal-Hadad temple bearing a bas-
relief of some winged animal with a man's head.

WHEN THE MAMLUKS took over, they legitimized their rule
through pilgrimage: not only as "protectors of the hajj,"
but by developing ziyarat throughout Damascus and Syria,
with the Umayyad Mosque playing a central role. This was
where pilgrims from Damascus to Mecca would start their
journeys, and the mosque housed its own ziyarat-worthy sites:
numerous Sunni, Shi'a, and Sufi shrines, including one where

Ayesha had allegedly taught hadith, a shrine to Ali, an 'Uthmanic Qur'an brought out once a day, maqams of Prophet Hud and Khidr, and the heads of John the Baptist and Husayn. Before veneration of the Prophet's tomb in Medina had fully blown up, many Muslims were treating the Umayyad Mosque as the religion's third holiest site. "The value of a prayer in Mecca is of a hundred thousand prayers," said Sufyan al-Thauri; "in the mosque of Jerusalem, forty thousand prayers, and in the mosque of Damascus, thirty thousand prayers." Legends added onto the mosque's importance, claiming that Jesus would make his return near one of the minarets.

I entered the courtyard and headed first for Husayn's shrine, in a corner far from the main prayer hall. Near jum'aa time it was impossible to get in there, as women filled the room and made it their own mosque, but I tried again after the prayer as the room emptied except for crying ziyarat people. First I saw the maqam, just a spot on the floor with a glass box over it, where Husayn's son, the Fourth Imam Zainul Abideen, used to pray one thousand rakats every day. Nearby, a small crowd huddled around the silver niche in the wall where you were supposed to put your head to be close to Husayn's head. It was mostly women in black abayas rubbing the silver and then their faces, but there were also men and couples and parents with small kids, touching and kissing and inserting their heads. I stuck my head into the niche and then went around the corner to the silver box with green light glowing out of the grille—a mutating-alien-ooze kind of nuclear-green glow—the same green light as in John the Baptist's shrine in the main hall and also minarets at night in Damascus and Lahore. Green was supposed to be the color of Islam; besides that, I didn't know why they'd put green light bulbs around the skull of Muhammad's grandson, but still I stood at a distance and trembled, losing myself in the light's promise.

I approached the grille and looked inside, finding a box under a shroud and a turban on top, ancient green cloth washed in fluorescent green light, a face under all of that somewhere but still anonymous, no face that I could see . . . and that was the Prophet's grandson, the one who came to me in a dream, and he didn't have a face then either. The Prophet's grandson, who was killed as an enemy of the Islamic State; that should tell you something. The grandson's great-grandson said that the tragedy of Karbala happened every day, in every land; but if it happened to Husayn when Islam was so young, what could Islam become? I brought my lips to the grille and kissed it, crying for Husayn and myself and Islam too, because Islam has also been butchered and trampled.

The green light wasn't real; somewhere in that tomb was an electric outlet and a light fixture put in by some people—to be specific, employees of the Waqf Department of the Syrian Arab Republic. But it was easy to forget because you couldn't see the bulbs or anything, just the glow. And you couldn't see the actual head either, which might have been a good thing. Maybe there was no head at all.

I sat in the corner directly facing the locked silver door of the tomb and looked at the living people around the dead man's head and at the people making prayers with their backs to it, facing Mecca. Some of them prayed with their hands folded across their navels and some prayed with their arms hanging at their sides; both Sunnis and Shi'as loved Husayn. A Shi'a man not far from me placed a small disc on the floor in front of him, touching his forehead to it when he prostrated. It was a turba clay, made from the soil of Karbala. I watched men take pictures with their phones of the tomb and their friends and wives in front of the tomb, and Iranian women caress the grille and weep, and it was real if you can ever believe in that kind of selfless pious love, hard sometimes because the other side of the equation never says anything back. But I wanted to believe in that green light like Gatsby.

39.

As the Mamluk campaign to religiously legitimize their power turned Damascus into a site of pilgrimage, the graves of various Companions and Ahlul-Bayt people became holy shrines. Other than Mecca and Medina, the Bab al-Saghir cemetery might have offered the most concentrated collection of holy bodies in the Muslim world, so I had to check it out.

Walking down the street in search of a taxi, I noticed that men selling posters had photos of the Nasrullah guy from Hezbollah right next to Christian art of Jesus and Mary like it wasn't a thing at all. It looked strange to me, only because American media made Syrians look like a bunch of insane religious fanatics. Pope John Paul II came here in 2002 and visited the Umayyad Mosque to pray at John the Baptist's shrine, the first pope ever to step foot inside a masjid. People acted like human beings about it, no one trying to blow him up or anything.

I found a driver named Ahmed, and we couldn't communicate easily with each other, but he understood that I was Muslim and it made him happy. He wanted to show me around and help explain things. First he took me to a shrine across the street from the cemetery, just for the heads of sixteen Karbala martyrs. They were bundled in shrouds and lined up in neat rows with donated Iranian rials lying between them, Khomeini's face staring up from the faceless. I didn't know their names or stories but prayed for them anyway.

Then we walked into Bab al-Saghir, a maze of raised tombs almost too close together to walk between, tall narrow headstones, and occasional big shrines with green domes.

"Ahlul-Bayt home," said Ahmad, pointing to a man's gravestone that bore the names of his ancestors, the Imams. In another corner of the cemetery rested Umayyad caliphs:

Mu'awiya, his grandson Yazid II, and al-Walid, builder of the Umayyad Mosque, but we kept it Shi'a. I prayed at the shrine of Ali and Fatima's daughter Umm Kulthum and kissed the tomb of Husayn's daughter Fatima Sughra, who had been kept away from Karbala because Husayn had a vision of the women being forced to march without their veils. Fatima Sughra, said Husayn, looked so much like his mother that to unveil one would humiliate the other.

I visited the sons of Zainul Abideen and Sixth Imam Jafar al-Sadiq, and more names and relationships honored with the same du'as. Because I didn't even know who some of the people were, it felt a bit like blind worship of a bloodline but I still kept up with the du'as out of respect for Ahmad, who seemed ready to cry each time he announced a tomb's inhabitant.

Bilal ibn Rabah, the first muezzin, was also at Bab al-Saghir, resting in his own green-domed shrine in the Ahlul-Bayt section, which had me trying to figure out where he would have stood during the schism. Bilal had a special bond with Abu Bakr and also Ali's sons and traveled to Syria as a soldier during the caliphate of Umar. Bilal was blessed enough to die while the ummah was still innocent, before the civil war and questions of Sunni or Shi'a. Inside we first found a reception room and were asked for a small donation. I put my money on the table next to some Iranian bills and went into the tomb. It was dressed in green with a big green ball on the end. Standing in front of it, dumbfounded that this place was actually real and that I was there with the real Bilal's bones, for a du'a I just repeated his own words to him: *Allahu Akbar, Allahu Akbar, Allahu Akbar, Allahu Akbar—Ashadu an la ilaha Allah, Ashadu an la ilaha illa Allah—Ashadu anna Muhammadan Rasullullah, Ashadu anna Muhammadan Rasullullah—Hayyal as-salah, Hayyal as-salah—Hayyal al-falah, Hayyal al-falah—Allahu Akbar, Allahu Akbar—La ilaha illa Allah—*

Then I sat on the floor and looked up at it.

"Bilal habishi," Ahmed kept saying. "Bilal habishi." *Habishi* was an old term for the black people around the Horn of Africa. Ahmed sat next to me and recited Bilal's story in Arabic mixed with improvised signs and gestures—acting out the whips on Bilal's back as his master told him to renounce Islam, then acting out a big boulder placed on Bilal's chest and repeating Bilal's *Ahad!* The One!

"American Muslims," I told him, my hand on my heart, "love Bilal." When Elijah Muhammad died in 1975 and his son Warith Deen sought to bring the Nation of Islam into the larger community, he needed something to ease the transition—a way to abandon racial supremacy without losing the empowerment of Elijah's message. Warith Deen coined "Bilalian" as a term not only for his Muslims, but all African-Americans endowed with the heart of Bilal, who withstood slavery and torture without ever losing his faith.

The book on Bilal that I had purchased in Washington, which I had first read as a teenager, was copyrighted 1977— the height of Warith Deen's move into Bilalian-ness—and contained an introduction by someone at *Bilalian News*, Warith Deen's newspaper after the end of *Muhammad Speaks*. For Elijah Muhammad's Nation, I would have been the Devil, but his son gave me Bilal.

Warith Deen knew what he was doing. Muhammad's Ethiopian companion spoke to something even deeper in American history, the dreams of redemption pinned on Ethiopia as Zion, the dreams that moved Abyssinian Baptist Churches and black liberation theology all the way back to slave preachers in the 1700s reading hope in the Bible, Psalms 68:31: *Princes shall come out of Egypt; Ethiopia shall soon stretch out her hands unto God.*

If I wanted to keep pursuing Islam as a Biblical thing, Jerusalem wasn't that far away. The third holiest city after Mecca and Medina, Jerusalem was where the Prophet stopped before ascending to heaven on the Buraq; his footprint's still there at another caliph's monument, the Dome of the Rock—which Abbasid historians dismissed as an Umayyad attempt to supplant Mecca as the site of pilgrimage. But I felt the pull coming from another direction; most Muslims didn't even know that Islam had a *fourth* holiest city, founded on holy land—as far as any land could be holy, a land with old African Judaism and its own African Christianity, the country that was home to the Ark of the Covenant and also the first hijra, where the Prophet sent his Muslims to seek refuge with a kind Christian king.

I was going to Bob Marley's Zion.

40.

During a layover in Cairo, the airport felt like a prison because I knew that I was somewhere cool and couldn't go outside to see it. Plus there was a strange old white man with a silver skullet (bald on top but long in the back, like Hulk Hogan) at the gate who kept hassling me.

"I'm a missionary," he said. "Ethiopia's a very religious country."

"They say that the Ark of the Covenant is there," I replied.

"Yeah, that's what they say. But they won't bring it out. If it's the real Ark, show it to me."

"Right," I said.

"I *used* to be Catholic, but now I'm Protestant."

"Okay."

He turned to another guy and said hello, but the guy wouldn't acknowledge him.

"Can't get a *hello* out of you?" asked the missionary. Finally the guy said hello and they talked a little bit; turned out the guy was from Russia, so the missionary started talking about the situation with Georgia and the treaty they had just signed. "That's good news," the missionary told the Russian. "I thank you for your part in it. I'm sure you had something to do with it."

Then the missionary turned back to me, wished me well, turned around again, put on his black sunglasses methodically and just stood there frozen straight, oblivious to the surrounding environment as though he was preparing for a beam to teleport him somewhere. When we landed in Addis Ababa, he'd be that guy who stood up and opened the overhead compartment while the plane was still moving, and they'd have to yell at him repeatedly to please sit down.

I got a room on the edge of town and then walked up the muddy streets past shacks selling bananas and Pepsi, reggae blaring from stores, men hanging around in green, yellow, and red caps with dreadlocks spilling out. I had coins in my pocket bearing the Lion of Judah. Addis Ababa felt like Jamaica, which was reasonable in the promised land of Ras Tafari. The story went that Marcus Garvey, Jamaican father of modern black nationalism, prophesied that a great king would rise from Africa. Jamaica later suffered a massive drought. The rain finally came with the arrival of Haile Selassie, king of Ethiopia, so people in Jamaica began revering Selassie as Garvey's black messiah and God incarnate. A new religion grew from it, combining Afrocentrism, Biblical fundamentalism, and sacramental marijuana smoking. Black skin became the mark of true Israel, while Jamaica became Babylon, the land of bondage, and Rastas looked to Ethiopia as Zion.

In those same years, a new religious movement took root in South Africa teaching that black men would come from America in airplanes to save Africa from its white oppressors. The leader of the "American movement," Wellington Buthelezi, declared that "American negroes have decided to fight the Europeans and will help the local natives," and told his followers to avoid the food of white people, especially pork.

I took a taxi to the Trinity Cathedral, which housed the tomb of Haile Selassie. My teenage driver wore a Bob Marley shirt.

"You like Rasta?" he asked. "You smoke ganja? There's lots of ganja here. For one hundred fifty birr, you get a big amount—" He took his hands off the wheel to illustrate. "Is that cheap?" It was. "Ethiopia produced the best ladies and coffee," he told me, making a sign of the cross to repent for his lust. Jesus and Mary stickers covered his dashboard and they were all white. "Ethiopia half Christian, half Muslim," he said, adding that they got along. "One god, it's okay."

The street leading to the church was crowded on either side of traffic with people, most in white, on their way to the weekly ceremony. On the way they purchased long orange torch-candles and little religious items, cards, rosaries, Amharic Bibles, and gave money to beggars. There were Rastas holding portraits of Haile Selassie, but the church was Ethiopian Orthodox. Christianity here wasn't a European slave master scheme, though it looked that way when Mussolini invaded and the pope wouldn't say a word against him. The Ethiopian church went back to a time before white empire could reach that far, Monophysites breaking off from what became normative Christianity in Europe and going their own way.

The taxi driver's name was Abraham; "not Ibrahim," he said, "that's the other one." He made a similar statement about the Moses statue outside Selassie's church, as though Moses and Musa were not the same person, but corresponding characters in parallel universes.

At the doorway of the church, girls curtsied and made signs of the cross, and men prostrated. Like the Pentecostal church in Lahore, this Christianity looked like Islam: you had to take your shoes off, men and women sat on separate sides, the women covered their heads, and menstruating women stayed home. I stood before Selassie's tomb with Abraham, who repeated the story about Selassie's trip to Jamaica, but assured me that Selassie rejected the people's attempts to worship him. From what I understood, Selassie gave ambiguous responses to the question of whether he was God, but Ethiopian Christians needed a way to keep their hero-king and remain doctrinally safe.

Selassie wasn't God to me, or even the black champion that they made him out to be. He was conservative, hostile to Islam, and overthrown in disgrace—as police whisked him away, crowds of angry citizens chased the car yelling "Thief!"—but it didn't matter any more than it mattered whether that cave in Damascus was really where Abel was buried or if there was even an Abel at all. For the Rastas, Selassie became a symbol of their own inner divinity, since Selassie's spirit resided in us all. I had to be okay with it. Selassie was a chicken who laid a duck egg, and it'd serve no purpose to be the know-it-all whining, "Well, yeah, this duck egg is cool, but it was actually laid by a chicken."

Outside the church I bought a crucifix for Sadaf, since she secretly appreciated Christian imagery from her trip to Italy, and the man put it around my neck. So now I was wearing Christian disguise and didn't like it, even hidden under my shirt it felt wrong. It took me back to my teen years, skipping mass at DeSales Catholic High School and skipping Christmas dinner with my aunts and uncles, sitting alone and defining myself by what I was *not*. I was a Muslim, not a Christian. Growing up in a small town with no diversity, I never had to do that with Hinduism or anything else; so even if Christianity was closer to Islam than most religions, I couldn't make a place for its symbol.

41.

I woke up the next morning and knew that something had changed inside me. A few years ago when I did my American Islam highway quest, riding Greyhounds for sixty-hour stret-ches, sometimes I'd get lonely but felt certain that something special and perhaps even holy was pushing me on, that any suffering on the road would nourish the truth and value of the book and it would shine through on every page. But ever since the dead dog at Abel's tomb, the loneliness had been too much. I had just thrown myself into Africa and didn't know a single person on the whole continent and felt terrible. It was even cold. Who knew that Ethiopia had a rain season?

Writing was my religious adventure, and religion my writing adventure; everything that I experienced became a book, but now the writing moved slow. Writing's supposed to be a lonely thing; you have to love being alone to really get into it, and most of the time I do, but I had reached that point where books had no meaning compared to a girl. Never been there before. At another time, a broken heart would have pushed the writing, but now it just shut everything down. Worst part about it, I could remember those times back home when Sadaf would call and I turned into a total asshole because she messed up my momentum and killed the sentence I was working on.

But you can't write a book just sitting in a hotel room with stacks of birr, you have to go outside and find your story. Maybe the funk would wear off and the sadness would ease when I reached Ethiopia's Muslim regions, and then I'd have to accept that yes, we're an ummah, all Muslims together. I listened to songs in Amharic outside, the end of a church service. It sounded like an adhan to me, since so much of Amharic came from Arabic; the Arabic word for paradise was *jannah*, the Amharic for heaven was *geh nedt*, the Arabic for mosque was *masjid* and the Amharic was *mahs geedt.* It was tempting to exoticize the beautiful song as holy just because I couldn't comprehend it, and was that really so bad? The content and form worked together, but my ignorance of language divided them, isolating the form, making the form its own content. The Icelandic band Sigur Rós used to sing in "Hopelandic," their own invented nonsense language, and their albums came with blank booklets so listeners could make up their own meanings and write them as the lyrics. Whatever the believers said, their sound was a comfort, so I hid under the blankets and fell asleep in peace.

My destination in Ethiopia was Islam's fourth holiest city, Harar, but I had to fly from Addis Ababa to Dire Dawa and then spend a night there before finding a ride. On the plane I read a *New African* article on Obama, which highlighted the influence of Malcolm X's autobiography on his early development. The article suggested that Obama understood Malcolm's anger and even felt it in a way that he could never let on, but believed that the path of militant rhetoric and outsider stances led nowhere. Remembering that George W. Bush spoke in coded language to evangelical Christians, I hoped with all my audacity for Obama's accusations that Hillary had tried to "hoodwink" and "bamboozle" voters to be *our* code, a secret reminder of the Harlem rally scene from Spike Lee's *Malcolm X.* That hope might have been as irrational as the Obama's-a-secret-Muslim paranoia of West Virginia crackers, but it felt good.

Stepping off the plane outside, Dire Dawa felt like real Africa, absolute darkness and quiet sky and hot at night, but it was also a little dirt town, the Geneva, New York, of Ethiopia. Riding around in a taxi trying to find a place to sleep for the night, I found myself with a choice between a $3 room and $30 room and took the $30 room—betraying the self-marginalizing punk rock ethic, writer-as-Action-Man-martyr ethic, even the religious ethic that kept me unhappy in soft, clean beds. In my

Greyhound days, I had turned travel into an ascetic practice: part fasting, part vow of homelessness, and spent the least possible, but I wouldn't have been able to afford that mission if I needed dinner and a room every night. Dire Dawa was another level. It seemed stupid to travel across the world to a place where $30 meant you were fucking loaded and still pretend to be poor; so give me my own toilet, a shower with hot water, let me get under the clean sheets and leave the AC on and relax with my own television.

I turned on BBC and learned that the Shi'a pilgrimage I had almost joined in Iraq was suicide-bombed, twenty-two dead. They had come to celebrate the birthday of the Mahdi, the invisible Hidden Imam who disappeared as a little boy a thousand years ago and had been in hiding ever since, waiting to return at the Last Times to set things right. Everyone had a guy like that. Johnny Cash sang about the Man coming around, even the Muslims said that Jesus would appear by the Umayyad minaret in Damascus, the Druze believed that al-Hakim was still alive and waiting to return, Rastas believed that Selassie would come back and deliver them from Babylon, and the Nation was still waiting for Master Fard and Elijah to fly in on the Mothership.

Sadaf emailed to say that she would pray one million rakats of thanks that I didn't go. I had skipped out on the Mahdi for the crying girl who begged me not to die, another choice I never would have made before. So now I had AC and I wasn't dead. Did that make me a bitch writer or bitch Muslim? The worst was that either way, I felt okay with it. I missed her more than the Mahdi anyway; she was the imam of *my* age.

42.

Nothing happened in Dire Dawa but a moment of transcendent defecation at the airport, so big and awesome that as it pushed out, I lost knowledge of myself . . . the kind of mystical poop in a public restroom from which I'd get up and feel that nothing was the same, that life outside the stall had changed. It came with the buzzing and trancing that I had felt at the Cave of Blood in Syria, and I found it briefly unsettling to know that one can get that experience anywhere. Maybe it was connected with the parietal lobe in my brain. I wondered if a study had ever been done on the cognitive effects of huge bowel movements in comparison to religious peak experiences.

A taxi driver took me to a parking lot, where he found a guy with a minibus who could drive me to Harar. The minibus went up winding roads through the mountains, and the land was all green, forests and steep hills turned into tiered cornfields. When the land became flat we drove along a shimmering blue lake. It wasn't anything like the Ethiopia I had grown up seeing on TV in the 1980s.

ETHIOPIA'S PLACE IN Islamic history reached back at least to the year of Muhammad's birth, and possibly further. Scholars have suggested that the Ka'ba's association with Abraham was influenced by Ethiopian Christians, for whom the Book of Jubilees was a sacred text. The Book of Jubilees mentions a "House of Abraham," a sanctuary that would establish Abraham's name before God forever. In pre-Islamic Arabia, some Jews and Christians regarded the Ka'ba as that sacred place.

In the year that Muhammad was born, an Ethiopian army invaded Mecca. The soldiers sought to advance to the heart of the city, the Ka'ba, and destroy it; tradition says that their elephants refused to approach the structure, and the Qur'an says that birds pelted the invaders with clay and left them like a field of half-eaten crops. A generation later, with Muslims suffering persecution and torture in Mecca, Muhammad sent a small group of refugees to the Ethiopian empire of Aksum, where a "righteous king" would give them asylum.

The Muslims lived peacefully with Aksum's Christians, but did not win many converts or establish a lasting presence. For the most part, Islam's later growth in Ethiopia came by peaceful means, but the Adal Sultanate in the sixteenth century grew strong enough to challenge the Christian state for trade routes. The sultanate's capital of Harar was protected with an outer wall, forbidden to non-Muslims, and marked with Islamic identity by countless shrines to local saints, the foundation for a claim to Islam's fourth holiest city. The people of Harar believed that the spirits of their hundreds of dead Somali, Oromo, Arab, and Turkish saints watched over them. The saints of Harar held assemblies on Mount Hakim to discuss the affairs of the city—almost like the forty invisible Abdals at Mount Qasiyun—but Harar's saint worship didn't look much like Sufism in the traditional sense. The saints weren't mystical masters, performers of miracles, or links in an order's lineage, usually just emirs and local historical figures canonized in civil religion—like America building a city of shrines to George Washington and Thomas Jefferson.

Throughout Ethiopia's history, tribal wars caused tension between the religions. In the 1800s, Christian emperors Tewodros and Yohannis IV tried to ban Islam, but this only helped Islam present itself as the voice of resistance against their regimes. The banner of Islam could have been raised against the Italian invaders in 1936, but the Italians built fifty mosques and convinced Muslim leaders to drop the cause of independence. Haile Selassie came to power after a wave of anti-Muslim hysteria from the ruling class; the crown prince, Iyasu V, had claimed descent from the Prophet and prayed in

Harar's largest mosque, and the Italians revealed that one of their Somalian agents had witnessed Iyasu's shahadah. The smearing of Iyasu as a secret Muslim ruined him. Positioning himself as the defender of Ethiopia's Christian identity, Selassie traced his dynasty back to Solomon, traveled to Jerusalem, and adopted forty children orphaned by Ottoman genocide.

That kind of antagonism seemed to be in the past, at least on the ground in Harar. My minibus driver Hamza was a Muslim, but he introduced me to a Christian tour guide named Hailu, and Hailu told me that all of his friends were Muslims. During Ramadan, Hailu would stay up with them chewing chat (known elsewhere as khat or qat), the local intoxicating leaf, and walk the streets after sunrise getting warm and tired and then sleeping all day.

"In Ramadan," he told me with a smile, "all the Muslims stop drinking beer."

I mentioned that I was Muslim. "Do you pray five times a day?" he asked.

"Not consistently," I admitted. "I just pray when I feel like it."

"You can pray all five in one," he said. "My friends do that." I could see that Islam in Ethiopia would be its own thing, and that was the only way to understand it.

43.

Hailu took me to the gate into the old city bearing the image of Harar's seventy-second and last emir, Emir Abdullah, who Hailu said looked just like 2Pac (he did), his favorite rapper.

"2Pac was very political," I said.

"That's because he was a *neegur*," said Hailu. He walked me through old Harar, first showing me the house of Arthur Rimbaud, the nineteenth-century gay French poet who came to the forbidden city, renamed himself Abdullah Rimbaud, and became a gunrunner, alleged slave dealer, and Qur'an scholar. He won a small following for his interpretations of the Qur'an but offended the local Qadiriya Sufis, who assaulted him with sticks and refrained from killing him only for Islam's compassion toward the mentally ill.

From there we went to the museum showing old Qur'ans alongside heavy iron chains and collars; at one time, Harar was a major post in the East African slave trade. "This is the history of rap," said Hailu; when I asked him to explain, he imitated the stereotypical hip-hop swagger. "In the slave days," he told me, "they had to walk like that because of the chains on their feet, and that's how rap started." I picked up a collar and observed the weight, imagining how it would feel on a neck. At first I confronted the collar as an American faced with my own country's history, but Ethiopia's slaves were taken across the Red Sea, not the Atlantic; this collar was a relic of the Arab slave trade. In my internal battle of Malcolm vs. Elijah, I scored this one for Elijah.

44.

I told Hailu that my main interest was the shrines, so he took me to Aw Ansar, a blue and white structure that had been built into a fig tree. The tree had been painted as part of the shrine, blending them together into one structure. To enter the shrine and see the tomb, I had to pass through a doorway formed by the above-ground roots.

A handful of devotees sat around the shrine, chewing chat, and a pot of burnt incense sat in the doorway. Even if it meant sleeping inside a tree next to a dead saint, I wanted to live in that shrine—it looked like a hut on Dagobah for nine-hundred-year-old Jedi masters.

We sat with the shrine people for a while. Since I didn't know much about the saint Aw Ansar, I kept the Dagobah image in my mind, like it was Yoda's coffin under the green shroud. The earliest influence on my religious thought was *Star Wars*, and I still got into Allah more as the Force than as any anthropomorphic God of Ibn Taymiyya with literal hands and feet and his literal throne. Ethiopia's Oromo people had their own native Jedi-like monotheism, with a god named Waaqa who existed in all things, binding them together. Waaqa created the universe in *safuu*, balance; chaos came from the loss of safuu, or a disturbance in the Force.

I've heard numerous people explain their idea of God as the Force, and a guy who wrote a book about surfing and religion said the same thing. There were even people naming "Jedi" as their religion on the censuses of English-speaking nations; on paper, Jedi was the third-largest religion in Scotland and the second-largest in New Zealand. In the United States, ministers in the Temple of the Jedi could legally perform marriages. George Lucas was supposed to have been influenced by Taoism, but I've never heard *Star Wars* geeks say that their god was like the Tao. People just use what's around them.

45.

Walking along the wall that surrounded the old city, Hailu pointed out the smaller gates and told me that they were specially made for the hyenas to come and go as they pleased.

The hyena lurked in a hazy place between human and animal—the Bedouin said that the Prophet wouldn't eat hyenas because they menstruated—and also between male and female: the female spotted hyena had an elongated clitoris and something resembling a scrotum, making it hard for humans to identify their sex. In local myth, the androgynous hyena fucked the bisexual moon. Hyenas lived on the borders. Various legends called the hyena a shapeshifter, going back and forth from one form to the other; blacksmiths were believed to belong to a clan of wizards who could change into hyenas at will, and Ethiopian Christians accused Ethiopian Jews of being *bouda*, were-hyenas. On the other side of the continent, educational tales often depicted hyenas as Muslims who rebuked old African animism.

America makes a favorable environment for shapeshifters. According to the Nation of Islam, Master Fard was born of a black father and white mother, which allowed him to travel among both the black gods and white devils. From his teachings came the Five Percenters, who also had a marginal man in their cipher: a white man born devil but made righteous, reformed by Supreme Mathematics. He was only a teenager in the 1960s, when he met the Five Percenters' leader, a man named Allah. They were patients at the same institution, Matteawan State Hospital for the Criminally Insane. Doctors and judges had called them both crazy, but they knew that they were at least more sane than a society in which the white man was God and black people were blasted with fire hoses for claiming their right to sit in a restaurant. Allah taught the white kid Master Fard's lessons and the Mathematics and then gave him the righteous name Azreal, after the Islamic angel of death. The first white Five Percenter, Azreal had a special place as a transitional being—neither the Original Man nor the Grafted Devil but holding the keys to heaven and hell, able to come and go through his own gate—passing in and out of the social construction of whiteness.

When I met Azreal, he was nearly sixty years old and still in the movement, even though most of his family had disowned him for the black-god talk. I've heard Azreal described by elders as the Five Percenters' human litmus test. Here's this homeless old white man with a history of addiction and institutionalization, waltzing into meetings of young black supremacists to ramble or sing or even make claims of being a white god; a Five Percenter's response to Azreal only revealed his own character and how he lived out the culture. Some dismissed him and called him a devil; others treated him with compassion, providing a meal and place to crash for the night.

Azreal gave me my own Five Percenter name, Azreal Wisdom. It breaks down in Supreme Mathematics as "Azreal 2." Like Azreal, I was a creature of the margins, lurking somewhere in the no-man's land between Muslim and non-Muslim. I could choose teams when it fit me, veiling and revealing my American-ness and my Muslim-ness, growing and shaving beards for the border. I even had two legal middle names, Edward and Muhammad, using Edward on my plane reservations and Muhammad on my books.

And like Azreal, I was a litmus test: a punky immature writer who published every terrible thought that ran through my head. Some Muslims made takfir on me without a second look, and some would say "It's nothing personal," while refusing to shake my hand or return my salam. I've also had quite a few conservative Muslim friends, pious and humble people who were equally mortified by my words but only reacted with love to their hurting brother. It's for them that I can even call myself a Muslim today—because *they* followed the example of the Prophet, who wouldn't even make takfir on the tribal chief who put his hands around his neck.

"Being Azreal is a lonely thing," Azreal had told me, and I found out for myself. I'm the spotted hyena with an oversized clit; I'm Azreal Wisdom on the border between heaven and hell, and I belong nowhere, but the beast who straddles the border becomes it.

46.

I went for an aimless walk the next day, hearing the teasing shouts of *faranji* (foreigner) and "You! You!" from kids. A man picked up his baby and held it in my face, demanding, "Ethiopian baby good, yes?" I gave him the thumbs-up and kept going, finding the chaotic crowded market and a yellow and white minaret rising up from somewhere in there. The market was built around the mosque, so to reach it I'd have to enter into the mess of little alleys and shacks selling auto parts, clothing, TVs, food, pens, whatever could be sold, going deeper and deeper in and unsure whether I'd ever make it back out. When I finally came to the gate of the mosque, a woman was sitting there with her three babies, hand open. I gave her something and walked up the hill. The front door was closed, but the women's side door was open and no women were inside, so I took off my shoes and walked through the curtain to the men's hall. I gave salams to the men with pointy beards and passed a few people sleeping under blankets to make my prayer.

I hadn't noticed it on my way up, but after leaving the mosque I saw the pair of turquoise domes with stars and crescents on top—another shrine. I took my shoes back off. Around the shrine were graves, some male and some female, and a moss-covered structure a little more than waist-high. The section under the smaller dome was just an incense room, but the bigger dome covered the tomb. There was also an incense bowl by the tomb, and the tomb's shroud had something that threw me off for a minute: the regular crescent, white on green, but the star was the Star of David. In the 1970s and '80s, when the Nuwaubians of Brooklyn called themselves the Nubian Islamic Hebrews, they used this same flag, claiming that it had come from the Sudan. After I made du'a, the men came out of the mosque to explain that this shrine was for Abadir's family. "Prophet's people," said one. Then they showed me inside the building next to it, just one room filled with Islamic banners, green and red and blue with shahadahs and crudely cut and sewn crescents and stars . . . and in the corner, a collection of big African drums. Thursday nights were special there, one of them told me: "Everybody goes and beats the drums and take the chat, all night long. It is holy place, you know?" I *did* know; it sounded like the Shah Jamal shrine in Lahore, like this was what Muslims did everywhere. Why didn't we have it in America?

It was like a genetic founder effect. The malangs in Pakistan usually didn't speak English or have much formal education or any money, so they weren't the ones going to America. The Pakistani-American community that I had known in Rochester was all doctors and engineers, professionals at Kodak and Xerox and IBM. Their Islam was intellectual, with shelves lined with pompous books like *Islamic Banking* and *Theories of the Islamic State*, written by stuffy Muslim PhDs—revivalists who sought to present Islam as something respectable to the modern world, with its own philosophers and intellectuals on a par with the Christianity of post-Reformation Europe. The revivalists wanted a Big Islam, Islam as Civilization—translating the Prophet's life into systems of economics and law that must inevitably prove superior to Western civilization and tip the balance again . . . so screw village superstitions and drugged-out Sufis banging on their drums. And mosques in America were so diverse, with Muslims from every country all in one room together, we needed to transcend cultural differences and go straight for the text. Not always a bad idea, but we lost something in the process.

Chat wasn't an efficient drug, you had to chew it all night to feel anything; I had a better chance with some old men by the road who were grinding it into a concentrated paste, enabling them to consume a whole bushel in a few swallows. "Chat?" I asked. One of them instructed me to open my hand and then scooped the chat out of the grinder with a spoon and gave it to me. I donated ten birr and went on my way with a bare hand full of cold, slimy green paste. Bought an apple soda and headed for my room.

Chat contains cathinone, an alkaloid comparable to amphetamines, and cathine, which has been compared to cocaine. They entered me through mucous membranes in my mouth and stomach lining. I held zikr beads in my hand and just kept saying *Subhanahu Allah*, glory to God. Back in the old days of Harar as Islam's fourth holiest city, only the emirs and imams were allowed to use chat, because it was believed to enable heightened communion with Allah. It was a sacred plant, an Islamic drug. Now everyone used chat, even the Christians, while a few Muslims opposed it. When the Supreme Islamic Courts Council came to power in Somalia, they criminalized chat. People protested in the streets. The council is now gone, but chat is still there.

It had me focused and dumb at the same time. I couldn't say how I'd do in a conversation with someone, but I could talk to Allah, feeling like I could pray one thousand rakats like the Fourth Imam used to do at the Umayyad Mosque—*Umayyad Mosque?* That place was far away enough to forget, along with the Islam of that place. I was in Harar with Harar's religion. On the veranda I listened to the animal sounds, the bugs and birds and goats, but also the angry Amharic sermon blaring from a megaphone somewhere, unable to tell if it was Muslim or Christian. The zikrs were a compulsion; I couldn't stop moving the beads between my finger and thumb and saying God's Name. It went like that for a long time.

Deciding that I wanted more chat, I left my room and went back down that road but the old men were gone. There was, however, a man walking by with unrolled posters of Jesus Christ and R. Kelly for sale, why not, it's all life in the sky. The colors of everything seemed stronger, the green trees and red flowers and the brown of the dirt, and it could have been from the chat or just Harar sunset. After searching around the market, I found a street kid in dirty shirt and bare feet and asked him for chat. He took me by the hand and led me to all the vendors he knew, but they only had bushels and I gestured with my hands that I wanted ground-up paste. He led me to an older boy who took us both down a side street.

The older boy spoke English. His name was Anwar and he said that the younger kid, Qadir, didn't know what he was talking about. Qadir stubbed his toe on a brick and they shared an exchange in Amharic.

"I ask him why he has no shoes and this shirt," Anwar told me. "He says his brother bought a car. He says a lie. I tell him, if his brother has money for car, why does he have no shoes?"

We found an old man in a tent with the equipment to mash chat, so Anwar bought a bushel, sugar, and apple soda and picked the best leaves with Qadir—you only wanted the soft green leaves, he said, not the dying discolored ones. Then some kids ran up to me and sang a song, Qadir joining in. One played an instrument made of Coca-Cola bottle caps. I gave them some birr and then a man came along telling Anwar that he wasn't grinding up the leaves right, so he sat down and did it and wanted some birr for his contribution. I paid him and the man whose equipment we used and then took the boys out for dinner, carrying the soggy chat paste in a plastic grocery bag.

Anwar asked me about America. It's good, I answered, but Bush was bad. Anwar liked Obama. "I think that Obama is from Kenya," he said. "He looks like a good man. He will be a famous president, freedom for the whole world." I didn't have the heart to break it to him—or to the self-righteous skinny white girl strutting around in her Obama shirt to let everyone know, "Yes, I'm the white girl in Africa with an Obama shirt."

I spent the night alone with my chat and did thousands of zikrs, intent on each one, reaching the end of my beads and then going right into another round. The next day Anwar took me to a chat ceremony at the Emir Nur shrine, a tall, aqua blue blob that almost looked like a cartoon creature that could smash through the gates and blob on down the street, smooth except for scattered protruding bricks like antennas or feelers or hairs. Anwar told me that they were for climbing to the top of the shrine for repainting every Ramadan. Emir Nur was a Somalian who had built the wall around Harar in the 1600s to protect the city from Christian tribes. It seemed possible that the prohibition of non-Muslims entering Harar originally had less to do with Islamic purity than tribal security. It could have become a religious ordinance later, as shrines popped up to give special meaning to the city and its wall.

"Every afternoon after Zuhr prayer," said Anwar, "men come to the shrine to read Qur'an and eat chat." The old man in charge of the shrine, Getachu, had legs so bone-skinny that it made the balls of his feet look huge. We had brought our own bushel of chat for him to mash up.

There were eight of us total, Anwar and I the youngest by decades. We had to communicate between Anwar, who told them that I was Muslim, and they all said *mash'Allah*. They asked where I was from and where I had been. I told them about Damascus and how I had visited the head of Imam Husayn. Even Sunnis can't deny the Prophet's grandson, so they all nodded their heads in solemn recognition. During their Amharic conversations I thought I heard "Karbala," but it was actually a phrase asking the man when he'd eat. When I explained what I thought I had heard, the place where Husayn was killed, they thought I meant "Ka'ba," but I explained that Karbala was in Iraq, not Mecca.

One of them went and got the key to the shrine to show me the inside, the walls decorated with Emir Nur's own sword and a shahadah banner and a built-in compartment for an old Qur'an. Beside Emir Nur's tomb was the grave of his mom and a bunch of water jugs for the annual celebrations. At the tomb of the man who built the old wall, I could understand the religious significance that Harar gave to its emirs. The wall wasn't anything supernatural or built with zikrs alone, but it kept the people safe, and what's more sacred than life? Seemed like a better reason to enshrine someone than their mystery-god powers.

We sat in a cipher around a bowl of hot coals, everyone with his own chat. Getachu placed lit incense sticks in the bowl and tossed incense flakes on the coals, then added a rusty old can on top as a chimney for the smoke. Before eating the chat, one of the men led us in an Arabic du'a with lots of *amins* and a rendition of al-Fatiha that I had never heard in my life, kind of jumbled in the middle. I ate my chat with a spoon right from the masher, and while we ate the adhan came, which almost put the conversations to a stop. One man put on his kufi and took his water bottle behind the shrine to make wudhu; he'd come back to the masjid section and do his salat alone while the rest of us sat around. I decided to pray too, touching my nose to the floor and breathing in incense, chat, weather, dust, animals, and Ethiopia. There was no mihrab showing the direction of Mecca, just emir flags on the wall and more drums in the corner and green specks of chat everywhere. I heard crowing roosters. Near the end of my prayer, another man joined me in the sitting position, so for two seconds we had the reward of praying in a congregation. After I finished mine, he continued his own and recited the prayer with a loud, almost pained groan.

I returned to my place with the brothers and Getachu showed me the coin on his keychain bearing the face of Haile Selassie, whose bitter history with the Muslims was long ago and forgotten. Selassie belonged to everyone now. Through Anwar translating, Getachu told the story of Marcus Garvey's vision of a great African king, which was fulfilled by Selassie bringing the rain to Jamaica. Getachu added a disclaimer to Islamicize the story, just like the Christians at Trinity Cathedral in Addis Ababa: though Jamaicans were ready to worship Selassie as God, the wise king denied them. He was only a creation, he told the people, not the Creator.

47.

"The hyenas' back legs are shorter than its front legs," Anwar told me. "Do you know the story why?"

"They never taught me that at the madrassa."

"One day, the Prophet was cleaning his teeth, and he saw a hyena run from one end of the world to the other. The Prophet said to the hyena, 'You are too fast, and your jaws are too strong; you will hurt my people.' So the Prophet shortened its legs to slow it down."

Harar's nightly hyena feedings took place near the Aw Ansar shrine. We came by after sunset and watched Hyena Man (his real name was Yusuf) appear with his basket of raw meat and call out the hyenas by their names: Shebo! Bichu! Qamar! Hello! The hyenas came from the darkness, furry and spotted with snub faces and black socks. They took scraps from Hyena Man's hands and even his mouth. If one got too anxious, he'd swat it and make the hyena yelp. He gave me some meat to toss them and even let me pet Qamar when it reached into the basket. The hyena, whose name meant Moon, flinched from my touch; these weren't carnivores with any integrity. The hyenas were cowardly and insecure, "savage in the pursuit of happiness" as Master Fard would have said. They came in packs and ate what was already dead and when they were full, they just lay down and slept.

"Look," said Anwar, pointing at one on its back. "No other animals sleep on their backs besides man, monkey, and hyena. That's another sign."

In the Sudan, hyenas were magic. A hyena tail would win a man the woman he desired, and a hyena's nose ensured a good harvest.

I watched the hyenas sleep. Anwar said that after midnight, the hyenas would enter the old city through their own gates and wander the streets in search of bones but never bothered anyone. The people and hyenas of Harar had learned to live together; "The hyenas' only problem is food," he told me. "Look at them now. If you feed them they're happy." Later that night I was sitting on the veranda in my boxers with more chat paste, looking out at the darkness behind the hotel, gulping mashed-up leaves with apple soda, and I found a new way to break it down: the hyenas were our nafs, our lower selves, the ugly spirit.

"Why did Moses have a hard time civilizing the Devil?" Master Fard had asked Elijah. The answer was that Moses had lost the knowledge of himself and was living a beast life; going among devils, he had become like them. One day, Moses had become so frustrated with the devils that he planted dynamite sticks on a mountain, told a group of them that they would find God up there, and blew them up. "If you only knew how much trouble these devils give me," he told the imams of his time, "you would do as I do."

No prophet or divine law could exterminate the hyenas, only shorten their legs and put them to sleep with controlled feedings. Muhammad understood this, possibly more than most figures in the heritage of world religions: while early Christians such as Origen saw the hyena in their flesh and chopped off their balls, Muhammad allowed us to enjoy our bodies in regulated ways. Buddha practiced uncompromising nonviolence, but he lived more as a model for monks than kings, and Buddhism had a body count anyway. Muhammad wasn't a world renouncer like Christ or Buddha; he lived in real life and had to put his hands in the same dirty things as all of us. Dealing with war as inevitable no matter how much he despised it, the Prophet tried to place restrictions on violence, limiting what a Muslim soldier could do and who he could do it to. Don't kill noncombatants, don't kill women or children. Sometimes it worked, sometimes it didn't. You can see the mixed results in the al-Qaeda manuals found in Mohamed Atta's luggage:

> If you slaughter, do not cause the discomfort of those you are killing, because this is one of the practices of the Prophet, peace be upon him . . . Do not seek revenge for yourself. Seek for God's sake.

The manuals tell the story of an unbeliever that Ali fought. During their confrontation, the unbeliever spit on Ali, but Ali refrained from killing him. "After he spat at me," Ali explained later, "I was afraid I would be striking at him in revenge for myself." But after correcting his intention, Ali did go back and kill the man.

On every Ashura in Harar, near one of the shrines or up on the holy mountain of saints, Muslims make a special porridge and offer it to the hyenas. First comes the master hyena; after he judges the porridge, the others take their shares. If the hyenas accept the gift, I was told, it means that Harar will have peace for the following year.

There was something to that, I thought. In the desert of Karbala, the hyenas rose up and ripped Husayn apart, leaving his body and blood on the hot sands and stealing his head. To mourn the prince of martyrs and the most innocent victims, some Muslims beat and cut themselves, writing their grief on their flesh; others come to the natural viciousness of the world with milk and butter, hoping to appease the ugly spirit for a time.

48.

Then came August 17, and the day's Mathematics was Know-ledge God, knowledge as a verb: you don't know God, you *knowledge* God, and then you can Build or Destroy (1 + 7 = 8). In the myth systems of Noble Drew Ali, Elijah Muhammad, the Five Percenters, and Ras Tafaris, the cause of the world's current inequality was the black man losing knowledge of his own divine self to worship false gods that didn't look like him.

"Either this is Revelation, or it is some made-up madness," Farrakhan said about what Elijah had taught him, "but tell me how made-up madness could raise a man from the dead . . . Tell me how could made-up madness make Malcolm X?"

I didn't know who Master Fard really was and would never know, but he might have been George Farr, an obscure figure mentioned in the archived papers of Marcus Garvey. According to government documents, George Farr surfaced in San Francisco, preaching pro-Japan rhetoric with a Chinese-American in Chinese cafés around the same time that Fard and his Chinese-American sidekick Ed Donaldson moved there from Los Angeles. In December 1921 Farr was interviewed by Office of Naval Intelligence informants at a Korean-run restaurant. The informants noted that in addition to a red, black, and green UNIA button on his coat, Farr wore a yellow flannel shirt suggesting that he had been in the U.S. army. As the FBI would later with Fard, the informants expressed confusion regarding Farr's background: "Though he claimed to be a Negro, his manner of talk, which had a little accent—not the Southern accent that is common to all Negroes, but the accent similar to that of an American-educated Hindu. He is rather small but stout. His facial color and the shape and structure of his face is also more like a Hindu than an American Negro."

"The white race has to go down," said Farr. "It has already

in a sense. It will go farther as we will witness before long."
Like Fard, Farr believed in the Bible not as a historical account,
but a foretelling of things to come: "Many of them have already
become facts and others will," he told the informants. "That is
one of the many things from the Bible we tell to the Negroes.
They have to awaken to those possibilities."

Someone wrote to me after reading *Blue-Eyed Devil* to say
that he went digging through genealogy services and found a
World War I draft registration card from 1917 for Wallie Dodd
Ford in Los Angeles, which stated that he was born on February
26, 1893, in Shinka, Afghanistan. The only Shinka that I could
find was a small village in the Punjab of modern-day Pakistan.

The Nation, of course, had the Master born on February 26,
1877, in the holy city of Mecca. No reason to accept Elijah's
version as actual facts, but part of me wanted to; Mecca
connected Fard to what I needed at the time.

BESIDES REPRESENTING Knowledge God, August 17 was the
birthday of Marcus Garvey, from whom all of this derived.
Garvey, the Jamaican-born father of modern black nationalism,
considered religion an essential part of his project. Rastas
said that Selassie was Garvey's prophesied black messiah,
with Garvey as the John the Baptist figure proclaiming his
arrival. Noble Drew Ali would also claim that he was the
one foretold. Noble Drew Ali was the likely foundation for
Master Fard and Elijah Muhammad, so Selassie-as-Jah and
Fard-as-Allah came from the same root. From Fard also came
the Five Percenters, who recognized all black men as true and
living gods—which even had a parallel with the Rastas, who
were their own divine princes. The Rastas and Five Percenters
often recognized each other as cousins on a family tree. In
Harlem, Allah B would take me to a Rasta juice bar where
they served no meat—Rastas lived by the Ital diet, and most
Five Percenters I knew were vegetarians or vegans because

Fard spoke of the mentally dead as "poison animal eaters"—and it was all peace between the Rastas and Gods. Outside the juice bar, a bearded Rasta in head wrap and red, gold, and green scarf sold Nuwaubian DVDs, and when I bought one called *The Creation of the White Race and Galactic History*, he greeted me with "One love."

Even as a white devil, I was the fruit of that tree too, as much as anyone: the primary historical force directing my encounter with Islam was the transatlantic slave trade. So in Ethiopia on the day, I had to celebrate Garvey. Anwar agreed and said that he could get some ganja grown at Shashemene, where some Jamaican Rastas had been living on a commune since the 1960s or '70s and fighting to have Bob Marley's remains reinterred.

As we wandered across Harar in search of Rastas that Anwar knew, he told me how much he loved this city and how special it was—"the only place where you can find all the nations of Ethiopia, the Oromo and everyone all in one place." And he told me the story of how he got there. He was born and raised in Addis Ababa, and when he was sixteen his sister got in a fight with their parents and left home. Some time later, a traveling businessman told their dad that he had seen her in Harar, so the parents sent Anwar out to get her. Anwar arrived in Harar on a mission but made tons of friends and blew all the money his mom gave him on chat and fun and had no desire to make it back home. His sister wound up returning home somehow, but Anwar stayed, making good money as a guide for faranji tourists and crashing at a different friend's house every night.

We met up with Qadir again but couldn't track down any Rastas, ending up stuck on a stoop wondering what we could do for Marcus Garvey. Qadir played with the zikr beads wrapped around my hand, and Anwar asked whether herb was haram.

"The Qur'an only forbids wine," I told him. "It says nothing about ganja."

"Ganja is better than wine," said Anwar.

"Nobody gets high and then beats their wife."

"Yes, ganja just makes you peaceful, happy people." Then another kid showed up, older than Qadir but younger than Anwar, fourteen or fifteen, and Qadir asked him how many names God had. Ninety-nine, the kid said, and Qadir tried to remember the ones that he knew. Al-Qadir was one of them, meaning the All-Powerful. I used to get into the name stuff; it was a good way to keep Allah in the brain.

Things looked hopeless, we had no ganja but could only talk about it. Anwar knew that the Rastas held ganja to be sacred, and I added some history: ganja wasn't native to Jamaica, it first arrived with indentured servants from India. The word *ganja* itself was Sanskrit, and the idea that it was sacred also came from the Indians. With a sacramental herb and Bible provided by colonialism, Ras Tafari shaped itself using materials from the same Babylon that it reviled. I tried to explain the Five Percenters to Anwar and told him that in Harlem, they called weed "equality." He appreciated that, because ganja made everyone love each other. Our conversation finally inspired him to make a last-ditch attempt, so we took our leave of Qadir, but the other kid kept tagging along. By Jah's Will alone we found one of Anwar's Rasta friends in a dark corner of a restaurant, complete with red, gold, and green Rasta cap, Lion-of-Judah dreadlocks spilling out, and a Haile Selassie T-shirt. We told him that it was a special day, and of course he loved Garvey ("Garevvy," they said in Harar), so he went to get the stuff, and then we all met up again on the road.

"To Marcus Garvey," we toasted, whether Garvey would have found it a fitting tribute or not, and also ignoring the real history—Garvey didn't even like or respect Selassie, openly calling him a failure. The Rasta took us to a bar to listen to reggae. The fifteen-year-old was still with us and ordering beers with no problem. I didn't drink, but it was still where I needed to be at that moment, my last night in Harar. I watched the men dance with each other and the women dance with each other, and the Rasta wanted to find another bar—one that didn't kill the good reggae vibes with Shania Twain—but when we went outside, Qadir was waiting for us. It was too late at night, and I couldn't leave the kid for another stupid bar, so we just walked around, Qadir holding my hand, which was acceptable male affection in Harar (like Lahore). Qadir said that if you believe in God, no one will attack you. I gave him my zikr beads and considered maybe that was the destined reason for me to eat the chat and do zikrs all night, to give the kid something magically endowed if you're into that kind of religion. It can be cool if you don't overthink.

How do you separate culture and religion in Harar? Someone could say that the remnants of ancestor worship, remnants of animal totemism, and intoxicating sacred leaves weren't "Islamic," but what else were they in a town of a hundred mosques and shrines? Anwar asked me if fig trees meant something special in Islam, because so many Harar shrines were built around or near fig trees; and even if there wasn't a buried saint to honor, people would still visit a fig tree to light incense and make du'a. Beyond the short sura in the Qur'an named "The Fig," I didn't know; it could have been an Ethiopian thing. There were Ethiopian Christians who believed that Mary lived in sycamore trees.

For this Rasta ganja merchant, the land itself was sacred. He taught me the symbolism of the Ethiopian flag: the red was the blood of the people spilled in slavery and oppression, the gold was the wealth taken from them, and the green was this holy country, the real Zion. I gave him a Fardiyya breakdown, with the red still blood, the gold being what the Trader promised the Original people, and the green as the earth, which Fard said was the home of Islam. It was coincidence that Marcus Garvey's birthday fell near that of the Mahdi—and just a coincidence for this year, because the lunar Islamic calendar was always moving—but maybe Garvey was the Mahdi, probably a better candidate than anyone else in recent history for all that came from him. And Ethiopia felt like the best choice for spiritual center of the world, better than Saudi Arabia. Ethiopia's Afar region was the cradle of humanity, where our cerebral cortex evolved to allow symbolic thought and we became the first ethical creatures—which also made Ethiopia the birthplace of religion, though we'll never find the remains of those old systems because they were systems without books.

Give me that old-time religion:

Spain was home to a fourteen-thousand-year-old cave sanctuary that housed deer remains and lumps of red ochre offered to a large vertical stone. The stone had been cut and smashed by its keepers to roughly resemble a face. One side of the face seemed to represent a man with moustache and beard, the other an animal with sharp teeth and whiskers. There's not much to help us know what it meant to have "religion" back then; it was still about one hundred centuries before the appearance of written language, and the lips of those big stone anthropomorphs remain sealed. From there it's a big jump backwards, roughly fifteen thousand more years, to a boy and girl buried in what is now Russia, both ornamented with thousands of beads, the boy wearing a belt of more than 250 teeth from the polar fox and ivory from mammoth tusks. In Qafzeh of modern Israel they found eleven *Homo sapiens* from maybe one hundred thousand years ago, stained with red ochre. The group included one skeleton with the mandible of a wild boar placed on its arm and a mother and child buried together. Drifting away from my friends' conversations into my own thoughts, full of chat and ganja, I tried to imagine the earliest Ethiopian prophets from much longer ago in the shapeless dreamtime, the first humans to point at a special animal and say that it was more, that it had *meaning*. What was the shape of their hands and heads? Did the first believer in God stand up straight? Did Khidr, our immortal earthly guide, look anything like us?

Returning to modern man: wherever I went, I seemed to find the right people. They walked me back to the hotel, finishing my Harar adventure. The next day I took another minibus through the green mountains to Dire Dawa and then a plane to Addis Ababa and then another plane out of Ethiopia, falling asleep above the clouds and dreaming in red, gold, and green like Boy George.

49.

Husayn apparently had two heads, because I visited one in Damascus and another in Cairo. Maybe there was a third head still attached to the body in Karbala, and even more; in the tenth century, shrines to the head existed in Aleppo, Baalbek, Homs, Raqqa, and Medina. For a time, there was even one as far away as Afghanistan.

The Cairo version of Husayn's head was enshrined about three centuries after his death. As in Damascus and always, the placement of a head in a silver box constituted a political act. Egypt's ruling dynasty at the time, the Fatimids—named for Husayn's mother—based their claim to power on a direct lineage from Husayn. The Abbasid caliphate called them out as frauds in the Baghdad Manifesto, and it was in the ensuing hundred years of credibility struggles that Fatimid caliphs littered Cairo with Shi'a shrines. Ali's daughter Ruqayya, whose alleged tomb I had visited in Lahore, received another shrine in Cairo, where people would come and pray for her intercession.

* * *

THE ULTIMATE BOON to Fatimid legitimacy was Husayn's head, which had been discovered in Fatimid territory, Ascalon. The location mattered. Ascalon hosted a shrine for Christian martyrs who had been decapitated during Roman persecution, and was one of the Fatimids' few strongholds left after the Sunni Seljuks took Palestine and Syria. The finder of Husayn's head was a Fatimid vizier who sought to make Ascalon a center of pilgrimage and rallying point for future military campaigns. During later instability within the kingdom, the head was brought to Cairo and put in a new mosque built next to the caliphs' palace.

As in Damascus, the head rested in its own room off to the side of the main prayer hall, but unlike the Umayyad shrine, this one was gender segregated, with separate entrances and a quarter of the room fenced off for women. I hung around for a while, watching the women wail and the men covering their own faces in their hands, one father with tears in his eyes recounting the story to his young son. Was it really Husayn in there or just some lucky dead guy whose skull had somehow become an object of veneration for nearly ten centuries? There was no telling based on energy or emotion, its vibe felt the same as the head in Damascus and looked to be real as far as anyone in that room knew or cared.

I didn't get as emo at the Cairo version of Husayn's head, but I did cry at my American ziyarat, the famous mosque where Malcolm X was photographed in prayer with the circles of spherical lamps like dozens of small suns hanging above him. It was the Muhammad Ali Pasha mosque, the big one with all the domes and half domes and the two long, thin minarets that appeared on Egyptian money. The mosque was a major tourist attraction, with tons of Europeans being carted in and out after paying forty Egyptian pounds. Examining my photos later, I'd notice white people walking through the mosque with their shoes on. At the Husayn mosque, I had seen two white kids get shoved out for dropping their shoes in the doorway, *inside* the mosque—but there was no kafr tourist money to be made at the Husayn mosque, so the rules could still matter.

It was from repeatedly watching the Cairo scene in Spike Lee's *Malcolm X*, where Denzel sits in Muhammad Ali Pasha's mosque and makes du'a, that I first learned to recite al-Fatiha. And I hadn't heard anyone pronounce the sura that way since, but after my prayer I sat on the red carpet under the round lamps and said it the same way with my hands open and couldn't stop repeating it and then rubbing the blessings and tears across my face. Can a movie be sacred scripture? Years ago, it was for me. Before I ever stepped foot in a mosque or even met a Muslim in real life, my conception of Islam came from watching Denzel on his knees, humbled before the Mercy, Malcolm transformed by the Truth (again), alone in this mansion of history and heritage, the creation reflecting on his Creator and everything that he's been through with voiceover narration: "All credit is due to Allah, Lord of all the worlds. Only the mistakes have been mine."

50.

As we left, my driver pointed out the neighboring mausoleum of Muhammad Ali Pasha. Another sidenote on religious sites as political gestures: in the Ottoman Empire, only a mosque with royal patronage was allowed to have two minarets. Muhammad Ali Pasha, who sought greater autonomy for Egypt from its Ottoman overlords, gave his own mosque a pair of minarets as middle fingers aimed right at the sultan.

51.

Islam, like Christianity, divided history into Before and After. It was easy to see that line in Arabia, in which Before was home to scattered, warring tribes who worshiped stones and had nothing, and After was the seat of a new civilization of kings, philosophers, poets, historians, scientists, doctors, architects. Arabia's pre-Islamic history, the Age of Ignorance, had meaning only as a contrast to the truth and power of what Muhammad would bring. I understood it as a convert, since converts drew that same line in our own lives, using the arrival of Islam to divide our biographies.

UNLIKE THE HIJAZ, pre-Islamic Egypt wasn't stumbling in the dark, waiting for a prophet to come and civilize it. Egypt had things to say to Islam; Egypt came with a challenge. I spotted the challenge from the road, just barely visible on the hazy horizon past the apartment buildings and office buildings and mosques:

The pyramids.

How did they look to Egypt's first Muslims? The glory of the pyramids came from men who believed in multiple gods, god-men with dog heads who begat more gods, men who worshiped the sun as a god crossing heaven in his boat. How do you show and prove your solo Allah's supremacy in their shadow?

Pre-Islamic Sabaeans used to make pilgrimage from Harran to Giza, believing that the pyramids were the tombs of Seth and Idris. Seth was the third son of Adam and Eve and had been the focus of veneration for a Judaic-Platonic gnostic sect older than Christ. Idris was a prophet mentioned in the Qur'an, and portrayed in classical Islamic literature as the father of astronomy, math, and other sciences; I could now forget the pharaohs Khufu, Khafre, and Mankaure and treat the pyramids as Islamic shrines.

The Qur'an says that Allah raised Idris high into heaven. Popular folklore placed Giza as the point of his departure or return, after which he revealed the new science of written language; Ibn Ishaq portrays Idris as the first human to write with a pen. But the Qur'an doesn't actually say that the ascended Idris ever came back to earth, leading some (Ibn Kathir, Hasan al-Basri) to believe that he never died.

Islamic tradition equated Idris with the Old Testament prophet Enoch. The Ethiopian Orthodox Church had its own extrabiblical scripture, the Book of Enoch, which also tells us that Enoch rose to heaven. In paradise Enoch was transformed into the angel Metatron, God's celestial scribe and the angel who brought God's Word to Moses. There was little threat to orthodoxy in building on parallels between Islam and other texts of the Abrahamic heritage, but the rabbit hole went deeper. Enoch was also associated with Hermes Trismegistus; one Arab response to the pyramids named Hermes Trismegistus/ Enoch/Idris as building them to preserve his libraries of secret knowledge. The prophet Idris now appeared as the offspring of a marriage between Judaism and Greek mythology. Lore surrounding Hermes Trismegistus portrayed him as a bestower of knowledge and wisdom to selected initiates, who would either receive revelation from him directly or stumble upon one of his lost tablets. This *hermetic* tradition manifested in Ibn 'Arabi's vision of Muhammad, who appeared to him holding the *Bezels of Wisdom*, and also the claim of Noble Drew Ali to have been initiated at the pyramid of Khufu before receiving his *Circle 7 Koran*.

Going deeper: the character of Hermes Trismegistus was a syncretic blend of Hermes, the Greek god of writing and magic, and Thoth, the Egyptian god of writing and magic—believed to be the inventor/revealer of astronomy, astrology, mathematics, numerology, geometry, medicine, alchemy, theology, ethics, law, and every branch of knowledge. Hermes' title "Trismegistus" was derived from Thoth's "Three times great, great." Like Enoch/Metatron, who was given a throne beside the throne of God, Thoth rode at the side of Ra in his boat that traveled across the sky, always holding his pen and scrolls. Thoth was usually portrayed as having a human body and an ibis head but sometimes appeared as a baboon. The choice of symbolic animals wasn't random: both the ibis and baboon had faces suggesting that they were thoughtful creatures, with something serious going on behind their eyes.

Apart from the relationship of Egyptian god Thoth to Islamic prophet Idris, some believed that Judaism, Christianity, and Islam all took their god from the Eighteenth Dynasty's short-lived experiment in monotheism. Pharaoh Amenhotep IV had founded an Aton sun cult, changed his name to Akhenaton ("Effective Spirit of Aton"), banned all images but a sun disk, and built his new capital as Aton's sacred city. The Egyptians refused to let go of their gods, and Akhenaton's reforms were abandoned after his death. Freud theorized that Moses was a priest of the Aton cult who led an "exodus" of Akhenaton's followers out of Egypt.

Back when I was a teen convert wearing the black turban and white robe, a Christian street-preacher downtown would see me and start yelling that Allah was not the god of Abraham, that Islam was only old Arab paganism, and that I worshiped a moon deity. If I wanted to, I could have drawn up some knowledge and slain him—where did he get his Christianity, his trinity, his god coming down to have sex with earth women and beget half-man half-gods? His Easter, his Christmas? In the sixth century, Pope Gregory the Great encouraged the Church to co-opt pagan holidays and temples and change their meanings. We could have gone back and forth on that forever. "Jewish history," says Jewish author Chaim Potok, "began in a world of pagans." Christian and Islamic history began in Judaism, but members of all three faiths have such a hard time with our pagan heritage. It's the same issue that believers take with Darwin's theory of evolution, stemming from a crucial need to be distinguished from this world, kept separate as God's highest creation. Like Adam, God's true message has to pop out of thin air, unsullied by the earth, but religion has its own fossil record, pentadactyl limb and molecular variance patterns. I've seen Christian missionaries argue that the opening sura of the Qur'an was just a rip-off of the Lord's Prayer, but you can dig deeper and read both against an ancient prayer to the Babylonian moon god:

I am kneeling; I tarry thus; I seek after you.
Bring upon me wishes for well-being and justice.
May my god and my goddess, who for many days have been
    angry with me,
in truth and justice be favorable to me;
may my road be propitious, may my path be straight.
After he has sent Zakar, the god of dreams,
during the night may I hear the undoing of my sins; let my
    guilt be poured out;
and forever let me devotedly serve you.

It wasn't all the same, but it was kind of the same.

There were other ways to see it, since an Islamic view of history did not limit Allah's guidance to one chosen tribe. The Qur'an said that every nation received a messenger speaking God's Word in its own language, which could mean both words and symbols. Allah knows best, but it was fun to speculate on Akhenaton as the messenger sent to his people, bringing Islam in a form they could understand.

Or you can deal with history by removing it from the map. I passed the Sphinx, human-headed lion guard of the pyramids with his nose blown off. Popular stories blamed the destruction on Napoleon, the British, or the Mamluks, but fifteenth-century Egyptian historians pointed the finger at a Sufi extremist, Muhammad Sa'im al-Dahr, who wigged out after watching Muslims offer sacrifices to the Sphinx with hopes of good harvests. Al-Dahr went Taliban-style on the Sphinx face and was hung by the Mamluks for vandalism. Centuries earlier, Saladin's son al-Aziz Uthman had attempted to destroy the Giza pyramids; he eventually gave up, but not before leaving his mark on the smallest one.

If only Islam was that easy, just a matter of tearing down the world's wonders—but that wouldn't purify religion any more than cutting off your arm could take the monkey out of your DNA. These things were too deeply embedded in what we had. Riding a tourist gimmick camel by the pyramids, I pictured these mismatched characters from different universes clashing together like *Star Wars* guys fighting He-Man guys and G.I. Joes meeting Transformers in my old toy box, animated like in a *Robot Chicken* sketch—I swear by the Pen and what the angels write, Qur'an 68:1—fully articulated poseable Muhammad on his Buraq, surrounded by plastic six-winged angels, flying over the Buraq's grandfather Sphinx, and Ibn Taymiyya riding a flying black-socked hyena across the starry night over Mecca where Ra's bird-headed scribe Thoth circles the Ka'ba . . . Thoth who's also Metatron, but I thought of Metatron as a robot with fusion cannon mounted on his right arm, shooting black hole antimatter like Megatron from the *Transformers*—because God brought Enoch into heaven and transformed him into Metatron, and the Decepticons' Megatron was floating through space half-destroyed when planet-eating cybergod Unicron made him into Galvatron with a new particle-accelerating laser cannon. So Enoch was a Decepticon. Thoth's secret mystical number, 4,579, could be digit-summed as $4 + 5 + 7 + 9 = 25$, symbolizing the 25,000-year cycle of every Qur'an written and renewed by the Original Man, who does all things right and exact, a year for every mile of the Earth's circumference, and 25 equals Wisdom Power but 2 + 5 = 7, and 7 = God, and the Noble Drew Ali action figure came with fez and robes and could stand with his feet together and his hand on his heart, forming a 7 with his body . . . Thoth puts his pagan hands on the Black Stone and Ibn Taymiyya descends upon the Ka'ba, wielding his huge Omega Prime Super God Sword (taller than he is, with its blade bearing the inscription TILL ALL ARE ONE) and chops off the bird head, but then Khidr/St. George/Utnapishtim with light-up laser eyes reveals that Thoth was really Idris the messenger of God, peace be upon him, and now Ibn Taymiyya bears the sin of murdering a prophet . . . half-original Ibn Taymiyya losing the knowledge of self and having a hard time civilizing the devil, he also decapitates his hyena but still rides it headless into the desert past al-Hakim's blood-soaked donkey, way out there past all the hiding mahdis and secret shrines for buried Abdals and Akhyars and nameless saints that no one ever knew, where more Bezels wait under the sand to never be revealed, and even a half-buried temple of Aton with trapdoors like Castle Greyskull, poor Ibn Taymiyya getting crazier in that mischief, and he's lost in the darkness that's only illuminated when the believers shoot at each other with red photon beams . . . make it Nuwaubian with secrets from the nineteenth galaxy, have Nibiru shining up above, add howling winds and Master Fard playing an Australian aboriginal didgeridoo while Killah Priest heavy-mental raps about building a synagogue on Mars for the royal seminars, boarding his spaceship with armfuls of solid gold bracelets.

Swimming with the mysteries, Islam feeling like a fucked-up Saturday cartoon, all the characters morphing from gods to Muslims to Muslim gods—like Man-E-Faces from *Masters of the Universe*, who could switch his face from that of a normal human to a robot to a monster, depending on the Divine

Attribute that he wanted to manifest—I wanted special-edition figures of all these guys and a Motherplane play set.

At least on Egyptian money, the distinction between systems seemed to be easier, with ancient pagan monuments appearing on the fronts of bills with English text and famous mosques on the backs with Arabic.

52.

From Cairo I headed back for Damascus and spent a few days looking at all the tombs again, just trying to pursue a straightforward Islam without getting spooky and neopagan about it. You can retreat into your brain and get dense, I thought, as long as you have a round-trip ticket; no good in getting stuck there.

But I also made my own relic: at the shrine of Fatima Sughra, the caretaker had given me a foot-long strip of green fabric for the purpose of collecting holy dust from the tomb and then rubbing it on my face. This cloth had gone with me through my travels, touching every site that I touched: the heads of Husayn in both Damascus and Cairo, the shrine of Mary at Sayednaya, the tombs of John the Baptist, Abel, Bilal, Lady Zaynab, Lady Sakina, sixteen heads of Karbala martyrs, the Ahlul-Bayt tombs at Bab al-Saghir, the handprint of Gabriel, the maqams of Khidr and Abraham, the meeting place of the Abdals, the cave of the Sleepers, shrines of Shaykh Abadir and Aw Ansar and Emir Nur in Harar, the tombs of Ibn 'Arabi and Ibn Taymiyya, the tombs of Seth and Idris at Giza. The cloth itself was worn and fraying with threads hanging off, looking much older than it was, which only helped its gravitas as a sacred object.

The last Friday before flying home, I went to jum'aa prayers at the Umayyad Mosque, the old mosque of empire. Saladin was buried somewhere in the immediate area, and his statue stood outside. I climbed onto the pedestal with him and did a Hulk Hogan pose. On the day of my flight, the Mathematics would read as Wisdom Understanding, which adds up to Power ($2 + 3 = 5$). The corresponding degree in Master Fard's lessons asks about Islam's reclaiming of Jerusalem from the devil—the answer building on Jesus as a prophet and righteous man whose name and face were used by the Ten Percenters as shields for their dirty religion. But it was the same with Muhammad and Mecca.

"Whoever has been given religion through God Almighty," wrote al-Ghazali, "must love his own emperor and remain obedient to him." Al-Ghazali took the pre-Islamic Persian concept of *farr*, the divine light of kings, and put it on his sultans. In Harar, they enshrined their dead emirs as saints. I was moving towards the anarchist critique of religion, "No gods, no masters," which felt pretty much the same as Master Fard's breakdown of society with the 5, 10, and 85. What would it take to wash my Islam clean after the dirty touches of kings?

In 1190 a Christian prophet told King Richard the Lion-Hearted that Saladin was the Anti-Christ who must be defeated to resurrect Jerusalem. We were dancing the same steps in our Republican theocracy, the Southern Baptist Caliphate—where George W. Bush declared that God wanted him to be president, John Ashcroft called the separation of church and state a "wall of religious oppression," and John McCain would soon pick a religious extremist to be his vice presidential candidate—where neo-Confederate theocons could sidestep their fear of Obama's insufficient whiteness by projecting it onto his questionable Christian-ness—

I was going home to the land where the Ten Commandments were given monuments on state buildings and we said "Under God" in our pledge to the flag. The words were added in the

1950s to mark our special country and special destiny from the godless Communists but could still help us against the minions of *Allah*. I belonged to God's Country, where we put God's Name on our money . . . and also where we ranked last among Western nations in our understanding of evolution, believed the earth to be six thousand years old, bullied our scientists into negotiations with theology and sabotaged our schools, argued Middle East policy using the book of Revelation, received coded allusions to the Bible in our president's speeches, picked apart the sermons at candidates' churches, and even half entertained the idea of electing clergymen as presidents—Pat Robertson, Jesse Jackson, and Mike Huckabee, though Thomas Jefferson had wanted to ban ministers from running for office. Maybe American religion only looked amorphous to me because I came from New York, not Mississippi, where Christian fundamentalists tore up rainbow pride flags and Qur'ans together at the state capitol building.

From the Damascus of Umayyad caliphs' vanity masjids, I'd leave for the nation of megachurches that followed Wal-Mart business models, the American empire still in White Christ's dominion. FBI agents and customs cops assessed a Muslim's loyalty by his beard or what she wore on her head, so I figured I'd shave and even wear one of the Ethiopian crosses I had bought for Sadaf. Jesus really does save, especially when you've stashed a Hezbollah flag in your carry-on.

BOOK 2

As no two people see the same view along the Way, all trips from here to there are imaginary; all truth is a tale I am telling myself.

—**BRION GYSIN,** *The Process*

Hajji Azreal Wisdom

1.

I came home just before the Democratic convention and the start of Ramadan. Walking through Brooklyn with hunger pains restored Islam as a religion of discipline and clarity, and I even imagined Ramadan as an anticapitalist gesture: No, Wendy's billboard, I will *not* try the Double Stack burger! I could see why Elijah Muhammad made his Nation fast during December instead.

Jum'aa at an Arab mosque almost ruined my good feelings. Those guys were Salafi style, the kind of place where men rolled up their pant legs because the Prophet's garments never passed his ankles, and before prayers a few men wrapped long skirts around their jeans because this meant something too. And the women did nothing, they didn't exist, no room there for my Muslim girlfriend. The imam gave a long, humorless khutbah all in Arabic, and even when the microphone stand kept falling down he couldn't crack a smile about it. He lectured us like an angry high school gym teacher, a style that failed to reach me in any language. Even the older Arab men who could understand him looked only half awake and bored out of their minds, like visiting the mosque was just a job, punch in, punch out, do your time.

Sadaf had shown me a YouTube clip of a miraculous child preacher somewhere in the Middle East, just four years old but standing firm in TV studios delivering fire-and-brimstone sermons with his little headdress and everything. There was no way that he actually composed the sermons himself or could even know what he was talking about. The YouTube comments lavished him with *mash'Allah* and such, but to me the kid looked like a parody. Even worse, most preachers now reminded me of him, especially the guy at this mosque. It was hard not to laugh at the imam as just another toddler acting righteous in his grown-up costume.

I considered walking out on the Friday service, a minor act of apostasy—listening to this guy ramble wasn't religion for me, it wasn't anything—but stuck it out on the odds that the actual prayer would feel better. It did, a little. Then I made my way through the crowd and past the door, outside to where the overflowing congregation prayed on sheets of cardboard on the sidewalk.

2.

I thought of New York in Five Percenter terms, since their renaming of the boroughs made train rides feel like hijras. Harlem was Mecca, and Brooklyn was Medina. But I also wanted to see the real Mecca, the heart of it all, to make the hajj and stone the Devil.

Sadaf had been to Mecca as a teenager, on an out-of-season pilgrimage with her parents.

"What was it like?" I asked her.

"A really beautiful place in the middle of a really ugly place. I wished it could have been somewhere else."

"I'm going," I said. She already knew, but it was still an intense thing to say. "I'm going to Mecca, is that some shit?"

"Are you going to come back all crazy?" she asked.

"I don't think so. Why would I?"

"Because that's what happens." Everyone had a story of an uncle or cousin who made hajj and came home as a "fundy." You go to Mecca, take a blast of taqwa to the face and let it explode your brain, and then you come home and can't let it go. You try to hold onto everything special that you felt at hajj, but it just doesn't work in the real world, and then you get touchy and uptight. I couldn't blame anyone for that.

BECAUSE ONLY MUSLIMS can enter Mecca and Medina, I needed a letter from a mosque verifying my Islamic credentials. In my whole Muslim life, I've only had a real relationship to one mosque, but hadn't shown my face there in more than ten years. I used to be the darling of the place, but couldn't face the brothers when I had a rotten secret, those murtad storms raging in my head; so I only went at night to avoid facing Dr. Shafiq, and then I lost my key and stopped going altogether. I remembered one of the brothers telling me that if I missed two Friday prayers in a row, I should make shahadah again as a symbolic reunion with the community; how many Fridays had it been for me?

Forget about the letter of endorsement, I still had to stand before Dr. Shafiq and man up to the past. Breaking it down mathematically: the year was 2008, Wisdom Cipher Cipher Build or Destroy, which *borned* back to Knowledge Cipher ($2 + 0 + 0 + 8 = 10$). Your cipher is your life, the Qur'an of your own history, represented with the cipher (circle) of 360 degrees. To have knowledge of your cipher meant that you've come full circle, going through the whole mathematics from Knowledge (1) to Born (9). Knowledge Cipher is closure, a reflection at the journey's end; but since 10 breaks down further as $1 + 0 = 1$, it's also a new beginning, the renewal of history and writing of your next Qur'an.

In one of Fard's lessons, the corresponding degree said that if a

Muslim kills four devils and presents their heads, his reward will be free transportation to the holy city of Mecca and a meeting with brother Muhammad. The degree was open to interpretation; some believed that the four devils were Lust, Greed, Hate, and Envy, which we had to slay within ourselves; another believed that it meant teaching the knowledge to four people, freeing their heads from the devil's grip. One scholar of the lessons understood the heads as an allegory for the genital, heart, throat, and pituitary chakras, the opening of which led to spiritual advancement ("meeting" or "becoming" Muhammad). There was also an underground Nation of Islam offshoot, the Death Angels, which actually went around killing white people in San Francisco in the early 1970s, and an urban legend of someone showing up at a mosque with four human heads in a sack.

3.

I planned to visit the Islamic Center for iftar, the breaking of the daily fast. Earlier in the day, I called Laury to ask about the old blue van still waiting for me in Toronto, and she told me that Warith Deen Mohammed had died that morning.

Elijah originally named him Wallace, after our master Wallace D. Fard, who had scrawled his own name on Elijah and pregnant Clara's door and told them it was the name of the baby. The boy would be special, Master Fard knew, the seventh child in the family and destined to become a master teacher.

Like the original Muhammad, Elijah died without officially naming a successor. Elijah had allegedly made statements in support of Wallace, but other hadiths pointed to Elijah's national minister, Louis Farrakhan, as the heir to the throne. Before Elijah's passing could spark a Muslim civil war, Wallace publicly declared himself the new leader of the Nation, pushing the rest

of the family and Farrakhan to come with him. In Harlem I
had bought a DVD of the 1975 Savior's Day convention held
just days after Elijah's death, with speeches by Muhammad Ali,
afro-sporting Jesse Jackson, and the new king Wallace in his
paramilitary Fruit of Islam uniform, hoisted on Fruit shoulders
in front of a giant portrait of his father. If Wallace wanted to
have everything that his father had, his own face on the walls of
mosques as *the Honorable* Wallace Muhammad, he could have.
The people were ready to give it to him, but he turned it down.

No one knew what he was going to do, that he planned
nothing less than to completely destroy the Nation. He sold off
his father's black capitalist empire, the restaurants and fisheries,
and disbanded the Fruit of Islam. He even changed the name
of Harlem's Mosque No. 7 to Masjid Malcolm Shabazz and
allowed white Muslims inside. Within just a few years, the
tradition as everyone had known it no longer existed.

As Imam W.D. Mohammed—not only renaming himself
Warith Deen ("Inheritor of Religion"), but altering the spelling
of his last name to achieve more distance from his father—he
gently eased the old ways into the background. Warith Deen
said that his father had given him permission and blessing to
teach whatever he wanted; Elijah knew that the time would
come to enter the world community of Muslims. And Master
Fard was not Allah, as Elijah had taught; Warith Deen told
his Muslims that he still spoke to Fard, but not in a "spooky
way"; he just picked up the phone and dialed Fard's number.

According to Warith Deen, Master Fard had even returned to
the Nation of Islam in disguise to help its reformation, undoing
his own work. That story had brought me to a Punjabi imam's
grave in Hayward, California, making Sunni du'as for him.
It could have been Fard in that grave (probably not), but the
story allowed us to reconcile our history and tie it all together.
In Warith Deen's retelling of the story, we could keep his father
and Master Fard as Islamic heroes but still name Malcolm

the winner, as though Malcolm's apostasy signaled the true fulfillment of Fard's mission. Going to Warith Deen mosques today, you still might hear Elijah quoted in a completely Sunni sermon, or old Nation terms like "grafted." You'll also hear call-and-response like it's a Baptist church.

Warith Deen was a diplomat, a bridge builder who shook hands with presidents and popes. As a leader of Muslims in a non-Muslim country, and a community comprised of converts or the sons and daughters of converts, he pushed Muslims to embrace America and find their way in. His father had equated the American flag with "Slavery, Suffering, and Death"—and he was right—but Warith Deen put the flag on his own newspaper's front page and delivered convocation before the Senate, and he was right too. Elijah's myths of white devils and black spaceships had uplifted thousands of people, but Warith Deen knew that a perpetual state of war couldn't move the Nation forward. He did the right thing with his moment in history; but still, thank Allah that Minister Farrakhan broke away from Warith Deen and revived the old Nation, just to maintain the legacy of self-reliance and that damning finger pointed at Uncle Sam. I thought of both men as Elijah's sons and heirs, the Isaac and Ishmael to our American Abraham, with the father wanting both of them to do exactly as they've done.

THE ORIGINAL Islamic Center of Rochester was now dwarfed by its addition, an elementary school still under construction. The mosque door was the same one that I had opened fifteen years ago and held for my mother.

At one time, this mosque was home for me, in a way that no other mosque could ever be. Its high ceiling, bare white walls, and gray and blue carpeting form my default image of mosques, what I expect whenever I step into a masjid. Red oriental rugs now covered the floor, but I could still see the old gray and blue at uncovered spots. A new trim of gold Arabic text lined the walls, but it wasn't overwhelming. The most significant difference inside the prayer hall was all the school stuff: washable marker boards, class rosters with kids' names and their accumulated sticker awards, model Ka'bas made with cardboard and permanent marker.

This mosque was where I became a Muslim in the social sense, sitting between Dr. Shafiq and my mom and repeating his shahadah in both Arabic and English. This mosque was where I learned to read Arabic and give the adhan and made my first Muslim friends, other teenagers at the Islamic Center Summer Camp. They were probably all married now.

Back when I had a key, I would spend whole weekends at the Islamic Center, scavenging meals from the kitchen and sleeping in the masjid. This mosque was where, when I felt the pain of apostasy coming, I'd come only at night, when I could be alone and really make it my mosque. This mosque was where I'd pray or read or write or just cry. During my stint as a backyard wrestler, I jumped off the women's balcony in imitation of Mick Foley's Hell in the Cell match against the Undertaker.

I had come back to Islam in the personal sense, knowing that I still believed in Allah and trying my best to follow the Prophet; but in the social dimension of religion, my oaths remained broken. It wasn't just my outrageous statements on the Internet or deviant beliefs; I used to be a friend of this mosque, but walked away. No one here at the mosque knew me anymore.

A handful of men were there for the breaking of the fast; we had our dates and juice and then prayed Maghrib. Lining up side-by-side with my brothers and looking at our bare feet, I could see that I was a white man standing between a black man and a brown man, and on down the line there were other white feet and black feet and brown feet. This was Warith Deen's work, bringing Malcolm's Mecca to our side of the globe. In my own thoughts during that prayer, I called myself a Bilalian, just for the word to survive in 2008.

It had been my dream to interview Warith Deen, to just sit at his feet like a wide-eyed grandson and hear the tales, capturing his stories before they were lost. Through Laury I had come into contact with a professor who knew the imam, and said she could forward my book on the Five Percenters to him. I had sent her a copy with a note for Warith Deen inside. He died less than a month before her planned meeting with him. Earlier in the year I lost my friend Barry Gottehrer, a former aide to New York mayor John Lindsay who was close with the Five Percenters' Allah. Malcolm's generation was going fast. It made me think of the Muslims of my generation, whether we had meaningful bridges to that history and how we'd add on.

After the prayer we went upstairs for dinner in the banquet area, rice and meat and bread all desi style. Everyone smiled and salam'd each other. I overheard a few African-American brothers discussing Warith Deen and the hard tasks that he had faced in his life. Allah forgive and reward him, *inna lilah wa inna ilayhi raji'un.*

I ate alone and went back downstairs. With the adults socializing in the banquet room, the kids had taken over the prayer hall for a game of freeze tag. I sat in a dark corner of the half-lit room and watched. Ramadan at the mosque was like a family holiday, and I missed that feeling . . . and I missed what I never had, my own Muslim family to share it with. Maybe with Sadaf, insha'Allah.

The mosque filled up again for Isha, the last of the five daily prayers, and we stood behind a strict hafiz—I only guessed that he was strict by the shape of his beard—who reminded us to make the lines straight and turn off our phones and "Control your children . . . this is a masjid, not a playground." But the little kids still ran around while the big kids and men prayed.

I wasn't even aware that when we all sang "AAAA-MMMMEEEEEEN" together, one of the voices belonged to Dr. Shafiq. After the prayer and du'a, he emerged from the congregation and took the microphone to address us. A slender Pakistani man, his beard was whiter than when I last saw him. He apologized for delaying the special Ramadan taraweeh prayers, but said that he wanted to talk to us about Imam Warith Deen. He had first met Warith Deen in 1977 at Temple University in Philadelphia, where Warith Deen had come at the invitation of Shafiq's professor, Isma'il al-Faruqi. It was early in the Nation's reformation, and Sunni leaders were reaching out to assist Warith Deen's efforts. That same year, Warith Deen would lead the largest-ever group of American Muslims—mostly members of his and his father's Nation—on hajj to Mecca.

Dr. Shafiq had helped Warith Deen teach proper prayers to Nation Muslims in Philadelphia and also supplied them with copies of Hammudah Abd al-Ati's *Islam in Focus*—the same book that I had used to learn my prayers. It almost felt like my life was bonded to theirs through our shared sources.

Discussing Warith Deen's reform of the Nation, Dr. Shafiq spoke of "*mainstream* Islam," not "real Islam" or "true Islam." A subtle distinction, but I clipped it. Dr. Shafiq was still an imam, *conservative* or *orthodox* or *traditional*, whatever you wanted to call him, but being conservative doesn't have to make you a prick about things. Dr. Shafiq was one of the good ones. Like Warith Deen, he understood the diversity of our community and knew to tread gently when navigating our differences. I wished that I could do that.

We made du'a for Warith Deen and then went into taraweeh— the prayers that would take Muslims through one-thirtieth of the Qur'an for every night of Ramadan, completing the book by the end of the month. It reminded me that Ramadan wasn't just about quitting food; we were celebrating the event of the Qur'an in the month that verses first came to Muhammad. I hadn't yet found my position on the Qur'an, but confused ones and doubters could still be *practicing* Muslims for whatever reason. It's a month-long holiday full of good feelings, no need to let dogma get in the way.

Taraweeh was divided into segments, allowing rest between prayers. After each segment of prayer, numbers of men filed out of the mosque, leaving gaps in the rows. I found myself always moving up to fill a gap between worshipers. By the end of the night I had made it to the front row, with just one man between myself and Dr. Shafiq.

He recognized me, and we shared a hug after the prayer. We walked together into his office, and he sat me down at the same table where I once sat with my mother, me still in my Catholic high school shirt and tie, a DeSales senior wanting to be Muslim.

"I've had some ups and downs," I told him.

"That's what life is," he said with a smile. I left the update at that and inquired about his sons, who had taught me to play cricket in Peshawar back when we were all teenagers. We talked about Peshawar (it's not going to get better, the sad doctor told me, no matter who's in charge over there) and then grad school; he said he'd help me get into Temple if I wanted. He even suggested the school in Michigan where I could study with Ingrid Mattson, president of the Islamic Society of North America. I wanted to tell him that he didn't know my story, that I've written some bad books and still wasn't acceptable to anyone, but people started coming in with other matters. Dr. Shafiq had been there for more than two decades, approaching three; he was the local figure of stability, a Warith Deen for Rochester's Muslims, and he carried that load without flinching. One quick question before letting him go: I wanted to make hajj. "It's very expensive," he warned me. "It's a business, you know, and there is so much money in the Middle East now. It is becoming very difficult for average people to make the hajj. It wasn't always like that."

I made more visits to the mosque for iftar and taraweeh.

During one of the dinners, I overheard a dismissal of scholar Kecia Ali as "too feminist." Kecia taught youths at her local mosque and did serious work with Shari'a—two indicators, at least compared to my position, that she approached her community and tradition as a pious, orthodox Muslim and legitimate reformer; but for these brothers, she had still crossed the bounds. It only showed how far gone I was, if only they had known. When the topic of Warith Deen's passing came up, my brothers mocked the Nation of Islam and Five Percenters while I just looked at my food and kept my mouth shut, a secret Five Percenter Shi'a feminist who prayed behind women and roamed the earth doing drugs at Sufi shrines. What could I say to them?

"You're becoming one of us," said Sadaf when I told her the story later. By "us" she meant the Muslims who were emotionally invested in the community, the ones who had to choose their battles. Instead of standing outside the mosque, pissing in, I'd rather stand inside and piss out; but success in the mosque depended on how much of my opinion I kept to myself, and I still couldn't hit the wavelength of true 85ers. Being a renegade Islamo-punk had run its course, but now I answered brothers' questions in a wonkish intellectual way, ducking and weaving around the truth claims. Even if I felt like a believer, I was sure that I didn't sound like one.

Making small talk with Dr. Shafiq about the brothers we knew back then—Iftekhar, Siddique, Qari Saheb and Mukhtar, kids from the summer camp—he mentioned brother Jonathon/Yahya, the other white teen convert from my era. Dr. Shafiq had no idea how he turned out; I had to tell him that Yahya became a patent lawyer and then stabbed his neighbor to death on the suggestion that he had molested his daughter. It broke the imam's heart to hear that. "Why did he have to do such a thing? When he was here, he had a hot temper, you know, but I thought that Islam would calm him down." Our conversation paused in a moment of silent regret for Yahya, and I realized that my own defeat could have been much worse. The place started to feel like home again.

ONE NIGHT AFTER taraweeh, the hafiz lectured the remaining few brothers about hadiths relating to the end of the world. He told us about the Mahdi, who would be doing tawaf around the Ka'ba at the time of his appointment. The forty Abdals would come to him, said the hafiz, and name him the Mahdi, and the Mahdi would refuse the call—"I cannot lead such a corrupt ummah," he'll say—until the Abdals threaten to kill him if he does not accept. He'll be thirty-three years old on that day, but for Shi'as, who held their Hidden Imam to be the Mahdi, he has already seen his thousandth birthday.

Near the end of the world, said the hafiz, there will be an increase in natural disasters, worth considering if you don't go insane with speculation: "Allah knows best, but just look around at all the hurricanes and tsunamis and earthquakes every year." The Prophet also said something about changes in time: a year equaling a month, a month equaling a week, and a week turned into a day, which some scholars have read to mean changes in travel and communication. In the future, said the Prophet, a man's hip will tell him what is going on at home. "It was difficult to understand the hadith in the time of the Prophet," said the hafiz, "but now, we see everyone keeping their cellular phones at their hips . . ."

There would also be an increase in killing, and sins like drunkenness, fornication, and musical instruments would become the norm. Again, Allah knows best, but still check out the current state of affairs. We lived in the age of fitna, the hafiz told us, and trying to remain clean of sin in this phase of time would be like diving into a lake and trying not to get wet. The Prophet had even said that in our age, someone who retained only a tenth of Islam would be regarded as a good

Muslim. Muhammad must have had a good understanding of what time does to oral tradition, I thought, and my own idea of Muslims today matched the sources used by this hafiz. The only difference was that he still had faith in what he followed as the uncorrupted Islam buried beneath the years, while I saw the Prophet, the Qur'an, and our perfected religion as a lost moment in time—like Picasso drawing pictures in the sand, only to have someone shovel the masterpiece into a plastic bucket and hand it to me: "Here is Picasso's greatest work." It's true in a way, the picture is in there somewhere, but it's also gone. So far from that moment, how could anyone be more than one-tenth of a Muslim? Once the Prophet died, all anyone had was *post-Islam*. If I was qualified to give fatwas, I'd make takfir on the whole billion of us.

After the lecture I went into the office to find Dr. Shafiq, and he introduced me to whoever else was around: "This is brother Mikail, he accepted Islam when he was very, very young. We sent him to Pakistan and then he disappeared! But he has come back, mash'Allah . . . and insha'Allah, he's going into PhD for Islamic studies, he'll take over the Islamic Center when I retire."

Finding a quiet moment alone with him, I offered a solemn statement with my head hanging low and sad: "It took me a long time to feel like I was ready for Mecca."

"Mash'Allah," he replied. I just hoped for a window to give my full confession, but he never took the bait. That was Dr. Shafiq's mercy to me. He knew, of course he knew.

He gave me the number of a brother who assisted local Muslims with the pilgrimage, and also typed up a letter endorsing my hajj:

It is certified that Michael Edward Muhammad Knight is a Muslim. He accepted Islam here at the Islamic Center in 1994. He is a good, practicing Muslim, and I wish him the best in his career and life.

He signed it and stamped it, and just like that, the gates to the holy city opened for me. A brother came into the office and Dr. Shafiq introduced us. "This is brother Mikail," he said, "the lost and found." Dr. Shafiq and I hugged again, and I left him to do his work. Walking out of the mosque to a dark parking lot, it felt like that same special holiday-time love as leaving Nan and Gramps's house after Christmas dinner. But I was also a coward, I had no balls whatsoever. God surround the dead and the living with care.

4.

A week later it was time for the Great American Muslim Punk Rock Movie, the adaptation of my novel full of Muslim drunkenness and fornication and even musical instruments to help bring on the End. Laury and her boyfriend were nice enough to deal with crossing the U.S.-Canada border to give me the van, even throwing a mattress in the back because they knew I'd be living in it. Between coming home from Syria and waiting for my next book check to pay for hajj, I was broke again (still no regrets about the $30 rooms in Ethiopia).

The film's director was a Syrian-American kid named Eyad who had worked as a director's assistant on that Brad Pitt movie about Jesse James, though they spelled his name wrong in the credits. To get to this point with him shooting DIY, he went through all kinds of pain and hassle with Hollywood people. He had some dumb haggling over plot with people at a big production company. They loved the novel but wanted my main character, a Pakistani-American college student, to instead be a white convert—they were only thinking of who they could put in the role and there weren't any genuine desi American movie stars, Kal Penn wasn't big enough in their eyes. Eyad told them about my personal back story and then they wanted that to be worked into the film, to have me as a fictional character in the house. Eyad explained that we had a clear line between the novel and the author on this one, so then they suggested making the film about some young Iranians who come to America and get into punk rock. Eyad said no, the story's about growing up Muslim in America. Finally, they suggested doing a film about a group of American Muslim punks living in a house together.

"That's the book you just read," Eyad answered. They couldn't grasp what we were trying to do. The problem was that Hollywood just loves white people, and we were presenting a story full of brown people. If we went with a production company, they'd end up taking out all of the Arabic, watering down the Islamic content, and even worse, turning it into an anti-Islam narrative, which could so easily be done. Non-Muslim readers of the script told us that we couldn't have a punk girl in a burqa, we had to show her face; that a woman leading men in prayer wasn't as shocking and feminist as we made it out to be; that no one could be punk and religious at the same time; and we'd have to move the story from Buffalo to Los Angeles. Besides, one asked, how can you make a movie about Muslims with no Arabs in it? Weren't all Muslims Arabs? It'd become a movie about Islam aimed at non-Muslim audiences, feeding into the Islam that they wanted to see, and a movie about punk rock for non-punks, which would reduce it to bad haircuts, just some stupid *National Lampoon's Islamo-Punk Rockers* with lots of big kafr tits.

The only real option was to strike out on our own, scrounging around to self-finance and do it the way it had to be done—which was closer to the spirit of the book anyway, originally self-published on photocopiers and spiral-bound and given away for free. Eyad said that he could leave Los Angeles and move back in with his parents in Cleveland and shoot the whole thing there; Cleveland and Buffalo were both miserable in the same ways.

The punk movie scared me to death. I had written the novel at a time when I had no hope of ever finding a place in the Muslim community; and now that people were giving me one, it was tempting to soften the characters and their words. We all had our doubts—Sadaf was never one of the kids that a story like this would speak to and questioned whether the balls-out punk approach would do more harm than good. Eyad would call me at two in the morning asking whether we should really include the scene where Rabeya crosses out the beat-your-wife verse in the Qur'an, afraid that we'd play into anti-Islamic agendas, feed the neocons and so on. It was a valid thing to worry about, but calls for united fronts always fucked over women. Someone, James Baldwin I think, said that a neutral position always sides with the oppressor. Eyad agreed, and I added that we could balance the crossing out of an ayat by smashing idols on the other side, fucking with the Stars and Stripes in some way. It was hard to know which would get us in more trouble, because Americans could get as violent over their flag as anyone else did for a book.

We always said that taqwacore was a middle finger aimed in both directions. America was still ugly and full of its own fundamentalisms, with a Christian extremist from Alaska potentially tipping the balance of the presidential election, and some fuck in a red state putting a sign in his front yard that read OBAMA HALF-BREED MUSLIN [sic]. Then came the news that earlier in the summer, George W. Bush had authorized U.S. forces to cross Afghanistan's border into Pakistan without Pakistan's permission, and I couldn't help but remember the words of that international bartender at the shrine in Lahore: *The Americans are coming.* No one knew at the time, but they were coming even as he said it. There were also reports that Pakistani troops had fired at U.S. helicopters over the tribal areas, sending them back into Afghanistan. Bush was accelerating the conflict either for another big trophy on his way out of the White House or the sudden panic that Osama bin Laden would outlast him in power or the realization that neglecting Afghanistan for six years was about to bite him in the ass. Or it could have been to make the War on Terror push economic issues out of the headlines, which would help McCain among voters who wanted America to bomb things. No matter who won in November, I assumed that we would in fact *capture* Pakistan in the decade to come and prayed that it would be everything that the bartender hoped.

It was a confusing time for the community. If the ultimate good was to see Muslims accepted as positive contributors to American life, did that mean keeping our mouths shut? What did it mean for the writers and rappers and filmmakers—should artists be held to the same concerns as activists? What should an artist do when truth disagrees with justice? Are you a bridge builder or a truth teller? Warith Deen or Malcolm?

Truth: there were American Muslims who saw themselves on the edges of both America and Islam, and I was one of them, and no one on either side wanted to hear our voices. America wouldn't know where to place us, Muslims who'd throw rocks at your soldiers not for a holy war thing, but a secular human rights thing; and Muslims wouldn't see us as legitimate, since our sisters didn't cover right and we viewed homosexuals as human beings, since of course America had brainwashed us. A mohawked Muslim downing a beer in front of my Hezbollah flag would make sense to no one.

"If we're right," I told Eyad, "we're right." If there was actually heart and thought behind what we did, it would shine through; so shit on everyone, let's go. Meanwhile, I signed off on an option with another company to make my Islamo-American road book into a movie, with a plan to have some douchebag actor pretend to be me riding Greyhound buses. My agent sent me a check dated 9/11, I cashed it and then drove my unregistered van to Cleveland.

5.

On the road, I thought about all the maqams of great holy men I had visited overseas, only to now drive through the wilderness of northern America, the real desert. There were no saints' shrines between Buffalo and Cleveland, but fuck saints; there is no god but God and why not entitle everyone to make their own land sacred? I toyed with the idea that if you made one thousand rakats anywhere, that spot could become your special maqam, even if it only mattered to you, and then I thought about where I would make mine—why not this road, the westbound side of the Interstate 90? I was already Sultan of the I-90 in the Moorish Orthodox Church, bestowing me a duty to the spiritual welfare of the thruway. Scholars have said that nafl prayers could be made while in a moving car; the Prophet used to make voluntary prayers while riding a camel, even if he wasn't facing Mecca. So I started to make rakats with one hand on the wheel, the other raised to my ear or placed on my thigh or the dashboard when I slightly lowered my head to make sujdah, eyes still on the road.

The intention was to perform one thousand nafl rakats, but I knew that I probably wouldn't make it and got distracted with thoughts anyway. I was on my way to the pivotal purple swing-state of Ohio and brooded on American religion. Thomas Jefferson had been accused of atheism by his opponents; if he were alive today, Fox News would pounce on him, and he'd never have a chance.

Jefferson owned a Qur'an—the first Muslim member of the

United States Congress, Keith Ellison, was sworn in on it—but I was more interested in his relationship to the Bible. Jefferson had made his own version of the Bible, collecting what he viewed as the best of the scripture and discarding what he considered to be outdated for the modern age. Jefferson's Bible contains no mention of angels, miracles, or any supernatural element to Christ's identity; Jesus is simply an ethical teacher, his only value resting in the wisdom of his words. After Jesus is crucified, his disciples bury him in a cave and block the entrance with a large boulder. And there, without a resurrection, is where Jefferson's Bible ends. Jefferson even left out the entire book of Revelation, which he mocked as "merely the ravings of a maniac." He never published the revised Bible in his lifetime, believing that it was not appropriate for politicians to speak on religion.

My fictitious Rabeya's crossed-out 4:34 was inspired by a real Muslim woman from history, Rabi'a al-Basri, who deleted a verse condemning the devil. Rabi'a justified the act by stating simply that her Qur'an had no room for hate. Too bad that more Muslims today don't know about her; she wasn't some bourgeois secular attention-monger calling for an enlightened and West-friendly Islam in *New York Times* op-eds, but a legit Sufi saint who cared about nothing but loving God. She came from our tradition, calling us to truth from the inside. Islam's heritage looked like a big palace to me, but most of the rooms were now locked; I just wanted to run through the halls with a crowbar, taking off doors.

At about 4:00 AM, I parked my van behind the punk house, a brick Ka'ba-looking structure that used to be a Chinese restaurant, and slumped into the mattress in back. The next morning, Eyad came through and opened up the house to show me our set. It was everything I needed a punk house to be, dirty and crumbling and walls covered with obscene murals.

The residents of the punk house called it Tower 2012 for their obsession with the coming shift in consciousness foretold by the ancient Mayans. The spiritual head of the house was this guy Nick who lived in what would be Rabeya's room, completely buried in books. We had some cool and strange conversations about Mayan calendars and spaceships. I shared the story of Louis Farrakhan on that mountaintop in Mexico in 1985, exploring the ruins of a Quetzalcoatl temple when the Mothership came down and beamed him up. Aboard the ship, Farrakhan was brought into an empty room, where he heard Elijah Muhammad's voice from a speaker in the ceiling. After foretelling that Ronald Reagan would soon drop bombs on Libya, the Messenger commanded Farrakhan to bring one million black men to Washington—the inspiration for the Million Man March ten years later. Farrakhan would additionally claim that while aboard the Mothership, a scroll descended from the ceiling and implanted itself in the back of his brain. Nick did not have a previous investment in Farrakhan or Islam in any form, but said he had no reason to reject the story.

We also discussed salvia, the entheogenic drug that inexplicably remained legal in most states. People who took it often reported seeing the goddess of the plant, a Green Woman who you could identify with the Virgin Mary or whoever. I would have called her Khidr, but when Nick put some salvia in a bowl with weed and had me smoke, I never saw her or even felt anything. He had me try a few times, and then he did some, flying off to another place where the plant wanted to teach him but refrained because then he wouldn't have returned to us. His whole trip lasted less than five minutes, but he treated it like a real visit to the mountaintop. I didn't know why the salvia gave something to him and nothing to me. Ibn Taymiyya had told the story of a person who thought that plants spoke to him, but it was really the Devil disguised as the plant.

Islamicizing the house, we added our own tags to the walls. I spray-painted "Rumi was a homo," a tribute to the Kominas. Marwan Kamel, singer for Al-Thawra, came through with a pile of stencils like "Osama McDonald," a Ronald McDonald with bin Laden's head. After purifying my niyya, I painted a black man with green turban and white beard, wielding a sword against a satanic skull that was already on the wall. Over the skull I painted a word balloon for him to say "Muhammad!" There were no scenes that focused on the picture, but this wall would be the background for our climactic concert scene at the end.

Doing interviews with Danish journalists, I have been asked for my opinion on the Muhammad cartoon thing. They seemed unable to register that a Muslim could simultaneously object to bigoted cartoons and still defend the cartoonist's freedom of expression; it betrayed their dualism of "good Muslims" (Westernized, secular, and liberal) and "bad Muslims" (apologists for al-Qaeda, supporters of Shari'a, bearded, mean). Even worse, they couldn't understand why I'd feel offended in the first place: "But your work is like that," they said. That pissed me off, but now they were right, since I stood staring at this punk house wall with no choice but to say yeah, I had drawn my own Muhammad cartoon, I was now one of those guys. But I wasn't. When I painted him, there was no joy of blaspheming, no *fuck-you-I'm-punk* about it, no begging for martyrdom fatwas. It wasn't even a "shit on him" moment. Muhammad was a human being and I painted him, no big deal, and it was worthwhile just for that. My real fuck-you was to paint him as a black man, Nuwaubu-style, defying an eighteenth-century Maliki jurist who had said that only unbelievers would claim that the Prophet was black.

We planned on smashing every idol. I searched stores in Cleveland's Arab neighborhood for the all-Arabic and somewhat fancy Qur'an that my Rabeya would attack with a black Sharpie and found it at a supermarket. The guy at the register touched the book to his forehead before handing it over. Back at Tower 2012, Eyad went through the house with his director of photography and blocked scenes while I found a secret corner to sit with that book. I cradled it like a sacrificial animal and then opened my Sharpie to slit its neck.

A tough choice. Which was more offensive: disrespect of the sacred object or violence against human beings? Which was the more urgent concern? Allah is the Protector and needs no protection. I'd rather protect my sisters and brothers, both victims of those words. It'd be an Islamic act to cross out violence. Yes. More Muslim than ever, because my actions were thoughtful and my niyya was right; also more punk-rock than ever, and a Five Percenter too, since I needed no Ten Percentin' theologian to do magic tricks with the verse, trying to make shit smell good. I can handle this myself as an ethical believer in God. Cross it out.

I found the verse and then killed it in quick motions, long black streaks over the words. There, done. I was the Qur'an's self-appointed editor, censoring the Creator and Sustainer of the Universe. It'd be a lot harder now to play the role of persecuted author.

And I'm still a Muslim: even after defacing the words, I still couldn't put the book on the floor; had to find a high place. What an inconsistent goofball.

6.

The cast and crew arrived in increments. I stayed with the crew at Eyad's house and the actors stayed in a hotel. Rabeya was played by Noureen DeWulf, who had appeared in *Ocean's Thirteen* and played Matthew McConaughey's girlfriend in her next project. She had also been featured in *Maxim*'s "Hot 100" list, which made it that much cooler that she'd be wearing a burqa through our whole movie.

The shoot lasted three weeks, and sometimes it felt like I was on another trip, like I had to go out and discover the native Islam of Cleveland. For my own experience, this was it, Tower 2012 the local shrine. The actor playing our red-mohawked Sufi drunk Jehangir Tabari was a Persian guy who used the stage name Dominic Rains. He had been Dr. Leo Julian on *General Hospital*, and in *Flight 93* he played Ziad Jarrah, one of the 9/11 hijackers who went down in Pennsylvania. Jarrah was believed to have been the hijackers' pilot. For him to play the mythical hero of taqwacore was like an alchemical transformation of Jarrah. Dominic got deep into it too, fully morphing into Jehangir Tabari—wearing the green-laced boots and red plaid pants for the whole shoot straight, no laundry, going to real-life punk shows in Jehangir's spiked jacket with Pakistan's flag on the back, getting himself legit drunk for Jehangir's plastered preaching, and walking around with a book of Rumi poems, pulling people aside to read stray lines. When we had a picnic by the lake, Dominic went out on the pier and sang the adhan. We'd build for hours on Islam and Sufism, Dominic probing me for Jehangir's religion, which turned out to match his own, a love for the divine expressed in boundless love for human beings and life. We'd talk about Bulleh Shah, Ibn 'Arabi, and Five Percenters. I told him that I was going to Mecca but couldn't begin to know what to expect.

These characters had all taken shape in my head, but now they had shape in real life, fiction born in reality and also reality coming to the fiction—since the novel's taqwacores now listened to actual taqwacore bands, Rabeya blasting Secret Trial Five, the Kominas' "Suicide Bomb the Gap" blaring from Jehangir's boom box. Marwan brought his whole band to Cleveland to play themselves in a cameo. One day I showed up on the set late (after getting meningitis shots for Mecca) and found Dominic in his Jehangir costume outside, playing in a drum circle with Al-Thawra. All borders were erased.

And then I entered the fiction myself, with a cameo as a skeevy old punk who yells at Yusef the clean-cut engineering student (played by Bobby Naderi) to keep his dick dry and read the Qur'an rather than get wasted and fuck whores, because then he'd wind up with orange testicles and cauliflowers on his asshole. My character was sincere and really trying to help the kid; Islam had these rules for a reason. Everyone on a path had a border that couldn't be crossed—a limitation that, when reached, would send them back in the other direction. For the old punk yelling at Yusef, it was venereal disease. I didn't know what my limit was, but felt that I had met it sometime ago and was now coming around. Maybe I'd know after hajj.

THE ACTORS FLEW out after finishing their scenes. Our last day of shooting, it was just Bobby doing his final lonely scene of Yusef putting on a burqa and masturbating. After shooting wrapped, we stripped the set for relics. I threw Rabeya's burqa, Al-Thawra T-shirt, and crossed-out 4:34 Qur'an into my van and waited for the crew to load up the grip truck that was blocking my van. As they rolled out, I said goodbye to the punk house, goodbye to punk itself, and headed for the I-90.

At the second-to-last exit before crossing the Pennsylvania–New York border, where the thruway became a toll road, I pulled off. It was the middle of the night in a small empty town. I went to a station with green and white lights, pumped gas, and then drove the van to a dark corner of the parking lot.

The headlights off, the engine off, too far away for anyone to see me in there, I took a breath and said a meaningless word, a *fuck* or *Goddamn*. It was a long way from Herman Street. Six years. A long way from the guy who wrote that novel, not even a good novel but it changed my life; a long way from typing my story at Buffalo State's Butler Library, since I could go there now and look up my name in the catalog. A long way from printing copies on Xerox machines and calling myself an ex-Muslim. Now I had a five-book deal and *The Taqwacores* paid my way to Mecca.

It was almost funny to look back at how tired and hurt I had been; Allah the Knower laughs most when good news is around the corner. Look at me, a Muslim, marrying a beautiful Muslim girl, insha'Allah with Muslim babies down the road. *Fuck*, I said again. It was all that I could say.

Fuck, Yusef.

I reached behind me into the plastic bin bearing the word PROPS written on a strip of masking tape, recognized the feel of Rabeya's burqa, and pulled it out. The light blue one, with her feminist patches and pins, the stained one that she had lifted up to spit semen (a vanilla-frosting-and-water concoction I had made in the punk house kitchen) at the Wahhabs. I put it on, looked through the fabric grid and the windshield to the parking lot—no one around. No gas station attendants, no Hollywood actors. The parking lot and the novel belonged to me. Made the mess into a spare T-shirt but it wasn't a sex thing, it was an author-and-character thing. Ritual is imitation. Then I took off the burqa and got back on the road to go home.

7.

Muslims are able to address the problems they face without feeling ashamed or that the topic is inappropriate to be discussing in a religious context. American culture has a similarly open attitude because we, as Americans, also have such a foundation—with the Constitution and Bill of Rights espousing freedom of speech, as well as our history of dissent and political expression. One of America's most treasured freedoms—freedom of speech—has a home in Islam too.

—ASMA GULL HASAN

Unless, of course, the problem a Muslim faced was Asma Gull Hasan. But we had good news on the taqwacore legal front: Hasan's lawsuit against me, claiming that *Blue-Eyed Devil* had falsely portrayed her as "wealthy, self-absorbed, insensitive, and acutely uninformed" and inspired the lyrics of "Rumi was a Homo" was dismissed. Allahu Akbar.

Meanwhile, we potentially faced more trouble as a Sufi shaykh threatened to sue us for Vote Hezbollah's TaqwaMan character, which had incorporated an image of him without permission. The logo had been used on the film's website and was about to appear on new editions of the novel. The funny part was that Vote Hezbollah gave a fake list of its members on the band's MySpace page, and the shaykh's lawyers took it seriously, addressing their complaint to "Jehangir Tabari." The fictional character was now real enough to be served papers.

8.

There are no punks or faggots in the Nation of Islam, the old saying went. But while we were shooting the movie, news came from Chicago of Louis Farrakhan's major announcement: the Nation of Islam would open its teachings to Muslims of all backgrounds, even white devils. I wondered if the news was related to the passing of Warith Deen Mohammed; perhaps Minister Farrakhan, who had already given a "farewell sermon," was thinking about his own legacy. Or it could have been another of his flirtations with the Sunnis; for at least a decade, Muslims have been speculating that Farrakhan would make a shift towards conformity.

Or maybe, just two weeks before the presidential election, he was adapting the Nation's black liberation theology to life in post-Obama America. There would always be racism and injustice, but it'd still be harder to hold up the grafted-devil stuff when all the white liberals named a black man their king. If white people could now join the Nation of Islam, what would happen to the old stories of Yacub the big-headed scientist? Old stories never died, I had learned that much already; they would just be understood in new ways.

I happened to have the phone number of Minister Akbar Muhammad, Farrakhan's right-hand man and one of the candidates named as a possible successor.

"I'm interested in what this could mean for me," I told him. "I have respect for the tradition, that's what brought me to the Five Percenters. I don't know if you're familiar with Azreal, but he gave me the righteous name Azreal Wisdom—"

"This is what I'm going to do," Minister Akbar answered. "I am going to give you the Minister's address, and you can write him a letter."

I also mentioned that I was making the pilgrimage to Mecca, and Minister Akbar wished me a peaceful journey.

So I wrote a letter to Louis Farrakhan and sent it to his house. This was tradition. Back in the day, converts were instructed to write letters to Master Fard, asking for their X. The letters were sent to Elijah Muhammad's Chicago mansion, which was now Farrakhan's home. Minister Akbar had to know that I understood.

I never knew where the Winds that Scatter would take me. Maybe it'd be the opposite of Malcolm's trajectory: I could go to Mecca first and *then* join the Nation.

9.

Election night, I went with Sadaf to Harlem to just walk through the street parties and share high-fives with happy strangers, and we thought about the kids we might have in a post-black-president America with no way of grasping how big this was in our day.

Barack Obama, regardless of the Christ that lived in his heart, was also our first Muslim president; not in the way that Conservapedia editors feared, but at least in the sense that Toni Morrison wrote of Bill Clinton as the first black president. It wasn't only that he carried the name of Muhammad's grandson and the hanging Iraqi dictator, or that he found inspiration in the greatest text of our native Islamic tradition, Malcolm's autobiography, or even that he attended Farrakhan's Million Man March. Like so many brown sons of immigrants, he lived in both America's Known and Unknown: at once alien and elitist, marginalized and privileged, like the rich doctors and engineers of the Muslim community, he lived white without looking it. His work and ambition pushed him forward until he saw that invisible line, the limits of the American Dream that he was never meant to reach. He came to the line and met its guards. The whispers over his name, father and childhood schools, the questioning of his church and his patriotism, Hillary pressing him to condemn Farrakhan, and *The New Yorker* cartoon were his detainment at a border, the experience of an American Muslim who travels through the Unknown and then comes home.

No, Barack Obama is not a Muslim. But even when he disowned Muslims—and denied accusations of secret Islam as a "slur"—and even when he dumped on Palestine, he would still be our triumph. We knew that our support would harm him as much as if he were Muslim; we knew that *our* hope must be whispered. Obama signs on Arab lawns would scare white people into voting for whiteness, clinging for fear of a black planet to Sarah Palin's Real America. While correcting so much of the old racism, the election also exposed the new racism, forcing the issue of American Islamophobia, bringing Colin Powell to say, "So what if he *is* Muslim?"

No, Barack Obama is not a Muslim. But in the histories of American Islam that have not yet been written, he will have his own chapter.

THE NEXT DAY I returned uptown with Ayad Akhtar, whose company had optioned the film rights for my *Blue-Eyed Devil*. Someone on the street was selling portraits of Barack Obama, Malcolm X, and Master Fard. I bought the Fard.

Just a couple blocks ahead was the current Mosque No. 7, the Farrakhan Nation's Harlem chapter. It was at least the hundredth time that I've walked past that place but the first time that I could knock on the door. Out stepped an older gentleman of ambiguous ethnicity and accent—maybe Turkish or Arab, I guessed, or "Turko-Persian," as one of Elijah's sons described Master Fard. He looked like the picture of Fard in my hands. The minister wasn't there, he told me, but I could leave a message and my phone number.

"May Allah guide you on your journey," he said.

From there we headed to the Audubon Ballroom, now the Shabazz Cultural Center with a life-size statue of Malcolm in the lobby and an upstairs ballroom with long mural telling Malcolm's whole life story—Malcolm as a boy in school, the teacher telling him that he couldn't be a lawyer, the Little home burning down, Detroit Red in his zoot suit, Satan in prison, Brother Minister Malcolm behind the podium, El-Hajj Malik El-Shabazz in his travels throughout the Middle East and Africa wearing a turban and holding a stack of Qur'ans.

There were still helium balloons drifting across the room from last night's Obama party, some listless on the floor, others with enough life to float knee-high, ribbons trailing behind them. The woman who ran the place pointed to the spot on the floor where Allah blessed Malcolm with martyrdom. From what I had been told, the original ballroom was in the section of the building that has since been torn down and turned into a parking lot, but then an Obama balloon grazed over what the woman had claimed was the spot, and I couldn't deny her.

Parting ways with Ayad, I became conscious on the train that my beard made me look nuts. I had stopped shaving to look holy for hajj, but it was a look that I couldn't pull off. Even when I shaved the moustache, it wasn't a proper Salafi beard, jet-black and groomed and oiled, only a mess growing in every direction and every color—mostly brown, but Sadaf could spot red hairs, some blonde and black, even a few grays. I could see my father in that beard, or myself as my father's son, especially with the blue eyes and blue flannel shirt-jacket and developing mullet. I wasn't a holy Semite of the desert, just a cracker of the West Virginia backwoods.

Time for the day's Mathematics: it was November 5, and 5 manifests Power and Refinement. Power is the truth but will only take you so far; sometimes you have to *refine* the power. The raw power is with the prophets out in the wilderness, the Jeremiah Wrights; the refined power belongs to the ones who negotiate with the devil's kingdom, the Barack Obamas. I wished that Obama could have come this far without ever apologizing for the reverend.

Brooklyn had history too. Five Percenters called Ft. Greene the head of Medina, and Bushwick was once home to the Nubian Islamic Hebrews who walked the streets in white turbans and robes selling incense and literature. In "H to the Izzo," Jay-Z mentions them when he says that he was "herbin' 'em in the home of the turbans." At home I had a big collection of their books, some even from the 1970s, with worn covers and dog-eared pages and sometimes even underlined passages or handwritten notes in the margins from faithful disciples so long ago. A few books had the owners' righteous Nubian names written inside the covers. The Nubian Islamic Hebrews ran Brooklyn for a time, but in the early 1990s they fled in a mass exodus to rural Georgia and became the Nuwaubians. The leader has since been sentenced to about a thousand years in federal prison for numerous counts of child abuse.

They don't make those books anymore. The Nuwaubian-era stuff doesn't have the Nubian Islamic Hebrew charm, the ironic Islamo-Americana camp that made me an Islamo-American hipster for hoarding them. The Nuwaubians still maintained their stores in New York, and their messiah's brother remained in Brooklyn, where he had led his own mosque on Bedford: the African Islamic Mission. Finding it became the day's quest, but after getting lost and taking the wrong trains or the right trains in wrong directions, I just submitted to wandering and reflecting on New York's Islamic history—sacred history as real to me as anything, and I couldn't shake it. I did find my way to Bedford, and saw only a Nuwaubian store where the African Islamic Mission once stood, but did find the Masjid at-Taqwa—the mosque led by Imam Siraj Wahhaj, the Kominas' target in "Rumi was a Homo." I was no friend of his, but a mosque's a mosque, and it was Maghrib time; so I went in, washed up and prayed and then went back to the street, sharing salams with a few brothers on my way out.

The original plan for this book was to leave all the American Islamic materials behind and come back to the greater Muslim World, rediscovering the Real Islam of historical and doctrinal authenticity, but I had given up on that a long time ago—building on Bulleh Shah as a Five Percenter with the taqwacores in Pakistan, building on Marcus Garvey with a Rasta in Ethiopia. These things all integrated too naturally. Maybe I'd build on Supreme Mathematics during hajj, wondering if anyone had ever done that before.

* * *

THE FIVE PERCENTERS never called their Mecca the holy city, because "holy" was for religious spookiness; Harlem was the *righteous* city of Mecca. I crossed the bridge again on Friday, bringing Volkan, the six-foot-six Turkish kid who had played Amazing Ayyub in the *Taqwacores* movie, to the righteous sites. He showed up with a big book of Rumi in a plastic bag, a gift from his parents to me.

First stop was Masjid Malcolm Shabazz on 116th Street and Lenox Ave/Malcolm X Boulevard. Established by Malcolm as the Nation of Islam's Mosque No. 7, it's now in the hands of the Warith Deen community, with a giant green onion dome. The men at the front desk asked what we were doing.

"Jum'aa," I told him.

"It started at noon." We were an hour late.

"So we can't go up and make salat?"

"What you got in that bag?"

"Rumi," I answered, showing him.

"Oh, you're okay." He nodded and we headed up the same stairwell that in 1972 was the scene of a big shoot-out between the Fruit of Islam and NYPD, back when Elijah was still alive and Farrakhan ran the mosque. We made our prayers separately as brothers filtered out of the room. In the far right corner, where chairs were set aside for those who could no longer kneel in prayer, some of the old-timers were still hanging out and talking. You had to respect the old-timers in a mosque like this, in a spiritual community that was still less than a hundred years old and had undergone so much turmoil in the last forty years: the Malcolm-Elijah war, Malcolm's assassination, the bombing of the mosque, Elijah's death, Warith Deen's reforms and the Farrakhan schism, and now Warith Deen's passing. I wondered how much they had witnessed. I couldn't make out everything they said, but I heard someone mention Elijah, then Warith Deen, and then Barack Obama.

"The Prophet said that even if your imam is as black as a raisin, you have to follow him," said one. "As *black* as a *raisin*! He's still your imam."

"He's talking about Bilal," said another.

"He's talking about *us*!"

Allah forgive me for allowing myself to be distracted in prayer, but in a mosque like that, history mattered. Those old men were part of my prayer.

Keeping my gaze focused on the floor, I couldn't know who said what. There were at least three of them, I thought, and before starting the prayer I noticed that one had on a blinding blue suit.

"Obama's like the Prophet Muhammad," said one. "*Barack* means 'blessing,' you know, and he's a blessing to all the worlds, like the Prophet."

On the other side of the world, al-Qaeda would release an al-Zawahri statement calling the new president a house negro, the audio set to pictures contrasting Obama with Malcolm. Al-Zawahri declared that Obama has "chosen a stance of hostility to Islam and Muslims;" the Muslims of Gaza, I'll give him that, but not the Muslims of Harlem.

We walked ten blocks uptown so that I could show Volkan the Allah School and introduce him to Cee Allah, another old-timer, his dreadlocks now gray.

"Peace, Mike!" he shouted when we came through the door. Big hugs, and I introduced him to Volkan. "I see you got that big beard," said Cee Allah.

"I'm going to Saudi," I told him.

"What you doin' there?"

"Mecca."

"You know, Old Man Justice went to Mecca!" Old Man Justice was the running partner of the Five Percent's Allah, the Father.

"Old Man Justice, for real?"

"I'll tell you the story," said Cee Allah. "He was walking up the street here and saw the Muslims selling *Muhammad Speaks*, and he wanted to buy one but he had no money. The Muslim says, I'll give it to you anyway. So Old Man Justice reads the newspaper and then he joins the Merchant Marines, and when he goes to Arabia the first thing he says is, 'Where's the imam?' So they lead him to the imam, and then Justice asks the imam, 'Where's Allah?'"

"What did he say?"

"The imam says, 'Allah's not here.' And when Justice comes back home, *that's* when he meets the Father."

"Oh my god," I said.

"I got the whole story written down somewhere; next time you're here I'll give it to you." Cee Allah's story seemed like a cousin of other stories I had heard about Justice and Allah's first meeting; in one version, Justice was the Muslim selling newspapers, and Allah was the one who wanted to buy a paper but had no money. As that story went, they traded a *Muhammad Speaks* for some of Allah's hash, and the friendship began. Allah knows best.

Old Man Justice went by other street handles: Akbar, Arbar, Four Cipher Akbar, Jesus, Jimmy Jam, and he was a maker of tradition but remained unremembered—no hardcover collections of his speeches and great statements because they were never written or recorded, meant only for the teenagers who'd buy him wine and listen to him on the corner. Old Man Justice died in '78 or '79 and hasn't been discussed in any academic papers; beyond brief mentions in the Five Percenters' FBI file and some *Amsterdam News* articles from the 1960s, there's not much proof that he ever really existed. But the young gods of the Five Percent Nation, receiving wisdom from the Old Man with his cane and brown-bag bottle, would in time become the old men passing his words on to me. I knew a Five Percenter who had been his student, and he carried the Justice name just like I wore Azreal.

On the train back to Medina, I thought of another Five Percenter from the early period, First Born Prince Allah, who syncretized Supreme Mathematics and the Lessons with Sunni Islam. He shared his unique interpretations by writing "plus-lessons," which he sold for $2 a copy. First Born Prince Allah was a complicated, contradictory, and uniquely American religious thinker, a Black Elk of the city. He should have been the subject of several books, but scholars of American Islam haven't even heard of him. I fell into deep sleep and dreamed about another elder. I didn't know who he was or what tradition he claimed; he could have been one of the Sunni old-timers at the Malcolm X mosque or a First Born god from the Allah School or even a Nubian Islamic Hebrew who stayed behind in Brooklyn and clung to that history. He worked at a convenience store, and I came in to buy eggnog. I put it on the counter and pulled out my wallet.

"You're trying to save money," he asked, "right?"

"Yes, I'm traveling."

"I'll tell you what," he said, smiling. "Sometimes you pay me, sometimes you don't."

"Okay." He was offering me the eggnog for free, but when I picked up the carton that I had put on the counter, it was now transformed, having shapeshifted into some shitty 10 percent fruit juice that I didn't want. The eggnog was gone.

I woke up with that ecstatic agitation that came sometimes from special dreams or odd coincidences or things happening for me in miraculous and unexplainable ways, the sense of it all being Real and deadly serious—the Qur'an is Real, the Prophet is Real, Master Fard is Real, Supreme Mathematics is Real. Sometimes Allah just gives it to you straight, no fucking around. The old black man behind the counter was Real too, even if I just dreamed him up. His message was Real: *Sometimes you pay me, sometimes you don't.* An experience was waiting for me to catch it in Real Mecca, but I had to keep a good energy and guard my intention; that was how I paid. If I didn't pay, if I tried to cheat my way through, it wouldn't happen for me.

The man behind the counter knew that I had a hard time holding onto religion with any consistency, it kept coming and going, and that I might have blown a whole year's worth of spiritual energy on travels before the time that I'd really need some. Hajj would be a heavy trip, heavier than anything, and deserved some real hype, but I had nothing left for it. That was why the Original Man came into my dream and switched my eggnog, sending the message: *This is what happens when you don't pay.* Dreams were just private myths; who said that? Jung or Campbell, I think—

10.

And whoever said it had also flipped it around: myths were public dreams. Hajj seemed like a public dream to me, shared with millions enacting a hallucinated version of what was really happening inside us—coming to the desert in white, circling the House of God, gathering stones to kill the Devil. Like a dream it'd offer no reasoned arguments, just symbols pounding and tossing the intellect.

Mecca was only days away, and I needed to prepare, read the right books to get my head right and *pay*. There was the Qur'an, of course, but Rabeya's edited Qur'an and the miniature book from my future mother-in-law were only in Arabic. All I had for English was a Pickthall translation, not the best. I had a biography of the Prophet, which was published by the big university in Medina and thus in line with the Saudi version of Islam. It'd be good for the plane and the city.

Besides the religious quest, hajj was also a walk through history, and I wanted to know the whole life of the city, how it became the Mecca that I'd find in 2008 and how many other Meccas it had been. Mecca was ruled by Zaydi Shi'as for nearly five hundred years. During their reign, adhans at the Great Mosque mentioned Ali's name. I couldn't digest everything in the time that I had, and I still hadn't read anything about the hajj itself, the basics of what I had to bring and do and say. Sadaf's dad mailed me a DVD of their hometown imam explaining the procedure, which I watched a few times with notebook in hand.

Then I started to read about meteorites. Looks random, but I knew what I was doing.

From heaven, I thought, a meteorite crater might have looked like the dot under the Arabic letter *ba*:

In the miniature Qur'an from Sadaf's mom, I couldn't even see the *ba* without a magnifying glass, let alone the dot. But within the dot rests the heart of the letter, within the letter rests the heart of the first words of the Qur'an, *Bismillah*—in the Name of God—and that *Bismillah* contains the heart of the first sura of the Qur'an, al-Fatiha, and al-Fatiha is the heart of the Qur'an. So a mile-wide *ba* dot made by a meteorite was like God's signature, written with the equivalent of 2.5 megatons of TNT and blowing out 175 million tons of earth.

Bismillah, I'd say, focusing my energy on the *ba*, pushing my lips together to build the tension and then ejecting my breath as a sound. In linguistics, *ba* is called a "voiced bilabial plosive": voiced because the vocal chords vibrate, bilabial because both lips are used, and plosive because the sound is produced by stopping airflow in the vocal tract. The *ba* came out with a kind of pop.

How much of the book can you stuff into your head when you get lost in the wilderness not on the first sura or the first ayat in the first sura or even the first word in the first ayat or the first letter of the first word but the first diacritical mark, just a dot? I said it again, only the *ba*, and kept saying it louder and stronger, *ba-ba-ba-ba-ba*, and I had my ninety-nine zikr beads so I counted each *ba*, and then I said them faster than my fingers could pass over the beads, turning *ba* into a forceful thing creative and aggressive, and I could understand the *ba* in *bang* and *bam* and *boom* and the primacy of *ba* in jazz scat singing and bebop and *hey ba-ba-re-bop* and *be-bop-a-lula*. Against peace and quiet, sound is violent, sound is anarchist, but only the first sound, the one you push out to break silence. *Ba* is a killer.

In the Supreme Sufi Alphabets of Shaykh Ahmad al-Ahsa'i, *ba* represented Allah's Divine Name *al-Ba'ith*, the Sender— which had me thinking about meteorites again. If Allah didn't send rocks from space, who did?

Meteorites were used in the first execution by stoning, God's annihilation of the dinosaurs. Sixty-five million years ago, the Earth was bombed with rocks from heaven, bringing on the apocalypse now called the Cretaceous-Tertiary Extinction Event. Debris in the atmosphere caused intense thermal radiation, leading to a short period—perhaps several hours— in which the Earth became, as one scientist put it, an "oven set to broil." Higher temperature and oxygen levels sparked firestorms all over the world, while the meteorite impacts created major dust clouds and kicked up sulfuric acid into the stratosphere, blocking out the sun. Plants died, followed by plant eaters, followed by predators. A third of the Earth's species were completely wiped out, but Allah destroys and then builds. Mass extinction created openings for new species to evolve and become dominant. And here we are.

Arizona was home to a big crater from the Barringer meteorite that hit fifty thousand years ago. Tens of thousands of years later, humans in the Paleolithic Age mined the crater for iron. In roughly the same time period, near Cape York, Greenland, the Inuit received a meteorite and used it for the making of tools. Meteorites were like heaven's parental nudges towards progress, and people knew it: Inuit shamans sometimes claimed discovery or possession of a meteorite as the basis for their powers. Archaeologists report that a piece of the Pojoaque meteorite gave evidence of heavy handling, and might have been kept in a medicine pouch. Bits of meteorite have been found in prehistoric burial sites throughout the Americas. A chunk of the Winona meteorite was discovered in a stone cist similar to those in which local peoples buried their deceased children.

The Babylonian king Gilgamesh, two-thirds god, one-third human, ruling Uruk circa 2700 BC, had a dream in which people assembled around a fallen meteorite to celebrate its arrival. In his dream, Gilgamesh embraced the stone as his wife. His mother told him that the meteorite foretold of a friend who would come to his aid. I also read about Egypt's solar temple in Heliopolis, home to the Benben Stone, which was sent from heaven by the gods and served as the basis for obelisks and capstones on pyramids. If it really came from the sky, who else could have sent it? The placement of the Benben Stone marked the exact spot where sunlight first touched the earth, but I also read that in Finland, a meteor crater dating to circa 500 BC was described to Greek scientist Pytheas as "the grave of the Sun, or the place where the Sun fell asleep."

Stones from heaven had me reading of ancient Rome, where—nearly two thousand years before the division of "sacred" and "secular"—stone gods were politically entrenched. In 204 BC, the Roman senate obtained Cybele, a Phrygian goddess represented by a piece of black meteorite, enshrined her in a temple, and made her the center of an annual holiday. Emperor Macrinus worshipped Heliogabulus, a "black stone fallen from heaven," as the sun god. Emperor Elagabalus worshiped his own black stone, taken from the temple of Syrian deity El-Gabal, and built a new home for it on the Palatine hill. With hopes of establishing El-Gabal as the chief god of Rome, Elagabalus planned a wedding between the black stone and a statue of Jupiter's virgin daughter Minerva, removed from the temple of Vesta. When this proved too controversial for the masses, Minerva was restored to her temple, and the black stone married lunar goddess Urania. After the death of Elagabalus, his El-Gabal was also returned to its rightful home in Syria.

The arrivals of holy stones were treated as special events well into the common era. In 1492 a meteorite that struck Germany caused Emperor Maximilian to convene a special counsel to properly interpret God's intended message. The stone was later hung in a church with specific orders to preserve and keep it. Chunks of meteorites that hit Japan in 1744 and 1850 were enshrined in temples. In 1771 Siberian Tartars revered their meteorite as a "holy thing fallen from heaven." In 1853 the Wanikas tribe in east Africa built a temple for the meteorite that struck Duruma, but sold their stone to missionaries after it failed to protect them from invaders.

India received four meteorites in the nineteenth century. The impact at Saonland left people so terrified that they recovered all of the meteorite chunks, smashed them into powder, and then scattered them in the winds. In Sabetmahmeti, however, they lavished a meteorite with flowers, ghee, and sandalwood. In Nedagolla a meteorite was carried to a temple, where believers offered it prayers, and in Durala the faithful aspired to honor their meteorite with its own temple; both specimens were later taken by the East India Company for the British Museum.

San Gregorio in Chihuahua, Mexico, was home to a twelve-ton meteorite bearing the inscription, *Solo Dios con su poder este fiero destruira pues en el mundo no habra quien lo pueda de hacer* (Since no one in the world could make it, only God with his power this iron can destroy). In Charcas, Mexico, an iron meteorite was built into the wall of a church and believed to cure sterility. In Wichita County, Texas, a meteorite was placed at the intersection of several trails and became a point of pilgrimage for the Comanche, who would leave offerings of beads, pipes, and tobacco. The Manito Stone sat atop a hill in Alberta, Canada, where passing Cree and Blackfeet gave offerings of wing bones or money, and pilgrims' loving caresses polished and smoothed the metallic surface. When whites stole the stone in 1869, old medicine men of the Plains tribes promised that the stone's removal would bring death and destruction; a few months later the local Christian mission was hit with smallpox.

For some, the myth wasn't in the meteorites' origin or sacred powers but their very existence. Thomas Jefferson replied to two Yale professors' reports of meteor showers with, "They may be right, but it is easier for me to believe that two Yankee professors would lie than to believe that stones would fall from heaven."

For those who witnessed them, meteorites at night could appear as bright as the sun. Sometimes they were yellow, red, or even green, with flashes of light as they fragmented. Trails of dust followed their paths across the sky, often lingering even after the impact. What's the proper response to watching the sky on fire?

I got into the meteorite stuff and found myself at this question, because I am a Muslim, and Muslims also have a stone from heaven. One tradition claims that our stone came to the earth around the same time as Adam and Eve. After their exile from paradise, Adam landed on Nawdh Mountain in India, and Eve ended up on the Arabian Peninsula, near the present city of Jedda. Then the stone came down, at the time whiter than snow, descending near Eve. Adam performed pilgrimage from India to the stone forty times. He placed the stone on a mountaintop, from where its light could shine upon the land.

This story is not in the Qur'an. I don't know where it came from, but that's how religion works sometimes: like messages in bottles washing up on the shore, and you have no idea who sent them your way.

Saudi Arabia's desolate Rub' al-Khali (Empty Quarter) region bears the proof of an ancient meteorite impact, named the Wabar craters as a mispronunciation of Ubar, the city that it erased. The Qur'an calls this city Iram. Between 3,000 BC and the first century AD, Ubar/Iram was the capital of the 'Ad nation, a major point in the frankincense trade, and may have been the first city to domesticate camels. It also gave rise to a prophet named Hud, who warned his people that God would punish them if they did not change their wicked ways. As those stories usually go, the Prophet Hud was ignored, and God's justice came at anywhere from forty thousand to sixty thousand kilometers per hour, with a total mass of 3,500 tons. It broke into at least four pieces before landing on the 'Ad, with the largest fragment causing an impact equal to the atomic bomb dropped on Hiroshima.

A caravan of frankincense traders might have arrived at where 'Ad had once been, finding only that the heat of the impact had transformed surrounding sands into lumps of black glass. I don't know what gods they believed in that could explain such a scene or how they understood the power that crushed a city. Perhaps, like so many stone collectors around the world, they gathered pieces of the meteorites and pellets of black glass and kept them as signs of the power, or ways to access the power for themselves.

A stone from the Wabar site may have been carried as far as one hundred kilometers to the north, to the Hijaz region—where a settlement named Makkah, or Mecca, had been made possible thanks to the discovery of water, the well called Zamzam. The stone was placed near Zamzam and given its own box-shaped shrine, the Ka'ba, which is believed to have also housed utensils for the well.

The desert and rocky steppes of the Hijaz offered little water or usable land, forcing nomads to wander endlessly in search of resources. The region saw frequent tribal skirmishes, as basic survival needs necessitated the *ghazu*, raids for food and materials. The presence of a sacred stone, however, would have discouraged fighting over the well, leading to Mecca's designation as a *haram*, a safe space where no blood could be shed. Marking a radical agreement of human beings not to kill each other, the stone encouraged further social interaction: trading, peace treaties, the kind of things that allowed a culture to build. Like the Inuit crafting harpoons from their Cape York meteorite, or the Monolith's arrival in *2001: A Space Odyssey*, Mecca's haram became an evolutionary moment.

In Semitic religion, stones were often used to designate holy land. We see it in the Bible, when Jacob falls asleep on a stone and dreams of a ladder reaching to heaven and hears the Voice of God. The next morning, he sets up the stone as a pillar and anoints it with oil. The pillar is referred to as God's House, but also commemorates the exact spot where heaven and earth were connected.

The ancient Middle East was littered with inviolable sacred cities. Along the Tigris and Euphrates rivers in what is now Iraq, each city-state was dedicated to its own patron god who protected the people in exchange for worship and sacrifice. Ur was the sacred city for Nanna, moon god and head of the Sumerian pantheon. Nanna's name meant "Illuminator" but he also wore titles like "father of the gods," "creator of all things," and *En-zu*, "lord of wisdom." The king Ur-nammu, who ruled the city from 2044 to 2027 BC, dedicated a ziggurat as Nanna's temple and sanctuary. The third terrace housed a bridal chamber for Nanna and his consort Ningal. After a safe return home from business trips down the Persian Gulf, Ur's merchants would show their gratitude with offerings at Nanna's temple. Scribes writing the receipts would note that a trader's gift came "from the prompting of his heart."

As in Mecca, the god's sanctuary could not be desecrated by violence and thus became the safest place to bring money and goods. Representing the stability and peace of a city-state, however, they became the prime symbolic targets of foreign invaders. Preparing for a Persian invasion, Babylonian king Namonidus ordered for all of his empire's idols to be removed from their sanctuaries and brought to the capital, either to protect them or be protected by them. Persia's King Cyrus accused Namonidus of taking the gods against their will, and after his successful conquest restored them to their homes. "May all the gods I brought to their sanctuaries," he prayed, "plead daily before Bel and Nabu for the lengthening of my days, may they intercede favorably on my behalf."

As kings asked for the support of gods, gods competed with each other for the attention of human beings. Understandably, a deity was often unwilling to share prayers and sacrifice with others. Nabu, god of wisdom and letters, assured his devotees, "Trust in Nabu. Trust in no other god." Nabu would have been a smart choice for an exclusive idol-idolater relationship; his role was to engrave the destinies of all humans on sacred tablets, and he held the power to shorten or lengthen life. For every New Year's festival, Nabu's devotees would transport him from his temple in Barsippa to Babylon, so that he could be with his father, another sun god named Marduk.

This was the world of Abraham, if there was an Abraham. His father was a maker of idols, a likely worshiper of Nanna and Shamash. Genesis places them in the city of Ur Kasdim, which might have been Ur. They are believed to have been Amorites. Early in Abraham's life, his father moved the family to Haran, another city dedicated to the moon god. Haran had its own sanctuary for Nanna, called E-khul-khul (House of Joys).

Dissatisfied with idols made of stone, Abraham searched for a better god. First he prayed to a star, but the star disappeared. Then he saw the moon and called it his god, but night became day and his god left him. When the sun came up, it was the greatest and brightest of all. This is my god, said Abraham; but at the end of the day, the sun was gone. Abraham then went to his people and told them, "I am free of all that you associate with him."

To prove his point, one night he took a stick and smashed his people's gods, leaving only the largest one. When they found their idols in pieces, they asked Abraham who had done it. Abraham replied that they should ask the last idol standing.

He left his father and their people. In Islamic tellings of the story, he was directed by God to the future site of Mecca. There they built the Ka'ba as the first temple of monotheism on the planet, placing the Stone in the corner.

Shortly after the Ka'ba's construction, Abraham and his son Ishmael were greeted by the king of the world.

"Who ordered you to do this?" asked the king of the world.

"God ordered us to do this," Abraham answered.

The king of the world asked for proof, for which Abraham provided five rams bearing witness. The king of the world then joined Abraham and Ishmael as they walked in a circle around the Ka'ba.

Ishmael maintained the Ka'ba after his father's death; but when Ishmael's own sons became men, they left Mecca to settle lands of their own. Each of them took a stone from the sacred precincts, leading to a future of stone worship across the Arabian peninsula. There were ka'bas at Narjan and Sindad. The ka'ba near Tabalah housed a white stone, and in the southern city of Ghaiman they worshipped a red stone. Worship of the moon god Nanna would be introduced at nearby Yathrib by exiled Namonidus, though the cult did not last long after him. Another temple to Nanna was dedicated at the south Arabian port city Sumhuram, with a sanctuary marked by sacred stones.

As the monotheism—or at least monolatry—of Abraham was abandoned, Mecca became home to the most popular sanctuary in the Arabian peninsula, the Ka'ba surrounded by 360 idols representing gods from throughout the region. Two idols, 'Isaf and Na'ila, were believed to have been a man and woman who turned to stone after making love in the sanctuary; they remained in the Ka'ba for some time before being moved near the hills of Safa and Marwah. Another idol, the goddess Al-Lat, was an uncut block of white granite worshipped at At-Ta'if, near Mecca. She formed a feminine trinity with Al-Uzza, a sacred stone south of Mecca, and Manat, the oldest of the three, another black stone and goal of pilgrims between Mecca and Yathrib. The goddesses were the daughters of Allah, the highest god, and worshiped through repetition of their names on ninety-nine-beaded strings, a practice connected to fertility rites ca. 800 BC. The Ka'ba itself was rededicated to a Nabataean god named Hubal, with an idol placed either inside the shrine or on top of it. When Hubal's right hand broke off, the ruling tribe made him a new hand of gold. A Yemeni king of Humayyur reverently covered the Ka'ba with a tent-like drape made from palm leaves, initiating a practice that continues today.

The Ka'ba's original meaning as a House of God was not entirely lost; many held Allah to be the same deity worshiped by Abraham. While Arabs predicted their futures by casting arrows in front of Hubal, inside the Ka'ba was a painting of Abraham with ritual arrows in his hand. As early as the first century AD, Arabs considered themselves to have descended from Ishmael, causing many to adopt Jewish beliefs and practices; Jewish historian Josephus Flavius noted that they used their lineage as a basis for circumcision. Four hundred years later, a Palestinian

Christian named Sozomenus reported the existence of an "Ishmaelite monotheism" that mixed Arab pagan concepts with pre-Moses Judaism. Some Arabs rejected both Judaism and Christianity, but considered themselves *hanifyya*, keepers of Abraham and Ishmael's lost religion. Among these hanifs was Abu Qays Sirma, a poet who declared, "I worship the Lord of Abraham," and constructed his own private sanctuary, from which he kept out the unclean. Some hanifs, such as Abu 'Amir and Umayya ibn Abi al-Salt, considered themselves prophets. Abu 'Amir issued revelatory utterances about the resurrection, and Umayya preached against idols and drunkenness; but for whatever reason, it never stuck.

On one of Mecca's feast days, a group of four hanifs gathered together and announced their rejection of the idols. "Find yourselves a religion," they told the people, "for you have none." One of the hanifs, Zayd ibn 'Amr, would lean his back against the Ka'ba and address his tribe: "O Quraysh, by him in whose hand is the soul of Zayd, not one of you follows the religion of Abraham but I."

The Quraysh were Mecca's ruling tribe, having taken control of the city in the early 500s. On a hot day late in the second half of that century, Zayd ibn 'Amr was approached by a Quraysh boy, an orphan named Muhammad, who was carrying a bag of meat. Muhammad was on his way back to Mecca from Ta'if, where sacrifices had been offered to Al-Lat. Muhammad offered Zayd some of the meat in the bag.

"Nephew," replied Zayd, "it is a part of those sacrifices of yours which you offer to your idols, isn't it?" Muhammad answered that it was. "I never eat of those sacrifices," Zayd told him, "and I want nothing to do with them."

"Then he blamed me," Muhammad would later confess, "and those who worship idols and sacrifice to them, saying, 'They are futile; they can do neither good nor harm.'" After that day, Muhammad never touched an idol again. He did not know it yet, but another ball of fire was about to hit Arabia, another shot from heaven to both destroy and renew, and it was him.

Muhammad would hear the Voice, but in language that he could understand: his spoken language, Arabic, and his cultural language, which informed him that sometimes men heard the Voice and received scriptures. When the Voice came, it spoke of things that Muhammad already knew: stories that he had heard, the black stone, the house of God that Abraham had built in his holy city. The Voice told him, as he knew it had told Abraham, Noah, and Moses, to teach his people.

Over the last fifteen years, Muhammad had become my language, my means of asking and answering. If this language had a physical heart in the world, if a trace of Muhammad could be found anywhere, take me to it. Take me to him. Time for the plane.

11.

At the by-now familiar airport in Cairo, we changed into our ihram, the two white towels that marked us as pilgrims. The place was filled with men in ihram when we arrived. Female pilgrims could still wear their regular clothes, but not veil their faces.

I put on my ihram in a bathroom stall, rushed because a dozen men were waiting in line. The bottom half was simple enough, wrapped like a regular towel and secured by rolling the top over my money belt. The other towel was harder to figure out, but I noticed that everyone had his own way of doing it. Stepping out of the restroom, I felt naked—the dictates of ihram meant that I was free-balling.

Pilgrims only wore the towels, but scholars have ruled that money belts, fanny packs, watches, and glasses were acceptable.

Sandals could not cover the top bone of my foot; my flip-flops were okay. Putting on the ihram garb was only a part of entering *ihram* status; I had to formally declare intention in my heart to make hajj. The airport staff had rolled out a large carpet to accommodate us. I found a spot and made two rakats, following the Sunna: in the first rakat, I recited Suratul-Kafirun, and in the second rakat I said Suratul-Ikhlas. There had to be a special meaning for those short suras, I thought. Suratul-Kafirun told Muhammad—and us—what to say to the enemies of Islam:

Say: O disbelievers,
I do not worship what you worship.
Nor are you worshipers of what I worship.
Nor will I be a worshiper of what you worship.
Nor will you be worshipers of what I worship.
To you be your religion, and to me, mine.

Suratul-Kafirun was a negation, declaring what Islam was not. Suratul-Kafirun broke us away from the old religion of Mecca, the idol worship that Muhammad brought to an end. In the next rakat, Suratul-Ikhlas gave the affirmation, a statement of what we do worship:

Say, He is Allah, One.
Allah, the Eternal Refuge.
He neither begets nor is born,
And there is nothing like him.

I waited until our plane was in the air before reciting the pilgrim's call to God: *Labbayk Allahumma labbayk, labbayk la shareeka laka labbayk, 'inna'hamda, wanni'mata, laka walmuk, la shareeka la.* I am here at your service, O Allah, I am here at your service, I am here at your service, you have no partner, I am here at your service, surely the praise and blessings are yours, and the dominion, you have no partner.

With those words, I crossed the line and became a pilgrim.

The garb and state of ihram erased our old roles, whatever we left behind. The doctors, generals, farmers, and scholars all looked the same. We entered a new category of person, above and beyond the maintenance of normal human society: pilgrims did not cut their hair or nails, and were forbidden from chopping down trees, killing or frightening animals, or even harming insects. As pilgrims could not have sex, ihram revealed itself to be a temporary position; if everyone stayed in ihram, the human race would die out. Preserving the tribe was no longer our job; for a time, we were removed from the world.

12.

Upon arrival at the hajj terminal of King Abdulaziz International Airport in Jeddah, I was asked my language and then given a free booklet: *A Guide to Hajj, Umrah and Visiting the Prophet's Mosque*, written by the government's Agency of Islamic Enlightenment in Hajj. In pre-Islamic times, hajj (our standing at Arafat and stoning the Devil at Mina) and umrah (pilgrimage to the Haram in Mecca) were unconnected; but Muhammad, putting two fingers together, told his Muslims, "I have entered the umrah into the hajj, until the day of resurrection."

While waiting for our bus to Mecca, I read the section "Things that Nullify Iman (Faith)." You could nullify your faith any number of ways, first and foremost by associating partners with Allah. Do not call upon the dead for their help, set up intermediaries between yourself and Allah, or ask for anyone's intercession. Do not consider the people who do these things to be Muslim, or you are not a Muslim. Do not seek guidance other than the Prophet's guidance, or hold manmade systems as superior to Shari'a. Do not doubt that Islamic law is "suitable for application in the twentieth century," or consider that Islamic law is the "cause of backwardness of Muslims." Do not believe Islam to be "only a personal matter between man and Lord, not connected to other aspects of life." Do not regard the judgments of Allah—the Shari'a demands of cutting thieves' hands and stoning adulterers—to be unsuitable in this day and age. Do not believe that it is permissible to rule by laws other than what Allah has revealed to us.

Do not hate what the Prophet has declared lawful. Do not mock Allah, his book, or his messengers. Do not engage in magic. Do not support polytheists against the Muslims. Do not believe that some people are entitled to deviate from Shari'a.

The final item on the list, simple enough: Do not turn away from Allah's religion.

13.

The bus ride from Jeddah to Mecca took forever. Our group leader Ahmad stood at the front of the bus and led us in labbayk chants. The chant was droning with no spirit at all, so I quit after a few rounds and looked out the window at the darkness occasionally broken by neon green lights of a minaret or the white lights of a gas station. We passed through some checkpoints and received Happy Meal–style packages from the Saudi government, snacks and small bottles of Zamzam water. If we were traveling by day, I might have seen the road signs reading NO NON-MUSLIMS BEYOND THIS POINT, but at night I couldn't tell where Mecca began, the point at which we were in a holy city.

I tried to contemplate the history of the Haram, the sacred precincts, knowing that all of it would leave my head once we arrived; it didn't seem reasonable to expect that in the Ka'ba's presence, a pilgrim could remember any books.

The Qur'an told me that Allah protected the Ka'ba—like when the Ethiopians with their elephants tried to advance upon the House, but Allah sent birds to bomb them with clay. Nonetheless, the Ka'ba has been destroyed and rebuilt numerous times. Before Muhammad became the Prophet, the Ka'ba was damaged by a flood. Upon completing its reconstruction, leaders of the various tribes argued over who should be the one to restore the Stone to its position. Muhammad resolved the conflict by suggesting that they place the Stone on a cloak and carry it together.

In 683, after the slaughter at Karbala, Yazid sent forces to Mecca to shut down his next rival, Abdullah ibn Zubayr. When Yazid's soldiers set fire to ibn Zubayr's tents near the Haram, the Ka'ba was burned, and the Black Stone cracked into three pieces. Abdullah ibn Zubayr cautiously demolished the remains of the Ka'ba, erected a temporary replacement with wooden frame and cloth curtains, and kept the Stone in his home, its fragments held together with silver nails. He rebuilt the Ka'ba according to what he considered the original designs of Abraham, but also added a door on the western side. After reclaiming the Haram for the Umayyads in 692, al-Hajjaj undid the western door and Abdullah ibn Zubayr's other innovations, but made the eastern entrance into double-doors, a practice that survives today.

In the hajj season of 930, Mecca was raided by the Qarma-tiyya, a fringe Ismaili offshoot, who two decades earlier had massacred twenty thousand pilgrims. They took over the city, stuffed hajji bodies into the Zamzam well, and carried the Black Stone to their utopian experiment in Bahrain. During the Qarmatiyya possession, the Stone was again fractured; this time into eight pieces, none larger than a date. The Abbasids paid a huge ransom to get the pieces back from the Qarmatiyyas, but Caliph Mu'tadid had one of them brought to Baghdad and placed in the gate of his palace, where it remained for a few centuries after his death.

After destruction by another flood, the Ka'ba was rebuilt in 1629. That was the Ka'ba standing today, I assumed. Men carressed its walls like it was the original Ka'ba touched by Muhammad, but they must have known that it was not. I would too, of course I would.

14.

Our hotel was barely a quarter mile from the Haram. After bringing my bag up to the room, I went back downstairs and exchanged my dollars at the front desk. My new riyals were covered with the drawn faces of kings, what a bunch of fucking hypocrites with stupid goatees. The school of Islamic law that ruled Saudi Arabia, the Hanbali madhab, did not allow the artistic depiction of living things. Drawing pictures was a link to idolatry and also an imitation of Allah's creative power. The Prophet had allegedly said that in the Jehennam fire, the artists will be asked to breathe life into that which they created; when they could not, Allah would then bring the drawings to life and make them torture the artists. That would make Ibn Sa'ud and Fahd and Abdul Azeez oppressors and tormenters in this world *and* the next, good for them.

"Are we free?" I asked Ahmad.

"You're free," he said. I bolted out of the hotel and rounded the corner, past a sign reading HARAM with an arrow and there it was at the end of Ajyad Street, the shining towers of the Great Mosque.

I joined the streams of people walking towards it, the men all in white ihram filling the street. The Haram looked like a palace of marble and light—like it was actually made of stars, there were so many blinding bulbs on that place, and stadium-style lights on the roof. It was a young building, most of it constructed after 1953 by the Bin Laden firm. The most recent expansions were completed in 1993.

I had no space or need to analyze that kind of thing, who built which parts when and how it changed from long ago, or the politics of it, or what this place meant in the conflicts of the modern world. As I approached the Haram, all internal dialogue shut off. I floated to one of the gates, took off my flip-flops and left them behind and walked in with my head down. I didn't want my first sight of the Ka'ba to be from around a corner or behind a wall, best to wait until it was right in front of me and take in its full power. I had a hard time making my way through all the people coming in every direction without looking up, but kept my gaze to the floor tiles. I walked down some steps and sensed that there was no longer a ceiling; I was back in the open air. Looking only at the white floor, I was already overstimulated, dizzy in the bright light and open night and the sounds and also the stillness, the sense that even with so much going on around me, the world was calm. People around me were making regular prayers or sitting with their families and tour groups. Ahead I saw a parade of legs walking in the same direction, and recognized the edge of scenes I had contemplated for my entire adult life, the generic photos of crowds swirling around the box. To keep moving forward, I knew, would have meant getting swept up in the pilgrims making their tawaf.

I remained hunched over. Standing at the Ka'ba was a mercy I could never deserve—not just because of a particular sin or rebellious word, but my whole life as a human, anyone's life as a human. We were small, we were *created*. Like Ali said, our lives went from semen to dirt. Knowing that I was semen and dirt, how could I lift my head?

It was an image waiting to be seen and understood, an image

when language failed. The Ka'ba meant so much that it meant nothing, it left *meaning* far behind. The explanations were gone, no pious history, no belief system to justify the feeling. When I stood there, knowing what was in front of me but still afraid to see it, there was no dogma, no doctrine, no book or prophet. I loved Allah and Allah's Mercy, and somehow this was Allah's House; but the rest of my religion fell away.

Then I looked up.

There was a plainness about it, empty in the good way. The Ka'ba was beautiful but not fancy like the rest of the Haram, blank enough to not impose a message. It was just a brick cube dressed in a veil, its blackness striking against the black night and blinding white stadium lights. It stood roughly fifty feet tall, much larger than in Muhammad's time, when Ali could reach the roof by standing on his shoulders. It remained inanimate, neither speaking nor moving to acknowledge my stare, but I loved the bricks as though they could love me back. I wasn't an idolater, but for the first time in my life I really knew the feeling.

They say that your first encounter with the Ka'ba is a good time for du'a, that Allah will grant anything that you ask for. I had thought about it on the plane and our long bus ride, and scholars suggested asking that Allah answer all of your du'as from that point on. Facing the Ka'ba, I forgot everything, and couldn't say a word but Sadaf's name. I said it a few times, remembering her, hoping that this might count as a du'a, and I cried. And then I began tawaf, moving with my brothers and sisters in counterclockwise orbit of the House.

A vertical tube of green light on the mosque wall indicated the corner of the Black Stone, where I'd start tawaf. From where I stood, I could see the Stone's silver frame as men swarmed around to touch it. Two religion cops in drab brown uniforms stood above the crowd, trying to manage the small riot around them.

About a hundred feet from the Ka'ba, I stood between the

Black Stone corner and the green light, and raised my hands to my ears like I was beginning prayer. I then extended my arms towards the Ka'ba and kissed my fingers. Bismillahi Allahu Akbar, I said. In the Name of God, God is the Greatest.

It was easy to weave through the people and get closer to the Ka'ba, much easier than I had expected. After passing the semi-circular wall around the Ka'ba's southern side—the Hatim, enclosing the spot where Ishmael and his mother Hajar were buried—I was close enough to the Ka'ba to rub the wall as I passed. To think that I could touch the Black Stone went against everything I had ever been told—it was too intense around that corner, people said, you can't get anywhere near it, and Malcolm X couldn't get within one hundred yards—but it didn't seem unrealistic.

Staying close to the Ka'ba, I passed the Rukn Yamaani corner, which was special for some reason that I never learned. I wasn't close enough to touch it anyway, but the next corner held the Black Stone. Most pilgrims continued around the Ka'ba, but I waded through until reaching the real mob, the ones who stuck around to see if they could touch the prize. Religion cops hung off the side of the Ka'ba, shouting commands and pushing people in an effort to keep things moving. An old woman cried out, on the verge of getting crushed; all I could see was her face, she was drowning in people. Tangled up in the mess of bodies, I wanted to get out, to retreat to the outer rim of the pilgrims. It wasn't an attractive moment for this religion. The Saudi booklet had told me that it was sunna to kiss the Black Stone, but not a required fard. Your real obligation was to protect the safety and dignity of your fellow Muslims.

Deep in the battle royale, to try and leave would have been just as destructive as staying to touch the Stone. I did what I could to keep my head above the crowd, even when brothers stepped on my calves to push me down, and arms wrapped around me and I wrapped mine around other men. I was near enough, and tall enough, to look over shoulders and see pilgrims as they put their heads into the silver frame around the Stone. Rather than join the fight to get closer, I watched. It seemed that as soon as someone kissed the Stone, he was pulled out and created a vacuum. In the next moment of vacuum, I shifted my weight and then something else happened—don't know what—and without any other moves or thought my body was drawn to that silver frame like a magnet, my face landing right in there. Seeing only a flash of black and brownish-red, I kissed the Stone with my hands around my face. Then a force pushed me from behind, causing me to head-butt the Stone hard, but it didn't hurt. I kissed the Stone again, took a step back and was then pulled away by the currents.

I had kissed the Black Stone in my very first circuit, but had six more to go and I felt dizzy. I moved away from the Stone and reentered the flowing tawaf, just moving along with the people around me, still unable to grasp what had happened. *I kissed the Stone*, I said, but language hadn't yet reclaimed its power. I kept walking around the Ka'ba in a daze, just knowing enough to lift my hands up when everyone else did and kiss my fingers and say Bismillahi Allahu Akbar.

I looked at the people, all kinds of people, all colors and nations. Indonesian, Turkish, Chinese, Iranian, Nigerian, Indian, Afghan. Young couples holding hands, men jogging like warriors, men with babies curled up in their ihram, old frail men with their backs bent at right angles, old women moving in packs. Tour groups following their leaders, long trains of pilgrims with hands on shoulders, repeating the leaders' chants. Afghan men with bright red henna-dyed beards, East African men with tribal scarring on their cheeks, women wearing their national dress.

After the seventh circuit, it was time to stand before the Ka'ba and make du'a, whatever would come out.

Allah, please don't draw me to that which is bad for me, and don't let anyone else hurt for my evil.

I then floated through the Haram until finding the place to pray my two rakats. Many people tried to pray directly behind the *Maqam Ibrahim*, a tall glass box containing the footprints of Abraham, but scholars said that you could do it anywhere in the Haram and it'd still count as behind the maqam. I prayed at the first space I found and then went to the hills of Safa and Marwah—which were now inside the Great Mosque, having been absorbed by the expansions—to make my *sa'ee*, the seven laps between them. It's easier now than ever, as the Saudis have given us two divided marble walkways to prevent injuries.

Sa'ee remembers Hajar, Abraham's slave and the mother of his son Ishmael. When Abraham's wife Sarah grew jealous of Hajar, demanding that Abraham cast her and the child into the wilderness, God sided with the wife. Abandoned in the desert by God's command, desperate to find water for her boy, Hajar ran back and forth between the two hills, at one point crying, "O Ishmael, die where I will not see you." This was the origin of Zamzam, the well that gave rise to the holy city. There were different stories of how the water came. One version had the baby Ishmael, left alone on the ground, kicking at the sand until suddenly uncovering the well. Another story said that the angel Gabriel came from heaven and approached them.

"To whom are you two entrusted?" he asked Hajar.

"We are entrusted to Allah," she answered.

Most of sa'ee was done at a regular walking pace, but green lights overhead signaled the parts where Hajar ran. I watched pilgrims in front of me pass the lights and pick up the pace and I chased after them, jogging until passing the next lights and slowing down. We walked and ran with each lap, some pausing at the water coolers to drink Zamzam in paper cups. But there was no water for Hajar, I remembered; I'd drink when she drank, when it was done.

Whenever the green lights told us to run, I felt Hajar's grief and panic, but it stopped being about her and Ishmael, or even this city or my ritual obligations. I thought of all the mothers and babies with no choices but to run wildly between the hills, the sad ones in a world where God didn't rescue everyone, and I remembered Mom. I was just a son with the best mother in the world, who had suffered in so many ways for my sake, and she always found the water. The great pre-Sufi ascetic Hasan al-Basri even said that honoring your mother had more merit than hajj. I just cried and cried for Mom because I had hurt her with this religion, I made my beautiful Islam into something hard for her and still she never said a word against it. She was what, five thousand miles away and couldn't hear me, but I was sorry and wanted to send that energy across the world to her.

TAWAF AND SA'EE completed umrah, the Mecca portion of pilgrimage. While in town, we could do as many umrahs as we wanted; but between two umrahs, we had to step out of pilgrims' status and then reenter it.

To leave ihram status, all I had to do was find a barber to shave my head. It was an old ritual to illustrate a crossing of the bounds. Long before Muhammad, pilgrimage ended with men shaving their heads at the idol of al-Uzza.

The shave only cost me ten riyals, less than three dollars. For the time being, I wasn't a pilgrim anymore, just a dude in Mecca at a five-star hotel with breakfast and dinner buffets and Internet access, and I could cut my nails and wear blue jeans again.

15.

They put us four in a room. The two beds were claimed by Mohsin, a computer programmer in his early twenties, and a brother in his fifties who hated on everything, so I called him Hater Uncle. They were both Pakistanis. The hotel staff brought two cots for myself and a Bengali uncle who snored.

"Uncle," I said softly, but couldn't bring myself to wake him up. *We're in Mecca*, I reminded myself, *don't be a dick.* I tried pulling the blanket over my head and squeezing the pillow around my ears, but he was too loud and close, our cots touching. I got up a few times and paced around. Mohsin was asleep. Hater Uncle was out somewhere, maybe at the Haram because it was mid-afternoon and not long before Asr prayer.

I tried to cool out by reading some pious literature about the history of Zamzam. The well had apparently been buried for several generations of the pre-Islamic era, only to be uncovered by Abdul-Muttalib, grandfather of the Prophet and Ali. When digging up Zamzam, he also discovered two golden gazelles buried in the well by the Jurhum, an ancient tribe. The Jurhum were first drawn to the area shortly after God's rescue of Hajar and Ishmael; while traveling in the valley, they spotted birds overhead and knew that they must have been near water. The Jurhum went to Hajar, who permitted them to stay; they gave Ishmael seven goats and he married one of their women, who bore him twelve sons.

After Ishmael's death, he was succeeded by his half-Jurhum son, Nabat; but in later generations, the Ishmael line was supplanted by its Jurhum cousins, who soon broke their trust with Allah. The Jurhum introduced idol worship to the Haram, horded wealth and mistreated pilgrims. If a couple in the Jurhum era couldn't find a place to fornicate, they just did it in the Ka'ba; among them were 'Isaf and Na'ila, who turned to stone and became the idols that once stood on the two hills, perhaps originally to remind pilgrims of the sex taboo.

We had varied explanations for the demise of the Jurhum. The historian al-Tabari said that Allah removed them from the earth with a plague of ants and nosebleeds; Ibn Ishaq said that another tribe overtook them. Near the twilight of their rule, a

Jurhum named Amr ibn al-Harith buried the treasures of the Ka'ba, the two gazelles. The uncovering of Abraham's sacred well and Amr ibn al-Harith's pagan treasure reminded us that Muhammad's grandfather, descended from Ishmael and a Jurhum woman, carried that conflicting history within him. And passed it on to his seeds. The reality of my religion, any religion.

LYING FLAT ON my back, staring up at the ceiling, I focused all of my psychic energy on each snore, trying hard not to snap. Then I rolled over and stared at him. He looked like a dead man with his eyes closed and mouth wide open. Why was I annoyed? A snore was breath, snores meant that my old uncle was alive. Snoring praised Allah like the chirping of birds, so I made his snores into a zikr. Every time the air went in loud, I said subhanahu Allah. I managed to fall asleep like that, until Hater Uncle came back and woke us all up for prayer.

Hater Uncle told us his stories from his shopping trip. When he asked an alley merchant if he sold sim cards, the guy answered, "I have everything" and then offered him weed.

"*Weed?*" scoffed Mohsin, either amused or disappointed, I didn't know him well enough to tell. "They have *weed* in *Mecca?*"

"People are people," I said.

"That's amazing."

"It grows wild in Pakistan," I told him. "I saw it along the road."

"*Really?*"

"Uncle," I said, turning to Hater Uncle. "You ever hear of bhang?"

"Sure," Hater Uncle replied, grinning and shaking his head. "We used to put it in the tea. Just a little bit, but it was so good."

"So you bought a sim card, uncle?"

"Yes, if you need I will go with you, I know where to go to get the deal. But do not buy from the Bengalis, they rip you off."

"Uncle," I said, pointing with my eyes and a sideways nod to the Bengali in the room. But he didn't get it.

"The Bengalis are thieves," he added. The Bengali uncle didn't say anything.

Staying optimistic, I recalled my own words. *People are people.* Even in Mecca. If pilgrims were better than human, I wouldn't belong here.

16.

Having achieved the ultimate goal of every pilgrim and kissed the Black Stone, I looked to other attractions in the Haram. Without ihram status, I went in my regular clothes. I lingered at the Maqam Ibrahim a few times, but religion cops yelled "HARAM ALAIK!" and shoved me along, lest I worship it. During one circuit, a regular guy took it upon himself to protect our religion—what would that make him, a religion vigilante?—and placed himself in front of the maqam with his arms outstretched, blocking pilgrims from kissing the glass.

I focused on the Hatim, the stone half-circle on the Ka'ba's north-west side. Islamic history held the Hatim wall to mark the dimensions of Abraham's original Ka'ba, before its destruction by flood. Islamic history held the Hatim wall to mark the dimensions of Abraham's original Ka'ba, before its destruction by flood. Ibn 'Arabi believed that the original Ka'ba had three corners, not four: the Black Stone corner, the Yemeni corner, and a third corner within the Hijr area. The Hatim was once connected to the Ka'ba, another change made by Ibn al-Zubayr and undone after his defeat. The space between the Hatim and Ka'ba enabled pilgrims to enter the enclosed space, which we called the Hijr (literally meaning "taboo," derived from *hejara,* "to deny access"). Because standing in the Hijr counted as being inside the Ka'ba, it was always packed with men and women trying to pray there, touch the Ka'ba wall or make du'a under the golden water spout (which Sufis called the "Spout of Mercy"). It has been suggested that before Muhammad was born, the Hijr was used to hold sacrificial animals. In Muhammad's time, it was a place to hang out and have visionary dreams.

Though we stood on it and prayed on it, many, maybe most Muslims regarded the Hijr as a grave, the resting place of Ishmael and Hajar. The order of events changed with the sources; but in the version that stuck with me, Hajar died before there was even a Ka'ba. Twenty-year-old Ishmael buried her and then his father showed up, flying in on the Buraq and accompanied by the Sakina, a creature that has since disappeared from the books. Alternately described as a two-headed cloud or a white vulture-like bird, with the head of a human or a cat, the Sakina was another hybrid, mixing Arab folklore with Jewish tradition's Shekhina, which was described as the "presence of God" or possibly Yahweh's feminine aspect. Shekhina descended among the people of Israel after they built the Tabernacle. Today, Sakina survives as a common girl's name, and a title of honor for Husayn's daughter back in Damascus.

Allah told Abraham to build where the Sakina rested, and she chose to land on the grave of Hajar. The Sakina indicated the area of the House by circling its outer perimeter, like a spider starting to build a web. Then the father and son went to work, Abraham building and Ishmael passing him the stones. They built the House using rocks from five mountains; one account named them as Mount Sinai, the Mount of Olives, Lebanon, Judi, and Hira. Conflicting versions of the story, both attributed to Ali, described the Black Stone as either revealed by the angel Gabriel or carried to Mecca by Ishmael. I liked the Ishmael version.

*   *   *

IT WAS CHAOS in the Hijr, more people squeezing in than the place could reasonably hold, especially since everyone wanted to pray rakats. People arguing and stepping on each other (with guards sitting on the Hatim making nothing better) was enough to get me depressed, but then I saw something different. Four people—one African man, two South Asian men, and one Turkish woman—stood together, holding hands in a circle around a brother as he prayed. When he finished, he joined the circle and someone else took a turn to pray. The team gained and lost members, and most of them were strangers to each other. I stepped in, and before long they invited me to take my turn. I entered the circle and made two rakats, but it was hard to make a mindful prayer while considering that someone could fall on me or step on my neck. It felt better anyway to stand and protect whoever wanted to pray. After our team eventually dissolved, I found others who needed help, like an old Turkish man trying to advocate for his wife while she prayed. I put my hand on his shoulder, the two of us making a wall to block one side of her, and then another brother joined us. The man and his wife both thanked us and I looked for someone else.

Amidst the violence of the Hijr—and it *was* violence, what else was it? The strong oppressing the weak, everyone wrestling and pushing, employing physical coercion to get a prize— there were also pockets of kindness and friendship between strangers who usually could not communicate with each other. Without explaining our intentions, we took each other by our sweaty hands and held tight. After watching over a Nigerian man through his prayer, he offered to do the same for me, so I jumped in and tried again. This time it was a real prayer, no fear at all. When I went to the floor in that crowd, the noises of the people were muffled, like I was going underwater at a noisy public pool and then jumping back up to the surface.

Staying in the Hijr for hours, I learned how to effectively

manage people around my praying brothers and sisters, both with my body (sticking out my ass to create more distance) and firm but loving insistence that the prayer is respected. I'd say it in different languages: salat, namaz, prayer. I was washed in the sweat of others, and tears stung my eyes. After a while, people in the Hijr started to acknowledge me as a positive agent. An Iranian brother's eyes opened wide when I said that I was American. An Indian brother smiled and told me, "I wish George Bush was like you, then I would love America." Some Pakistanis complimented my strength and called me a *pewhlan*, a wrestler, and I told them that I knew what it meant. Two West African sisters in bright purple gave me serious thanks for pushing people back while they prayed together. One Iranian woman thanked me, and then we had an awkward moment where it seemed that both of us wanted to shake hands, but were afraid of offending each other. I did see a Turkish woman and Kenyan man shake hands after cooperating, both of them wearing their flags.

"American?" asked a brother, and I nodded, just as I noticed the water jug hanging by a strap over his shoulder, bearing the flag of Iraq. Then I looked in his eyes and lost it.

"*Staghfur,*" I cried. We held each other in the Hijr, brothers at the grave of our common ancestor in the spiritual sense . . . and I squeezed tighter, repeating the only Arabic word I knew that seemed appropriate. *Staghfur, staghfur.* Forgive me.

Sometimes I'd stand over a brother and sister and have my back to the Ka'ba, enabling me to watch everyone as they faced the House to make du'a. People stood in a row around the Hatim wall, men and women together, some of them bawling. They were all staring up at the Ka'ba, so no one caught me looking at them; but while watching people, I was also trying to hold my balance against all the pushing, protect the Muslim on the floor and also avoid falling on him or her myself—an epic battle against the unending human flood. When wrestling an unbeatable opponent, victory could only mean an end to the fight. The end came when religion cops and a team of shaykhs in their own uniforms, red and white kifeyyehs and white thobes burst in and cleared out the place. Then the blue-uniformed janitors came in to sweep the floor. Fajr prayer must be soon, I thought. During congregational prayer, the Hijr had to be empty, otherwise people would be inside the Ka'ba and praying in front of the imam.

How long had I been in there? I couldn't know. But I blended back into the tawaf, and then drifted out to the edge, found the King Abdul Aziz gate and left the Haram, even if they were preparing for Fajr. Walking away from the white ihrams and white lights up Ajyad Street to the Ajyad Hotel, I felt dizzy and sleepy but still mentally clear, like my sense of the world after a really great punk show that kicked my ass in the right ways. There was supposed to be another Ka'ba directly above us in the starless Saudi night. The Baytul Mamoor, it was called. The Prophet went there on his journey to heaven, and so did Ibn 'Arabi, finding Abraham leaning against it. According to a clip from Arab television that I had watched on Youtube, the earthly Ka'ba and celestial Ka'ba were connected by a "magnetic equilibrium zone" like that between the North and South poles. This explained the short-wave radiation that NASA had discovered emanating from the earthly Ka'ba, said Dr. 'Abd al-Baset Sayyid of the Egyptian National Research Center.

The doctor also suggested that this radiation caused the residents of Mecca to live longer and healthier, and be less affected by gravity. It was the kind of thing that Master Fard would have told Elijah, setting up the poor Apostle to be shattered later in life. "Circling the Ka'ba," Dr. Sayyid said to the curious news anchor, "you get charged with energy." But at least that part was true.

17.

The next night I was looking out at the Haram through a shopping center's window. Superimposed on the mosque in the reflection, in white letters on red:

BURGER KING

I ordered a Beef Royale combo meal. The LCD message at the register read, HOLY MOSQUE HAVE IT YOUR WAY.

It was easy to feel like the Haram had lost something in the modern era, landing somewhere between the Stone Age and Saudi Disney, but it wasn't all gone. Pilgrims shared a modern myth that summed up the truth of this place, if not the facts: the kings had attempted to redirect the flow of Zamzam into their palaces, but the ancient spring would not conform to their plan. The water refused to betray us. Even if it was made up, the story had a legit moral: as hard as they tried, the Saudis could not kill what was real in the Haram.

The real was still there, and I hoped that I could unlock it, insha'Allah, if I was willing to get weird.

THERE WERE ALWAYS thousands of people at the Haram, even at night, but at least at later hours it wasn't too crazy. After my Beef Royale, I went back over, took an escalator to the second floor and found the green-light corner. *My name is Azreal Wisdom*, I said to Allah. *I came to your House by myself.* I watched pilgrims around me stretch out their arms towards the House, and pilgrims below swarming around the Stone.

And what is my paradise other than you, and it is you by yourself that covers me . . . if you have entered paradise, you have entered yourself.

—ALLAH, QUOTED BY IBN 'ARABI IN THE
Bezels of Wisdom (Ishmael chapter)

Sit yourself in heaven at once!

—ALLAH, WHO APPEARED IN THE PERSON OF
MASTER FARD MUHAMMAD

Finding a quiet corner and lying down with a cup of Zamzam water, gazing up at the dozens of ceiling fans, it felt like maybe I really could have it my way. Something was happening inside me: I sensed the Ka'ba of my heart opening up, and the Prophet and Ali calling me inside.

I'm not a mystic or a schizophrenic, but I believe that semi-deliberate imagination games can get you somewhere, like a free-write without the pen and paper, so I played along.

Should I go in? Not long after the Prophet's death, it became a matter of serious discussion whether Muslims could enter the Ka'ba. Those first Muslims were converted pagans, crossing a border and afraid to look back. In the jahiliyya lives they left behind, a man tore off his clothes to rub his navel against a nail in the Ka'ba floor (the "navel of the world"), and people climbed on each others' backs to reach the "firm tie" or "sure hold" in the Ka'ba's ceiling. To close the Ka'ba would have looked like the natural way to govern those impulses. Muslims who believed that praying in the Ka'ba was acceptable, even a practice of the Prophet, did not go so far as to see it as a required act of the pilgrimage. One scholar notes, "It is as if even its defenders feel some uneasiness about it."

In Ibn 'Arabi's time, the Ka'ba was opened on Mondays and Fridays; in later centuries, pilgrims could enter into the Ka'ba for a fee; in modern times, the doors were solid gold and access was limited to guests of the King of Saudi Arabia, who opened the Ka'ba once a year to personally wash its floor. But this wasn't that Ka'ba, no royalty allowed in the Haram of my heart.

In my heart's Ka'ba, it looked like the inside of the real Ka'ba. I knew what the inside of today's real Ka'ba looked like from a photo that circulated on the Internet. It had marble walls and floor, like the rest of the Great Mosque, and three wooden pillars with gold trim. The upper portions of the walls were draped in green curtains. Lamps hung from a rod running through the pillars. To the right of the door was another door, the Door of Repentance, which covered a winding aluminum stairwell that went up to the roof.

Lying in a fetal curl on the Haram's floor, I closed my eyes and imagined its marble to be the floor of my heart's Ka'ba. "What is it that seekers find inside the Ka'ba of the heart?" asked the Urdu poet Jamiluddin Aali. "One finds an idol, one a man, and one a deity." No Muhammad or Ali, I was alone.

In real life, I heard the slapping of someone's chupals, and worked it into this waking dream, asking myself questions and going with the first response to pop into my head.

Whose chupals are they? A young Arab boy in bright Indian clothes, looking at me.

Is he curious? Afraid? Does he know me? I don't know yet.

Who is he? Ishmael. Or Ismail, as we say.

The chupals' slapping grew distant and faded out. *Where could he have gone?* The Ka'ba wasn't that big a room, but Ishmael would have known the secret places.

Who's Ishmael? Son of Abraham who almost didn't make it—first abandoned to the desert, then placed on the altar by his father holding the knife. Both by God's command. Ishmael lived to father the Arab people, which would make him the antecedent of Abdul Muttalib, grandfather of the Prophet and Ali. For the Arabs who followed Muhammad, Ishmael's life was more than religion, it was genealogy. Pilgrims revolved around the House, the site of Ishmael's grave; they prayed behind the footprints of Ishmael's father, *their* father, builder of the House; and they walked the path of Ishmael's mother, their mother, who found the water. Umrah told the story of racial origins and survival.

Every generation was a miracle. Abdul Muttalib had vowed that if God gave him ten sons to protect him, he would sacrifice one at the Ka'ba. After his tenth son came of age, he told the boys of his vow and made them cast lots with arrows to determine who would be killed. The winning arrow belonged to Abdullah, his youngest and favorite son, the future father of the Prophet. Abdul Muttalib was prepared to cut Abdullah's throat by the hills of Safa and Marwa, but took the advice of a female seer to bet his son against camels, ten-to-one until the boy won. Abdul Muttalib finally saved his son—and his unborn grandson—at the price of one hundred camels.

To further stress the point: Ali was born inside the Ka'ba, near the graves of Ishmael and Hajar, marking the cycle of death and life that connects us with those who came before us and those who came from us. For Shi'as, Muhammad and Ali were themselves sacred ancestors; the marriage of Ali to Muhammad's daughter began a whole new line, the Infallible Imams. According to one of those Imams, no less than seventy prophets were buried at the Ka'ba.

Leaving the dream play, I stood up feeling like Dave Bowman in *2001: A Space Odyssey* after he went into the Monolith, and weaved through people in tawaf like I was the new Starchild. I passed women who were cloaked head-to-toe in black abayas with gold headbands, ornamented like walking Ka'bas. Did they know that the portion of the Ka'ba's veil that covered its door was called the *burqa*?

Reaching the edge, I could see the real Ka'ba below, where men struggled to put their faces inside the Ka'ba's silver frame and kiss the Black Stone, like I had done. I remembered Ikbal

Ali Shah saying that in early times, when worshiped as a goddess, the Stone radiated a greenish hue.

It was too far away to see, but I had been closer and knew that the silver frame around the Stone—let's be honest—was shaped like a human vagina.

The House was where Ishmael buried his mother, but also a womb itself. The Ka'ba was a woman, a mother, standing by a sacred well in the desert, in an area vulnerable to floods, and now guarded by nine (Born) minarets that looked like erect penises. Its perimeter had been drawn by the flying Sakina, who looked to me like a female version of the Ruh, the Spirit. *She* was the resident of what we called the House of Allah, and she wanted her House at the grave of Mother Hajar. Before Islam, pagans commonly made tawaf naked, shouting, "We shall go before Allah in the same condition in which our mothers gave birth to us."

The House was a shrine, but to what?

Tales of Muhammad as a child had him at the Ka'ba with his uncle, Ali's father, praying for rain in a drought year. A story from his later career portrayed water gushing from his fingertips, enough for all of his companions to wash for prayer. Water was a miracle in the desert, and life itself was a miracle, and the miracle of life came with water too, semen and vaginal fluid and amniotic fluid; the Qur'an even says, "We have made from water every living thing." And Ibn 'Arabi said that Mecca was the womb of the earth.

The Black Stone was where my interpretation went off the chart, but I was glad to have read that meteorite stuff before getting on the plane. In 2001, scientists examining meteorites in Australia and Kentucky found traces of extraterrestrial sugar, possibly formed by an interaction of ice, ammonia, carbon monoxide, and starlight nearly five billion years ago. The findings led some to suggest that sugars and amino acids—the building blocks of life, DNA and RNA and cell membranes—had come from outer space, via meteorites that *fertilized* the world. True or not, it helped my understanding. The Black Stone was proof of cosmic sex, sky father and earth mother, heaven's intercourse with the world.

In my T-shirt and jeans, I moved with the white-toweled pilgrims in tawaf, reciting no labbayk but the Rakim song "The Mystery," where he raps about God who chose Earth as the home for new life and then "let off his resources in the water"—but it's an allegory for his own parents conceiving him. From Rakim I went to the RZA, whose song "See the Joy" spoke from the perspective of a sperm cell "going through a struggle so I could exist." RZA described the womb as a "state of triple darkness," the phrase coming from Elijah Muhammad; sixty-six trillion years ago, it was triple darkness from which the first god created himself.

A million motherfuckers tried to race ahead / but I was the one that fertilized the egg. Life is a struggle, said the RZA, life is a struggle. How many lotteries did we win to be here—how many Hajars among our foremothers, how many blessed babies who almost didn't make it? I gazed up at the House as I passed its southwest corner, the Rukn Yamaani, still feeling the shock of my own existence, and then saw the southeast corner where the men in white fought for a chance at the Black Stone like sperm around the egg. Between the Stone and the Ka'ba's door was the Multazam, the "place of attachment," where pilgrims rubbed their bodies against the wall to have their prayers accepted. Women at the Multazam traditionally prayed to become pregnant, asking Allah to renew the miracle for another round.

I'm here, I thought. Here meaning Mecca, but also *here*, a soul in this body, a human being alive in the world, even if I shouldn't have happened. I knew why Ali said that he was the dot under the *ba* in *Bismillah*, the Pen, the Guarded Tablet, the Throne, the Chair, and the seven heavens and earths—and his great-great-great-grandson the Sixth Imam, Ja'far as-Sadiq said, We are the prayer that is mentioned in the Book of God, we are the charity, we are the fasting, we are the pilgrimage, we are the sacred months, we are the holy lands, we are the Ka'ba, we are the qiblah, we are the Face of God, we are the signs, and we are the clear signs.

I added one: *We are the mystery*. It's all about us. Umrah is ancestor worship, and water worship, and life worship. Our trembling at the odds against anyone having ever been born.

18.

The Haram gave me the truth of creation, presented in the form of a story. The story reached me through a man who sat in a cave until an angel came and told it to him. Allah created man from a clot, said the angel. The man was Muhammad, and the cave was just a taxi ride from my hotel.

Our group leader advised Mohsin and I against visiting the Mountain of Light. "Just stay at the Haram and make tawaf," he said, following the advice of our handbooks from the airport: "Do not burden yourself by visiting places for which there is no reward, or for which there might be some blame for doing so."

At the bottom of the mountain was another reminder, a billboard placed by the Saudi government:

> Brother in Islam:
> The Prophet Muhammed [PEACE BE UPON HIM] did not permit us to climb on this hill, not to pray there, not to touch its stones and tie knot on its trees and not to take anything from its soil, stones or trees.

> The good deed is to follow the path of the Prophet Muhammed [PEACE BE UPON HIM]. So do not oppose that. Allah said "Indeed in the Messenger of Allah you have a good example to follow for him." [AL-AHZAB: 21]

ANOTHER INDICATION OF Saudi disapproval was their complete neglect of the place. While the Haram remained immaculate, and constantly maintained by a large custodial staff, the Mountain of Light sparkled with thousands of discarded Aquafina bottles, and human litter sustained the wild animals.

"We gotta watch out for baboons," said Mohsin. "Supposedly they'll wave at you if you give them salam, but they're still mean."

"They have baboons here?" I asked.

"They might be jinns that got turned into monkeys. There was something in the Qur'an about that."

Along the climb up there were merchants selling zikr beads, water, and posters of the Ka'ba, and beggars showing their deformed limbs, and pilgrims greeting us on their way down, always asking my country and smiling when I said America. And there was a pack of baboons with bare asses and skinny red dicks, one drinking from a discarded water bottle, another posed on a rock looking thoughtful like the Egyptian knowledge-god. When they came close, I calmly picked up a rock and they knew enough to run.

I wondered what this mountain looked like in the Prophet's time, and what the climb would have been like for him. Now the place was covered in graffiti in Arabic, English, Hindi, and Korean, and we occasionally found man-made steps. There were some brothers with tools and bags of cement who asked for donations, so we gave each one a riyal or two. "Imagine the blessings of that," said Mohsin; "everyone who comes to the Cave uses a step that you helped build."

There was a makeshift outdoors mosque, really just a smooth

floor covered with a carpet, no walls or anything, for us to make Asr. Mohsin invited me to lead the prayer, but I insisted that he lead. If my brothers knew what was really in my heart, they wouldn't want to pray behind me.

It took forty-five minutes for us to reach the Cave, on the side of the mountain and decorated with calligraphy in red and green. Above the crowded entrance, someone had painted the earliest verses revealed to the Prophet:

READ! IN THE NAME OF YOUR LORD WHO HAS CREATED, HE HAS CREATED MAN FROM A CLOT. READ! AND YOUR LORD IS THE MOST GENEROUS, WHO HAS TAUGHT BY THE PEN, HE HAS TAUGHT MAN THAT WHICH HE KNEW NOT.

The Prophet used to come here before he was the Prophet, back when he was just Muhammad ibn Abdullah. His wife Khadija would accompany him to the cave on annual retreats in the month of Ramadan; our taxi driver had told us that Khadija ran up the mountain three times a day to bring him food, for which Allah personally greeted her with salam. The mountain had poor people begging then too, and Muhammad would feed them.

This was where the angel Gabriel came and brought the Words.

Sure that he was insane, Muhammad decided to throw himself off the mountain; but then the voice spoke again: O MUHAMMAD! YOU ARE THE MESSENGER OF ALLAH AND I AM GABRIEL. Muhammad saw the angel standing on the horizon and turned away; but the angel was there too. Wherever Muhammad looked, the angel greeted him.

The city below was filled with *kahins*, soothsayers, and *sha'irs*, poets—the word literally signified one with awareness beyond the natural realm—who relied on information from jinns. Employed to tell fortunes and settle disputes, the kahins and sha'irs would consult with their personal jinns and then deliver statements in rhymed prose.

By the grace of Allah, the Qur'an later assured Muhammad, *you are not a soothsayer or a madman*. Muhammad brought something new to Mecca's spiritual life, a book that fell heavy upon the old ways and crushed them. He did not deny the fortune tellers—the jinns were real, of course, and a jinn might whisper a secret into the kahin's ear, which the kahin then mixed with one hundred lies—but denounced their vocation. Rather than pay oracles for the confusing words of a jinn, men and women could read commands directly from the Lord of the Universe. The Qur'an marked the Arabs' launch into what we call civilization: the supplanting of tribal custom with codified law, the death of folk mysticism and birth of scripture-based authority, religion's move from disorganized to organized.

INTERACTIONS AT THE Cave felt like a more relaxed version of wrestling at the Black Stone, with everyone pushing and squeezing around the entrance, selfish but not desperate or mean. People did get angry at some Iranian and African women for taking too long with their prayers. When I reached the front, I saw that the cave's white-tiled floor only had room for one person at a time. A woman snuck under my arm and got in, and immediately started to pray so that no one would remove her. I crawled in and found a space at her side to make one rakat, though I couldn't do the standing part.

This was the Cave where it all went down, where I got the story that I use. I couldn't know what that meant for Muhammad, what he experienced in there. Our whole way up the mountain, I had tried to get it. Nothing quite worked. Not the Mystery God with long beard handing him a stone tablet, not an angel coming to him from beyond himself, and not even a writer-mysticism view of revelation like it was F. Scott Fitzgerald's typewriter in there. Cognitive scientists could tell me that Muhammad had a parietal lobe like any of us, and that if you quieted down the lobe, something "holy" happened, but the world was filled with people having visions, and most of the time they failed to bring new ethics and meanings to a place. I knew that I wasn't going to get it, at least not in the time that I had.

I made the prayer quick, no concentration or heart, just to get it done and let someone else have a chance, and then backed out of the cave. It was even more crowded than before I went in, no way that I could leave as I came; so I climbed on top of the cave and sat above the crowd for a while, watching them struggle with each other and women draw circles with their fingers on the cave entrance.

Then I saw a baboon about three feet away. We noticed each other at roughly the same time, but before I could react, he ran around me, snatched my big water bottle and darted off with it. A group of old Iranian women, watching from below, laughed at the dumb American who had his water jacked by a monkey. I smiled to show that I wasn't upset.

I climbed around and met up with Mohsin on the other side. The experience of the Cave was too quick and hassled to be fulfilling for either of us. I only thought of the people fighting for a chance to sit there, expecting some magical power from the spot, and my own hypocrisy, since I had only added to the crowd. Maybe the Saudis were right in discouraging visits to this place, since it seemed to bring out the superstitious bullshit side of religion, pure 85 percent. And then I heard a voice of my own: *You have something that they don't have.* I took refuge in Allah from that bad whisper and kept walking. Along the way down I bought some postcards from a brother, glossy photos of the Ka'ba at different times in history. One of the pictures showed the Haram in the late 1800s, near the end of the Ottoman era with all the clutter of structures around the Ka'ba, like a shrine over the Zamzam well nearly as tall as the

Ka'ba itself, and the Banu Shaybah gate named for the Quraysh clan that maintained the Haram. The surrounding mosque was simple and just ground-level, none of the overwhelming King Fahd and Abdul Azeez extensions. Another postcard showed the Ka'ba during the big flood of 1941; it looked like brothers were swimming their tawaf.

The sun had just finished setting when we reached the bottom, so we hit up a mosque right by the mountain for Maghrib prayer. The imam recited one of my favorite short suras, at-Tariq (the Night Visitor). *By the heaven, and the night visitor*, the imam recited in Arabic. *And what will make you to know what the night visitor is? It is the star of piercing brightness. There is no human being but has a protector over him. So let man see from what he is created! He is created from a water gushing forth . . .*

19.

My failure to understand the Prophet's experience in the Cave had more to do with Allah than Muhammad. I could bear witness to Muhammad as the father of my knowledge, but the traditional view of prophethood did not speak to my view of God, no tablet-engraving old man on a cloud.

My Allah came from more than just prophets. There was that other branch of my Allah's family tree, going back only to 1958, when Arthur Lipsett was hired as an editor by the Canadian National Film Board's animation department. Collecting discarded scraps of footage from the editing room, Lipsett mashed them up into a nine-minute collage, *21–87*. The film has no narrative, just a sense of things, expressed with images of trapeze artists, machines, old people walking the streets of Montreal and New York, and monkeys. The audio material includes a clip from a conversation between Warren McCulloch, neurophysiologist and pioneer of artificial intelligence, and Roman Kraitor, the filmmaker who developed IMAX. When McCulloch insists that human beings were really just machines, Kroitor responds:

> Many people feel that in the contemplation of nature and in communication with other living things, they become aware of some kind of *force*, or something, behind this apparent mask which we see in front of us, and they call it God.

The film *21–87* happened to be life-changing for George Lucas, who would place hidden tributes to it in *Star Wars*: when Luke Skywalker and Han Solo sneak into the Death Star to rescue Princess Leia, they learn that she is held in cell 2187. Lucas married his own dabbling in Eastern philosophy to Lipsett's sampling of Kroitor to conceive the Force, which I then married to Islamic tawhid and the Sufi concept of *wahdat al-wujud*, the "unity of being." That's where I conceived Allah, and also Muhammad the Jedi Master, imagining the Prophet's experience of Allah as Yoda's experience of the Force. Ashadu anna Yoda rasulullah.

20.

There was another place in Mecca where the Prophet interacted with the unseen, a place which had also become a site of pilgrimage: Jinni Masjid, built on the spot where he had accepted conversion from a group of jinns.

Because jinns were made from smokeless fire, like the Devil, Muslim thinkers debated whether Shaytan/Satan was a jinn. Ibn Taymiyya held the opinion that the Devil was the father of all jinns, their Adam. Tradition contained a wealth of information on the lives of jinns: the animals they rode, the ways that they organized their tribes, and encounters between jinns and prophets like Solomon.

Muhammad's teachings on jinns pushed humanity forward on the most basic level. After using the toilet, he instructed, do not use bones or dung to clean yourself, because these are the foods of jinn. Do not eat with your left hand—the hand used in his time for unclean things—because the Devil eats with his left. And do not spend unnecessary time in bathrooms, garbage dumps, or graveyards, because the jinn like to frequent these places. Popular folk belief placed jinns at the bottoms of dried-up wells.

Keep your children close to you at night, said the Prophet, so the jinns do not snatch them away.

In the modern world, Muslims viewed jinns primarily as mischief makers; when I told Mohsin about the discovery of extraterrestrial sugars on meteorites, he answered that it "sounded like something the jinn would do to trick us." In the Prophet's time, they were something more, the source of authority for kahins and sha'irs. The jinns also had their own religions and jinn prophets, but Muhammad was the only human prophet sent to them. Converting to Islam, *submitting* to Muhammad, the jinns too were abandoning the old ways. That seemed like the key to understanding this mosque.

Jinni Masjid did not have a section for women, so they sat on the ground outside and waited for their men to finish praying on soft carpets. There was no chivalry in mosques; but when these thoughts came to me during prayer, I remembered that distraction was the work of devils, and one devil in particular, Khinzab.

Mohsin and I sat after our prayers for some time. I couldn't tell what ran through his head, but I was trying to feel the history of Jinni Masjid, any remnant of the smokeless fire creatures who came here and bore witness to Muhammad's mission. What kind of jinns were they? The Prophet said that there were three types. One class of jinn had wings and could fly through the air, another resembled snakes and dogs. The Prophet is said to have advised against killing a snake in your home, because it may be a Muslim jinn; first give the snake three warnings to leave. But if the jinn comes as a black dog, kill him. Ibn Taymiyya said that the black dog was the devil of dogs.

The third type of jinn had the strangest description; all we knew was that it stopped for a rest before resuming its journey.

Jinns lived much longer than humans, so it wasn't impossible for a jinn from that day to be alive and even lingering in the mosque: a jinn Sahaba, a companion of the Prophet, still among us today. Too bad the Saudis had to rebuild everything; the mosque didn't even feel old. I still walked up and touched the smooth mihrab like everyone else, and didn't know why.

IBN TAYMIYYA BELIEVED that humans and jinns frequently intermarried and had children, and that if we could "pull off the veil" we'd see that most people in society were possessed by jinns, like the disguised aliens in *They Live*. Makes you wonder what kind of world he lived in, and what his days were like. Seems like Ibn Taymiyya had a hard time with things.

Preoccupied for a day or so, I hit up the Ajyad Street stores for books on jinns and exorcisms. One of the books looked like serious field research, the author interviewing various imams about their experiences with jinns. One informed the author that jinns had names, all kinds of names; he once met a jinn whose name was 36. Another imam claimed to be a great daw'ah worker among the jinns, having converted a number of Buddhist and Christian jinns to Islam.

I learned that any jinn, male or female, could possess both men and women, and more than one jinn can enter into the same person at a time. A jinn usually entered you through your feet, then climbed up inside you for a home. Jinns liked to hide in the hearts of men and the wombs of women.

Then I looked up jinns on Youtube in the hotel's Internet café. One video claimed to show a jinn praying in a mosque. It looked like a prayer rug manipulated to stand upright with an almost human posture, surrounded by watching men. There was also an innocent home video from Syria, showing a sudden flash of light behind a child—a passing jinn? And footage of a soccer player flipping and contorting on the ground, the result of jinn possession.

A clip from Lebanese television in 2006 showed a shaykh who claimed to perform exorcisms. Holding what looked like a rolled-up dishrag with string wrapped around it, he told the program's anchors, "If I showed it to all the doctors of the world and told them that this had come out of the womb, or the vagina, of an ordinary married woman, they would never believe it—let alone when it came out of a girl who is a virgin, at the blossoming age of thirteen or fourteen." Then he brought out a shopping bag filled with them, rags and towels rolled and bound to look like thick black snakes.

"All this just from one girl?" asked one of the anchors.

"All from one girl," the shaykh answered, "but on different occasions. It did not all come out at once. Today, her mother contacted me and said that the last piece had come out of her daughter, causing her no problem."

"Excuse me, Shaykh," the anchor interjected, "but is this girl still a virgin?"

"God be praised, God be praised. Like I said earlier, I will never forget this girl. It is a miracle." The girl was possessed by jinns, he explained. "The jinn used to send out small notes from inside her, on which it was written: 'This girl will never marry. This girl is destined to do abominable things.' It wrote repulsive things, God forbid."

Youtube videos showed women in white hijabs screaming

and bellowing with gravelly voices, the jinns speaking through them, while shaykhs forced them out with the shahadah. Across the spectrum of religions and cultures, anthropologists have found demonic possession to primarily afflict women. Possession, like modern stories of UFO abduction, served as a coping mechanism, a new way for the survivor of abuse to understand how she was taken against her will. Deprivation theory would explain possession as a way for women without physical or social means to switch identities and shift the balance of power in their homes; a man might beat his wife, but not Satan. In Egypt, a woman had used jinns to obtain divorce—not by her own possession, but accusing her husband of marrying a jinn without her permission. Unable to deny the existence of jinns, since they were mentioned in the Qur'an, the judge's hands were tied. He accepted the testimony of the woman's witnesses, who stated that while they were in the house, they saw a vase fall off the table for no reason.

Egyptian folklore told of jinns and ghuls who lived in the desert, coming to villages at night with a thirst for blood. One found a young woman on the street at midnight and asked her, "Shall I eat you here or carry you on my horns to the desert?" She then allowed him to carry her on his horns to his hut. Another story told of a jinn who took the form of a man and sucked blood from a maiden's finger, prompting her brothers to kill him, dismember his body and sell the meat as fish to the jinn-man's family.

Jinns even interfered with the early Muslims, the greatest generation. One night, when the Prophet left Ayesha's home, she felt jealous over him; he later explained that her jinn had come to her. The Prophet told her that every person had his or her own *qareen*, a jinn companion. The Prophet himself had a qareen, though Allah helped Muhammad "deal with him until he became Muslim."

21.

Hater Uncle opposed our wanderings around the city, since just a regular prayer in the Haram counted for one hundred thousand prayers anywhere else; why miss the reward? But Mohsin and I took taxi rides around the city, making our own ziyarat tours. Our driver was Bengali and Mohsin built with him in Urdu to get the story: he worked in Saudi to send money to his family in Dakka, he said. He had been away from home so long that he didn't even know his kids.

He drove us by the Prophet's birthplace, which was a library now so we didn't go in, just making du'a as we passed. And we stopped at the Jannatul-Mowla, an old cemetery, but the Saudis closed it after sunset.

We could see the newer section from an overpass. The cemetery looked like a vacant sandlot, except with rocks arranged neatly in rows. Jannatul-Mowla was a clan cemetery, holding Muhammad and Ali's family: their great-great-grandfather, Abd Manaf (his name, "Slave of Manaf," recalled one of the pre-Islamic gods), Abd Manaf's son Hashim, Hashim's son Abdul-Muttalib, and Abdul-Muttalib's children, the Prophet's mother Amina and Ali's father Abu Talib. The first convert to Islam, the Prophet's wife Khadija, was also here, with their son Qasim, who died before his second birthday.

Suspect narrations said that whoever was buried in Jannatul-Mowla was guaranteed paradise, but Muhammad's ancestors had all died as idolaters. The issue was especially complicated for Abu Talib, who had lived to see his nephew become the Prophet. Sunni sources placed Abu Talib in Hell, with fire under his feet that caused his brains to boil. According to Sunnis, Ali didn't even refer to Abu Talib as his father when informing the Prophet of his death: "*Your* old, misguided uncle has died. Who will bury him?" Ali initially refused to bury his father, but

Muhammad insisted, after which the Prophet told him to wash off the dirt. Then the Prophet made a du'a that Ali described only as "more precious to me than everything on earth."

Many Shi'as insist that Abu Talib died a Muslim, and that claims otherwise stem from an Umayyad conspiracy to slander Ali. At an Ashura lecture, I heard a scholar admit that Abu Talib kept to the idols, but that we could never find proof of his disbelief harming Islam. That was the only approach for me, a convert always facing Muslims' dissatisfaction with my kafr mother: *Al-hamdulilah that she accepts your chosen faith, brother . . . has she taken shahadah yet? No? You work on her, insha'Allah . . .*

Just riding around at night, our taxi driver pointed out holy sites, like the place where the Prophet pulled a tree towards him, and a mountain that was owned by Umar. The Saudis were tearing the whole mountain down, he told us, to build luxury apartments or something.

We had completed our umrahs at the Haram, but the distinguishing rites of hajj actually took place outside Mecca. Hajj was fulfilled with our visit to the Arafat plain, where we'd accept Allah's forgiveness, and then our stoning of the Devil in Mina. Knowing that Mount Arafat (also known as the *Jabal-e-Rahmah*, Mountain of Mercy) would be too packed at hajj time, Mohsin and I checked it out a week early.

The Jabal-e-Rahmah was 150 feet high. On the top stood a fifteen-foot obelisk of whitewashed lime and granite, representing the place where the Prophet had stood during his last pilgrimage to give the Final Sermon. Garbage and litter, demonstrating a lack of government approval, indicated that we weren't supposed to be there. Besides that, the Saudis left another sign:

> Dear Muslim Brother!
> The prophet Muhammad [PEACE BE UPON HIM] did not come here except the day of Arafat. He did not climb

on the hill, not commanded to touch its stones or trees, not to pray or inscript or construct anything else on that. He did not order to tie knot on the trees or rocks; but he said: "You can stand anywhere in the Arafat."

Dear Pilgrim!
You should follow the sunnah of your prophet [PEACE BE UPON HIM] who said: "Learn your rituals of Hajj from me." May Allah accept deeds of you and me.

As at the Mountain of Light, there was no evidence at the Mountain of Mercy that anyone cared about the Saudis and their signs. The hill drew a good crowd in the days before hajj.

Besides the regular litter, the ground was covered with discarded photos. Some brothers stood around with Polaroids offering to take people's pictures, but the photos on the ground were different: wallet-size studio shots of children, like the pictures we got back in elementary school. Boys in their crested uniform-shirts and ties, girls in white hijabs. There were also pictures of adults from various corners of the world. Some looked like they came from South Asia, others the South Pacific. I took out my camera and arranged several of the photos to fit within a single shot, while a brother looked at me like I was nuts or doing something inappropriate; but this was the real story of the place.

Leaving photos at the pillar wasn't covered in my Saudi hajj manual. I saw a posed picture of a young man, early twenties I thought, in green turban like I had seen in Pakistan, and wanted to know the photo's journey. Had he brought it there, or had someone brought it on his behalf? Was he alive when the photo found its way here—was it a rememberance of the sick or the dead? In leaving the photo there, what did someone think would happen? Next to him I found a Polaroid of a family, a husband and wife with their three kids. The architecture behind them suggested that the picture had been taken wherever they came from—Indonesia, I thought, or somewhere in the region. The wife was sitting in the foreground with white hijab. Standing at her side was a girl three or four years old, and behind them stood the husband and the two big kids, a boy around ten and a girl who could have been twelve or so.

I circled the pillar, which probably looked like another inappropriate act, since innovators have actually made tawaf around Arafat, but my eyes were to the ground, to the hundreds of photos. They reminded me of the tin feet and hands that people left at shrines in Pakistan, acts of magic and rememberance at a place of power. An attempt to compel the divine, a special tug on the god's heart? *Ya Rahman, this is my dear son; please keep him in your thoughts.* I looked up and saw men and women rubbing the pillar, even kissing it, while mouthing prayers.

The Prophet broke lots of stones in his time, and I couldn't guess what he would think of this scene. The pillar itself wasn't anything special, even in secular history. It wasn't there in the Prophet's time, he didn't make it or touch it, and no one knew who put it there or when; but people rubbed that stone like it contained Muhammad frozen in carbonite and they were looking for a way to release him.

As for his words at that spot, his farewell speech to the human race, the Prophet told us that our lives and property were as inviolable as that sacred day. He abolished the old ways of usury and blood vengeance, told the men their rights over women and reminded those present to repeat this sermon to the absent. And he said that despite the Muslims' victories, one enemy still ruled them.

O people: the Devil has despaired of ever being worshipped in this land of yours, though he is content to be obeyed in other works of yours, that you deem to be of little importance.

22.

Keeping up with the five daily prayers made me conscious of the sun's position. I didn't have a watch, so we made plans by prayers: "After salatul-Asr, we'll go eat, insha'Allah."

Since it was easier to visit the Haram late at night, the prayer I made most often there was our pre-sunrise Fajr, and then I'd walk back to the hotel while the sun came up. Prayer at sunrise and sunset were forbidden, the Prophet said, because the sun rose between the two horns of the Devil. There was a wisdom behind that, since pagans used to worship the sun at those times, and Muhammad wanted to move us away from those things.

He also told us not to sit between the sun and the shade, because this was where the Devil sat.

I thought of the Devil, and what it would mean to stone him. I could focus on the Devil as my ego and desires, but the Saudi books warned against treating him as a mere metaphor. Shaytan was a real thing, they said, an actual living creature who waged unending war on the children of Adam. I tried to get into that Mystery Devil. If he was real, the Devil was slick beyond any of us. The Devil would convince a man that he was the one sent to save Islam; he'd tell him, "The sign that you are the Mahdi is that a mole will grow on your body," and then cause a mole to grow.

There were lots of unfortunate ones who heard those whispers and followed them over cliffs. The Devil can get you just by acting as your hype-man. Sitting alone in the hotel room as the sun descended, I found myself dwelling on past travels and the way that brothers reacted to a blue-eyed American Muslim. It really had nothing to do with me, but sometimes it still became embarassing, an uncomfortable thing to carry. It was the same in Mecca. At the Haram, an African man had asked my country, and when I said "American" he had tears in his eyes. A good moment for the Devil to sneak in and whisper, *You are something.*

I jumped out of bed and headed back to the Haram. Making the post-sunset prayer, I stood between two brothers that I did not know and made sure that my feet touched their feet. The Prophet said that any space would allow the Devil to come between us.

23.

Pilgrims are allowed to make umrah on behalf of the deceased, and Azreal may or may not have returned to the essence—you never know with that guy—so I decided to make one for him, just in case. First I had to leave the city limits and reenter after visiting a *mikat*, a designated station for assuming pilgrim status. Mohsin and I put on our towels and took a taxi to Masjid Ayesha, a mosque built on the spot where Ayesha had entered ihram for the Prophet's Farewell Hajj. Because she was menstruating at the time, the Prophet told her to perform all rites except tawaf, which she'd make up later.

Just outside the mosque, conical pillars marked the boundary between sacred and non-sacred ground. Inside, everyone was dressed like us and there for the same reason, performing their two rakats of intention. While making my own prayer I remembered Azreal, my teacher who said, "Thanks Mike, for everything," though I had given him nothing and he gave me his teachings and name. And then I thought of his teachings, which were essentially just two items:

1. Arm Leg Leg Arm Head (A.L.L.A.H.) reveals the divine in all, and nowhere in there does it say "penis" or "black."

2. Lessons and Mathematics are only part of your cipher; the other degrees are the "life lessons" that you pick up along the way.

I made proper intention that this umrah was for Azreal, and then got up and took the taxi back over the boundary. I was a pilgrim again.

It seemed appropriate to do Mathematical Tawaf—seven circuits around the Ka'ba, it was too easy—breaking down each circuit the way that Azreal would have if he was there. The first laps were Knowledge (1), Wisdom (2), and Understanding (3), and the structure itself had three floors, and I was on the Understanding level. Everyone had different degrees of Knowledge, Wisdom, and Understanding, and the hajj brought us all together. Allah willing, we could do it in harmony—or Equality (1 + 2 + 3 = 6). The fourth lap was Culture, so I just looked at all these cultures around me coming together, long lines of pilgrims with hands on each others' shoulders and following their leaders. The men were restricted to ihram garb that wiped culture away, but you could still see our differences in the ways that men shaped and dyed their beards, or the tribal scars that some African men wore on their cheeks. Female pilgrims wore their regular clothes—writer Mohja Kahf had told me that Ayesha made hajj wearing brilliant red, though conservative translators tried to make it yellow—so there were brightly colored shalwars from India and solid black abayas from Iran, and many women covering their faces though they weren't supposed to. The women often wore distinguishing items to make their group recognizable to anyone who got lost—a square of purple cloth safety-pinned to the back of their veils, or an Iranian flag. The women of an Indonesian group wore bright saffron scarves over their white hijabs.

In Supreme Mathematics, my fifth circuit manifested Power, the easiest one to build on because power was everywhere in this place. We entered the Haram through gates named Fahd and Abdul Azeez, and the kings even put their names on our holy things: on the Ka'ba's rain spout, it read, "This water outlet has been refurbished by the Custodian of the two honorable Haramains, King Fahd bin Abdul Azeez of the family of Saud, King of the Kingdom of Saudi Arabia." King Fahd's name was also on the lock of the Ka'ba's door, while the door itself bore the names of his father and brother. The Ottomans did the same thing when the Ka'ba belonged to them.

The religion cops manifested Power with no Refinement. Besides the teen cops, some of these guys were supposedly former convicts who had earned reduced sentences for memorizing the Qur'an, and then found employment as Protectors of Virtue and Preventers of Vice.

Power ruled over people because they had no knowledge, slaves to mental death—the Saudis fed them something and they just took it—but if you add Knowledge (1) to Power (5), you get Equality (6). Passed the green light and began the sixth lap. Equality was what Malcolm found here, praying with blonde devils. Azreal found his Equality at Matteawan State Hospital for the Criminally Insane, where he met a black man who called himself Allah; and then on the streets of that other Mecca, Harlem, where Allah told his teen militants that if they had a problem with Azreal, they had a problem with him too.

Imagine Azreal in the Haram, what a catastrophe—he'd run around in my old Doug Flutie jersey and some gym shorts showing off his scars from kicking through sanitarium windows. He'd either get lost among the masses and end up homeless on the Mecca streets for twenty years, or he'd tell the wrong guy that he had met Allah in New York and they'd take off his head. After Equality came God (7), and Azreal said that God was equally in everyone, but most Five Percenters wouldn't recognize a devil as God, and Azreal could never come to this city and honor God with the Muslims. Which was fine, because

I was Azreal's Muslim son, smuggling him across these borders in my heart. For my seventh circuit, I remembered Allah—not the one feared by Abraham, but the one loved by Azreal at Matteawan State Hospital for the Criminally Insane, the one honored by a young disciple with a gift of seven Milky Way bars (symbolizing the seven heavens), the one who let Azreal and hundreds of Harlem and Brooklyn's fatherless call him Father. So he was my grandfather. Imagining the Ka'ba as a mother, I remembered the Mothership, and the Allah of 1960s Harlem who said, "The Mothership is the mother's hip."

During my seven runs between the hills, remembering how Azreal loved his mom, I pretended that I was carrying Old Man Azreal on my back, fulfilling the son's duty. Though I prayed for people all the time, I wasn't entirely comfortable with the idea that we could aid others in that way. Nor could I offer the umrah as a prayer to something outside myself, which would betray Azreal's Five Percenter beliefs. Azreal knew better than to sweat those theological mischiefs—one of the *life lessons* he gave me—and he'd know what I meant by running around the black-veiled box and between two hills for him: just an act of love for someone who didn't get a whole lot of love in this world. Repeating his name on my beads, I remembered him and hoped that he was happy, warm, and well-fed, whether at the Allah School in the other Mecca or a shelter in New Jersey. He might have been somewhere worse, a jail somewhere, or maybe a jail disguised as a hospital or buried with a number instead of a name. Azreal's wish was to be cremated, he had told me, so that his ashes could be spread with his mom's (and Allah's) at Harlem's Marcus Garvey Park.

In case there really was such a thing as performing umrah on behalf of someone, I meditated for good energy on Azreal's behalf, whether living or dead, and then I thanked Allah for Allah.

24.

After finding a barber to officially end that pilgrimage, I came back and entered the Haram on the ground level. Beyond the outer rim of tawaf, men and women were finding places to sit and wait for Fajr prayer. I took a seat and watched. While I stayed in one place, the pilgrims making tawaf went around and came back again, mastering the four directions and 360 degrees. The cipher moved counterclockwise, like the earth's orbit when viewed from the sun's north pole. Master Fard said that the Original Man was the maker and owner and knew every inch of the earth, the best and poor parts. In pagan times, men and women also made tawaf around the Ka'ba, which they had surrounded with 360 idols, matching the 360-day year of many ancient calendars. And one for every degree.

> I was born underwater
> With three dollars and six dimes
> Yeah, you may laugh
> 'cus you did not do your Math
> —ERYKAH BADU, "On and On"

The Ka'ba held too many layers of meaning and I wasn't qualified to dig through any of them, neither as an anthropologist, nor a student of Islam, nor a wizard. My stray readings smashed together. I knew that Sephardic and Hasidic Jews made seven circuits around a cemetery before burials, but I didn't know what to do with it. Buddhists circumambulated stupas, Hindus went around lingams. Allah made the electrons do tawaf around the atoms, and our solar system joined 400 billion other stars in tawaf around a supermassive black hole, center of the Milky Way. To the birds overhead, pilgrims around the Ka'ba must have looked like a human prayer wheel or NGC 5457, the Pinwheel Galaxy. It all sounded cool.

THE BROTHER TO my left—young black man with scant goatee, Arab kifeyyeh and camouflaged pants, sitting alone— looked like he might have been American. How can you spot an American? His posture? Might have been just a feeling. But I cooked up a fantasy bio for him: he converted as a teenager after reading about Malcolm, just like me, and now the two of us were together at the Ka'ba reenacting the moral of Malcolm's hajj.

Just to see if he had an accent, I turned and asked him a question.

"Brother, do you know what time's the Fajr adhan?"

"It's coming up, insha'Allah." He was American.

We got to talking. His name was Mikayel, he grew up in Philly and converted after getting into Malcolm, holy shitballs, and now he was a member of the Warith Deen community. We built all the way to Fajr time, sharing our thoughts on the Nation of Islam. "I think that Elijah misinterpreted what Fard was really teaching him," he said, so I dropped the bomb that Fard had returned in disguise as an Ahmadi imam to help Warith Deen reform the Nation. Mikayel didn't buy it. I told him that it wasn't necessarily true, but still a good story. I looked up at the thing in front of us, the big black box, another good story. He did too, neither of us saying anything. We were in Mecca, I realized, sitting in the shade of the Ka'ba, talking about Master Fard.

We asked each other the question that all converts get asked, *How did your family react?* but without the implication that they'd go to Hell unless we brought them to Islam. Our families were cool. We asked each other if this was the first hajj. It was, for both of us. Mikayel said that he had mixed thoughts about it, having seen some things that he didn't like. "People are fighting," he said. "I thought it'd be different."

"People are going to test you here," I told him, "but they tested the Prophet worse." He smiled and shook his head.

"I'm glad you told me that," he said.

We sat in silence for a long time. The birds chirped. I noticed women sitting in front of us, women were everywhere. While men and women remained mostly separate within a tour group, the group itself stuck together—which meant that the Haram as a whole was not arranged by gender. The handbook that we were all given at the airport said that women were supposed to pray behind men, but no one here seemed to care and the religion cops couldn't possibly reorganize a crowd of this size. It wasn't completely integrated—there were lines of men and lines of women, the spaces between often bridged by married couples—but still went way past the limits of any other mosque on the planet. I wished that language and etiquette would have allowed me to speak to these women, to ask what it meant to them. One American woman, Asra Nomani, was inspired by her hajj to push for gender equality in mosques back home.

The typical argument against men praying with women, claiming that men couldn't handle the distraction, provided one of Islam's more pathetic modern embarassments. If Muslim men were correct to live in such fear of women, then Muslim men weren't men; but at any rate, these guys had issues. Muslim men were devils in the way that white Americans were devils, trained and conditioned to a devil's state of mind.

Behind us, an uncle mentioned to his friend that he had seen women right up near the Ka'ba during prayer.

"It's okay," said his friend. "Al-hamdulilah; nothing wrong. It is a good thing for her."

"Yes, brother, I was not saying against it. She is lucky, al-hamdulilah."

The second adhan came and we stood up, black Mikayel and white Michael and the uncles behind us and the women all around us, and we prayed together. Intergender prayer back home felt like an activist event, but it seemed more natural in Mecca. This was where Malcolm felt like a "complete human being" for the first time in his life, and I felt that too, in a different way: transcending not only whiteness but also maleness, becoming more than my penis.

After Fajr, we stood again for a funeral prayer. They did junazza after each of the five daily prayers at the Haram. As we filed back onto the streets, I caught a glimpse of the coffins leaving the Haram, carried above the masses like they were floating down a river.

25.

"You see the difference between the kuffar and the Muslims?" Hater Uncle asked me by the hotel elevator.

"What's the difference?"

"Here when time come to pray, everything close. All the stores, they close and pray."

"That's because it's the law, uncle. They have religion cops running around making sure that the stores are closed."

"The kuffar, they have no . . . no *power in their souls*. They have nothing."

"Do you think the Saudis have power in their souls?"

"Allah gave them the House." That was all that mattered. Allah honored the Saudis with custody of the Ka'ba, so of course they must have power in their souls. Hater Uncle tried to break it down with a verse of the Qur'an, basically implying that if you were in charge of the House, it was because Allah chose you for it. But that wouldn't hold for five seconds.

"What about the Quraysh, uncle? They ruled the House for a time. By your logic, the Prophet was wrong to fight them."

In Muhammad's time, the Quraysh had also claimed that as custodians of the Ka'ba, their blood was as sacred as the Ka'ba itself. Muhammad respected their sanctity, refusing to fight them, until it became clear that the Quraysh and Muslims could not coexist.

Hater Uncle shook his head.

"But he won, you see? And nobody has kicked out the Saudis, so . . ." He let his words trail off like that was all the proof we needed, no reason to keep talking.

The Iranians had opposed Saudi control of Mecca and Medina for years, pushing for the holy cities to instead be administered by a joint alliance of Muslim countries. In 1987 clashes in Mecca between Iranian protesters and Saudi police led to four hundred deaths and over six hundred injuries.

Apart from Wahhab-Shi'a hostility, the Saudis had enemies because they promoted an extreme Sunnism that also served as the most essential critique against them. You can't be a Wahhab and have dozens of wives and solid gold bathtubs, you can't enforce Wahhabism in your own country while running off to Europe and blowing the people's fortune away on casinoes, wine, and hookers, and you can't call yourselves the protectors of Mecca and Medina while allowing kafr soldiers from the United States on your land.

In 1979 an organized force of armed rebels seized the Haram in Mecca and took pilgrims as hostages. They were angered by the Westernized royals, who had poisoned the country with television and educated women. Though the Qur'an forbade violence in the Haram, the Saudi government obtained a fatwa from its scholars allowing a violent recapture of the mosque. After a successful seige of the Haram and execution of the rebels, the Saudis granted more power to the country's religious leadership. The royal tightrope act continued, with Wahhabism further entrenched as the ruling Islam of Saudi

Arabia, and the Saudis using their money and prestige to push Wahhabism around the world, while real Wahhabs wanted the hypocrites destroyed.

"Those chickens will be roosting," I told Hater Uncle, "insha'Allah." And then I looked around, nervous that some-one had heard me.

26.

Allah willed that we'd be in Mecca on a Friday, allowing us the reward of attending jum'aa prayer at the Haram. The pilgrims willing to arrive hours early were able to pray inside the mosque, but I had to join the thousands outside. The reward should have been the same, since it was still the same congregation, but all I really have to say about that Friday is that Arab men outside the holiest mosque in the universe were calling black men "Abd," which means "slave." In my life as a Muslim, as much as any prior disillusionment, this moment really drove it home: childhood was over, no turning back. Sorry, Malcolm.

27.

Ibn Taymiyya distinguished between visiting graves and making ziyarat to them. He said that if you happen to find yourself at the Prophet's Mosque in Medina, you should perform a prayer in the masjid and greet his tomb with peace—but if you journey to Medina solely to see the grave, you are a "deviant innovator." Medina had no connection to the rites of hajj, and to make unnecessary efforts to visit a dead body—even the Prophet's—constituted a serious sin, especially if you did so with the idea that it'd give you spiritual benefit. Ikhwan shrine-razers had targeted the Prophet's tomb long ago, but most Muslims treated Medina as a crucial part of the pilgrimage.

Even on the plane from Jeddah to Medina, I missed Mecca. Mecca was Islam, but also bigger than Islam. Mecca was the root, Mecca reached back into the darkness before the Prophet. Mecca was where the truth stood clear from error. In Mecca, Muhammad was like Jesus, only a warner and preacher and a voice of justice and compassion in an immoral age. In Medina, Muhammad came like Moses, he brought the laws and took heads. Medina was where truth became religion, the institution of future scholars and jurists and pious universities. In Medina, Muhammad built his own society; Medina was the birthplace of political Islam.

Again, our bus arrived at the holy place at an odd hour of night. Our hotel had us even closer to the Prophet's Mosque than we had been to the Haram in Mecca. After making our way through the hotel's welcome—with a loud band of drummers and black men dressed in costumes from another time serving us dates and tea—we deposited our things in our rooms and then headed over to the mosque outside.

Nothing at the Haram of Medina looked anything like it had in the Prophet's time. The huge gold-and-marble Prophet's Mosque wasn't here—the original mosque was adjacent to his home and the apartments of his wives. Because prophets were buried where they died, Ayesha's apartment became his grave. On his deathbed, Muhammad told us not to make his tomb into a place of worship, and cursed the Jews and Christians for having done so with their prophets; but over the years, expansion of the Prophet's Mosque led to its swallowing up the Prophet's tomb.

I walked in like it was just another shrine, which it was, but it wasn't. It was Muhammad, Muhammad the body, waiting at the far end of a vast red carpet. In my mind I ran through all the

Muhammads there had been, more masks for the Prophet than Rey Mysterio; this was the Muhammad who appeared to Ibn 'Arabi in visions and handed him the *Bezels* praising idolaters, and also gave Ibn Taymiyya the basis for endorsing war on unbelievers (which included Shi'as). Which Muhammad was waiting for me at the front of the Mosque?

Muhammad, I said to myself. *Muhammad, Muhammad.* I repeated the name enough times to run through a ninety-nine-beaded tasbih and then some. *Muhammad.* You can say a word so much and so fast that it doesn't mean anything anymore, it becomes gibberish. Muhammad wasn't a person or even a philosophical concept like *insan al-kamil.* Muhammad could have meant a tortoise shell, or a floating transparent dodecahedron of light.

Walking to where the crowd was, I found a solid gold chamber with a barricade that prevented us from touching it. I couldn't really see through the grille to the tombs inside, but knew that there were three: Muhammad and the heirs to his politics, Abu Bakr, and Umar. Space for a fourth tomb was reserved for Jesus, who would be buried there after his return.

That's Muhammad, I reminded myself. *Behind the gold.*

Between the chamber and the barricade stood religion cops to make sure that no one took pictures or went overboard in love for the Prophet.

"Hajji, hajji," said one of the cops, waving me to the door. I didn't know how long I had been standing there, but apparently my time had run out. I thought a pious thought, moved along and before even knowing it, I was outside the Mosque with no feeling, no sense that the big golden box contained anything at all. It might have been better with bhang, but the cops might have been meaner.

28.

At the hotel they had us two to a room. I was roomed with Hater Uncle, who made sure to wake me for all the prayers. Mohsin was roomed with a chubby Egyptian uncle who seemed to always have a smirk on his face.

"What is your name?" the Egyptian asked when I stopped by to visit.

"Michael," I told him.

"What is your good name?"

"Michael."

"That is your *good* name?"

"That's what my mother named me."

"You never changed it?"

"Brother," I said, ready for this after hearing it from Hater Uncle, "who was the first person to accept Islam?"

"Khadija," he answered, then muttering the Arabic wishes for Allah to be pleased with her.

"Who was the first male to accept Islam?"

He hesitated. "Ali," I answered for him.

"No, it was Abu Bakr," he replied. "Ali was only the first of the children."

"Okay." That was a Sunni-Shi'a thing, no point arguing with him. "Brother, what were their names before they converted?" Abu Bakr had changed his name only because his original name, Abd al-Ka'ba (Slave of the Ka'ba) suggested idol worship, but Ali, Khadija, and most of the Prophet's companions kept their birth names.

"Yes," he said, "but those are Arabic names."

"Brother, I didn't convert to being Arab."

He laughed at that.

"I like you, Michael."

"Just so you know," I told him, "my middle name's Muhammad." He laughed again.

"*Michael Muhammad?* You are an unusual brother."

AFTER SEEING THE Prophet's Mosque, my real interest in Medina was Jannat ul-Baqi, the cemetery that housed some big names from our history: all of the Prophet's wives except Khadija, the caliph 'Uthman, the Prophet's grandson Hasan, and three other Shi'a Imams, the fourth, fifth, and sixth. The Prophet's infant son Ibrahim was there, his uncle Abbas and some of his aunts, including Ali's mother. The founders of two schools of law, Imams Shafi'i and Malik, were buried next to each other.

Even Muhammad's daughter Fatima was supposed to be there, though the exact location was debated. She had died during the reign of Abu Bakr, who she never forgave. According to Shi'a narrations, she had been fatally injured by Abu Bakr's supporters as they stormed into the house to demand Ali's allegiance—and she was pregnant at the time. Knowing that her end was near, Fatima asked her husband not to allow their enemies at her funeral. Ali buried her alone at night, guarding her privacy against the oppressors, and reportedly made three false graves to keep her true location a secret.

For Shi'as, Fatima was the "Eternal Weeper," crying still. Her pain and sacrifice matched that of her husband, and her sons, and the sons of her sons, and those stories made me so sad and angry that I almost went *ghuluww*, becoming a heretical exaggerator in my love just to balance the injustice.

I didn't have a sense of Medina geography and had no idea where to find the cemetery, but discovered it while walking outside the Prophet's Mosque after Fajr. Seeing crowds of Iranian women standing around, reciting and crying, I knew that some holy graves must have been close.

Even if Fatima's grave was known, those women could not visit her; women weren't allowed in the cemetery, since their crying bothered the corpses. There was no logic to it, since women were allowed to bother the corpses of the Prophet, Abu Bakr and Umar. I made my way up the ramp and through the men. The sun was just above the brown earth. The graves were only mounds and rocks, regular rocks of random shapes, nothing with a name to show who was where. In Ottoman times, the cemetery was home to numerous domed shrines for the celebrated Sahabas and Ahlul-Bayt—including one for Fatima, even if it wasn't really at her grave—but on April 21, 1925, the Ikhwan razed them and the shrines of Jannatul-Mowla. Shi'as commemorate the date as the "Day of Sorrow."

As much as I grieved for Muhammad's daughter, I understood the Wahhabs' shrine-razing. For the superstars of our history to be placed in the dirt with the same anonymity as Jannat al-Baqi's thousands of other bodies felt like pure Islamic reality: in death, there's no fame, no special status for wealth or family. Of course, this was betrayed by the marble and gold shrine of Muhammad, Abu Bakr, and Umar behind the cemetery, and even within the cemetery by the elevated cement walkway built around 'Uthman's grave.

The section housing the Shi'a Imams was fenced off and blocked with tall blue signs giving the same advice in several languages:

• DEAR VISITOR •

This is the Prophet's way of visiting the graveyard:

Graves are to be visited for introspection and learning a lesson. The Prophet said, "Visit the graves for they remind you of death."

Upon entering the graveyard the Prophet used to greet the people of the graves saying, "Peace be on you O people of the Abode of the Believers. We are surely going to join you insha'Allah. May Allah show mercy to the former and to the latter. We ask well-being for us and for you, O Allah, do not deprive us of the recompense (that You may grant us for our bereavement), and do not subject us to temptation after their departure."

The Prophet has forbidden to perform salah towards the graves, and also to sit on them. He said, "Do not sit on the graves nor perform salah toward them." (Reported by Muslim)

The Prophet has forbidden addressing supplications to the dead, and asking them to procure for us what is good and ward off what is evil. Allah says, "And those whom you call upon beside Him (Allah) cannot help you nor can they help themselves" (al-A'raf 197). And the Prophet said, "If you ask, ask Allah; if you seek help, seek Allah's help."

I went up and down the aisles trying to see it their way, since there's no God but God and no helper but God, but they ruined it by installing shaykhs and religion cops to harass everyone. The religion cops were generally heroin-skinny teenage boys, gesturing tough but afraid to really assert themselves beyond a wave of the hand. *Hajji, hajji,* they'd say, gesturing that you've stood too long at a grave and needed to keep walking. The shaykhs had more confidence, standing proud in their white jalabs and red and white kifeyyehs above the pilgrims. Along with the cops, they served as a boundary between us and the graves, keeping us from getting too close. The shaykhs lectured and debated while the cops stood around, sure that they looked badass.

Only so much you can do in there, just follow the walkways and stand with an Albanian or Turkish group making du'a until the shaykhs come and scold the group leader. This wasn't Lahore. Even if I was intellectually opposed to grave worship, the shrines in Pakistan still had heart and I missed the pink flower petals.

Back outside, I saw a religion cop shouting at an old Indian auntie, and she looked at him with tears in her eyes like she couldn't understand this in a dozen lifetimes. A few feet away, some Persians and South Asians argued with a Nigerian decked out in red and white kifeyyeh. I had seen him in the cemetery, scolding grave-worshipers on behalf of the government.

"We respect the Arabs," he told the circle around him, "because Allah gave them the Qur'an—"

"But you are speaking *against* the Qur'an!" exclaimed a brother practically jumping in his face. "Allah says the Arab is not better than the non-Arab, nor is the non-Arab better than the Arab, except for good deeds—"

"YOU ARE NOT LETTING ME FINISH!" snapped the Nigerian. "Please let me explain, and understand that I cannot argue with all of you at once. Listen: Allah gave the Arabs the Qur'an in their language, and we give them respect for having that language. There is no language in the world like Arabic, and when they come to our country to teach us Islam, we at least respect them for that much." Some other brothers jumped into it and they went back and forth yelling over each other, but I lost interest.

Marcus Garvey, whose statements on religion made the Nation of Islam and Malcolm X possible, found discomfort with a blonde-haired, blue-eyed, pale-faced Jesus Christ. You can't pray to a god who doesn't look like you, he said. Islam was supposed to be better, a universal religion for all the world. Since we didn't have pictures of Allah, Allah's face couldn't empower one skin tone over another; but we still knew how Allah spoke, who he spoke to and what language he used, and what nation he preferred for his final message to mankind. The Qur'an was like a white Jesus for Arabs.

Back in the room, I found Hater Uncle sitting on his bed with the Qur'an, reading under his breath, wearing his new red and white kifeyyeh over his shoulders.

"I am memorizing," he explained.

"Do you know a lot of Qur'an?" I asked.

"Thirteen, almost fourteen paras." Nearly half the book.

"Do you understand Arabic?"

"No, I do not. But Allah makes me to understand." He looked at me like I was supposed to be amazed. "I do not *know* the words, but Allah gives me the *wisdom*."

Five Percenters would argue that if you want to be Mathematical, Knowledge (1) comes before Wisdom (2), and only then do you get Understanding (3); but I let it go.

29.

At Mecca's Haram we prayed in the open air on a marble floor, but at the Prophet's Mosque we were inside, breathing shared air with our faces all pressed into the same carpet. Everyone got sick. During the quiet parts of a prayer, you'd hear dozens of men coughing, even the imam on the microphone.

Returning to the hotel after Fajr with a sore throat and pounding headache, I closed my eyes and pulled the blanket over my head. When I was a little kid, I used to put myself to sleep with visualization exercises, pretending that I was Han Solo frozen in carbonite, carried across the galaxy in Boba Fett's Slave I. This time, I went back to the Ka'ba of my heart. Muhammad and Ali carried me inside, both of them faceless; I couldn't even fathom the skin on their hands, it was like being carried by two ghosts. They delicately lowered me to the floor and buried me under blankets. Then they left me. I imagined three million people doing tawaf outside, but the inside remaining quiet and calm like the pilgrims were a galaxy away. Though its dimensions were like those of the regular Ka'ba, the marble room still seemed more spacious.

The only sound in the hotel room was Hater Uncle on his bed, gently turning pages of his Qur'an, and I worked it into the scene. I visualized young Ishmael again, now sitting cross-legged before the Qur'an on a wooden stand; but when Hater Uncle began his recitation—reading in the sweet desi uncle way, almost feminine, not the mighty and joyless kick-your-ass Saudi tone—I gave his voice to Ishmael, who now became Old Man Ishmael with wrinkled face and soft white beard. To build the scene, I asked myself what he was reading, going with my first response: the portions of the Qur'an about him and his father and that terrible day with the knife and the Stone. The day that Abraham had a vision in which he killed the boy—a clear order from God. Ishmael was an ancient spiritual master but also a traumatized boy, and the boy still lived inside him somewhere, searching the text to understand why things had to be that way. Even if Ishmael had lived to be 140 years old like the books said, or was really here in my heart's Ka'ba four thousand years later, I'd assume that he never found an answer.

Hadiths had Muhammad saying, "The person who recites the Qur'an most beautifully is the one who recites it in a solemn sadness," and "The Qur'an was revealed in a sad fashion." I could hear the sadness in Hater Uncle/Ishmael's recitation, right for reliving those moments when Dad says, *O dear son, I have seen in a dream that I must sacrifice you. What do you think?* And you reply, *O my father, do what you are commanded. If Allah wills, you will find me of the patient ones.* And then Dad puts you facedown, and you close your eyes and wait for it, only to have Dad back off because a voice tells him, *This was a clear test.* Only one way to read those words, if it was you.

Maybe the book in Ishmael's hands wasn't even the Qur'an. Perhaps, while the rest of us struggled to comprehend that day, Allah bestowed a mercy on the boy who had to live it: a special scripture just for him, with the secret answers made plain.

Lying under my blanket on my Ka'ba's marble floor, watching

Old Man Ishmael read, I wondered how it felt to have one's childhood hell put in a holy book. He was a prophet and poor righteous teacher but also a survivor of abuse, probably PTSD.

30.

The Prophet said that whoever made wudhu at home and then went to Masjid Quba to make two rakats would receive the full reward of umrah. Hater Uncle usually preferred to stay in harams, but he went with us for those blessings. The Prophet had laid the first stones in Masjid Quba's construction, but that mosque no longer existed. The Masjid Quba that we visited was built in 1986.

Our group's Medina ziyarat tour also brought us to the grave of the Uhud martyrs, which was surrounded by a tall fence that kept us from improperly honoring them. The Greatest Martyr, the Prophet's uncle Hamza, was in there somewhere, but unmarked as always.

Last on the ziyarat tour was Masjid Qiblatayn, the Mosque of Two Qiblahs, where Muhammad interrupted a prayer to change its direction. Up to that point, the Muslims prayed facing Jerusalem. Muhammad asked Gabriel to change the qiblah to Mecca; Gabriel answered that he was only a slave, and the Prophet should ask Allah. When the new verses came, Muhammad walked into the mosque and recited it to all the Muslims in prayer. They obeyed him and turned, performing the second half of their salat facing Mecca. It was more than a ritual change; Muhammad saw himself not as the founder of a new religion, but a prophet in Abraham's line, restoring the old religion to its true form. When it became clear that Jews and Christians would not accept him as such, Islam broke away and became its own path.

As a turning point in Islam's history, the switch loses power if Muhammad had also prayed towards Mecca *before* Jerusalem. He most likely did, since the hanifs, the monotheists of pre-Islamic Mecca, prayed facing the Ka'ba. Early historians such as Ibn Hisham held the Jerusalem qiblah to be a post-hijra move, a brief symbolic turn from Mecca's pagans to the city of Jews and Christians.

It's some messy history, but time has cleaned it up. Muslims today assume that Muhammad originally prayed facing Jerusalem, and only changed the qiblah once, by Allah's command. If prophets moved back and forth between qiblahs, it might look like God didn't have his shit together.

31.

The biography from the Medina university gave Muhammad as the Saudis needed him. It started with a lengthy treatment of his genealogy, going back to the Arabs' blessed origin as sons of Ishmael, lots of clan and tribe history and racial essentialism— *yes, the Arabs valued honor and respect above everything, I get it, and they were so generous and known for their hospitality.* Discussion of Muhammad himself focused on his time in Medina, the Prophet as divinely guided legislator and leader of an army, head of the first Islamic State to which the Saudi royal family imagined themselves the heirs. The biography wasn't a pious work, or it was but also something more, a national history. Muhammad was the first man to unite the tribes; the second man was Ibn Sa'ud.

Instead of reading about the Prophet's emotional life, his disillusionment with society that caused him to go up on the mountain where he'd hear the Voice, or even his internal conflicts about war and punishments, the book fed me a chronicle of military campaigns and treaties. And I read of the individual Jews and whole Jewish tribes who betrayed or tried to sabotage the Prophet's mission, all highlighted as Jews. It was their nature to oppose righteousness and cause mischief, the book explained. When they broke their treaties, Muhammad did what he had to. I visited that history while in Medina, hiring a taxi for ziyarat to the Masjid Khandaq, where the Muslims fought the Battle of the Trench.

Masjid Khandaq was a large white mosque in front of some rocky hills. On the outside it looked like a mansion, the kind that I'd imagine for a Colombian drug lord. Inside it was quiet and spacious and felt like a church to me, probably because of the blue and orange stained-glass windows. There was no plaque or anything to give the background of the place, but we knew. Everyone who came here knew; they sought out Khandaq as part of their tour through the Prophet's miraculous life, like Masjid Qiblatayen or Masjid Quba or Masjid Ghamama, where the Prophet had prayed for rain, or Hudaybiyyah, where the Prophet had spit into a dry well and caused it to flow again. Due to increasing development, the holy sites were going fast; pilgrims used to visit the special "Seven Mosques," each of which was built as Muslims dug the trenches, but only two of them remained.

The nafl rakats were a compulsion, like something pulled me to the floor and made me do it. Then I left, nothing at Khandaq that I needed to dwell on. I want to tell the story but I've thrown that book away. Something about a Jewish tribe that signed a treaty and then broke it, and then there was a battle in which the Muslims defended themselves by digging a trench. After the Muslims won, the commander of the army ordered all of the Jewish tribe's men to be killed, and the women and children sold.

I understood the jihads of that time, and even the verses of the Qur'an telling Muslims to fight the unbelievers. It wasn't religious intolerance in the way that we'd undertand it today, in the age of secular nation-states. The Muslims were a tribe, and did what tribes sometimes do. I had no problem with the raids on caravans; among the tribes of the Hijaz in Muhammad's time, that was a legitimate way to eat.

The Battle of the Trench was something else. Perhaps back home, there were progressive Muslims who had gone into the history and either picked apart the narratives, or found a new way to understand what had happened. But I wouldn't find those articles in Medina, and had to deal with the story as it came to me.

Even if I could dodge the Masjid Khandaq, Medina represented parts of my Prophet and religion that I wanted to cut away, an Islam burdened with jurisprudence. If people could only defend Islamic law by turning away from our time and facing the past, then I had no use for it. If its rationale is dependant on the past, leave it in the past. Bury it in Jannat ul-Baqi, say peace and walk on before the mutaweens hit you.

When the Prophet brought wisdom ahead of his time, and gave orders that elevated his people above their cultural setting—*don't bury your baby girls alive*—we showed it off as proof that the message came from God. But when faced with things like the Battle of the Trench and fifty-something Muhammad's sex with a nine-year-old, we brought out "historical context." You have to understand how it was back then, we'd say. Trying to have it both ways felt so cheap, but I didn't know what else to do and Medina threw it in my face. I was at least sure that in my own setting, a modern pluralist society in which religion was divorced from official power, I had no use for Muhammad as a source of law. I more or less needed him to just be a pretty cool guy. I wished that I could go back in time, on behalf of my modern cool Muhammad, to warn seventh-century Muhammad of where Islam would go, what it would become. Modern Muhammad should program me and send me into the past to save him for the future, like *Terminator 2*. But the Prophet already knew that we'd fuck him over, and he told us that he knew.

There was a way around the Trench. A Sudanese scholar named Mahmoud Muhammad Taha saw a distinction between early verses of the Qur'an revealed in Mecca, where the Prophet was powerless, and later verses after his rise to leadership in Medina. For Taha, it was in Mecca that the Prophet, detached from any worldly position, was free to preach a universal message for all humankind. In Medina, however, the Prophet-as-politician was forced to deal with the specific circumstances around him. Allah revealed the Medina verses to guide Muhammad's commuity through the particular challenges of seventh-century Arabia. By this view, a verse from the Medina period telling Muslims to fight pagans would not be a call of eternal holy war, but a response to a specific political environment which no longer existed. Prophetic policies and punishments for crimes were not meant to be our models today, but worked on the tribal level a millenium and a half ago. Mecca is religion, went Taha's argument; Medina is history.

It was a dangerous idea. Though Taha never went so far as to reject the Medina verses, he came close enough for the authorities to charge him with apostasy and put him to death; again, a case of political power deciding which relationship to the Qur'an is correct. As an American Muslim, the state would also affect my relationship to the text—freeing me to cut up my Qur'an on the floor of the Jefferson Monument. I was starting to think that when I got home, I'd really do it, building my own Qur'an for my own life. Reading only the Mecca suras would still allow me the sections that I loved, like ar-Rahman, just reminding me of all the Mercies; and ignoring Medina would free me from verses like 4:34.

The thought took me far out of bounds. Acceptance of the complete Qur'an was like those stone pillars outside Masjid

Ayesha, marking whether you were in the holy land or out. There was no place between. You can't toss part of the book and stay in; but Hater Uncle recited long suras without even knowing what they said, and that didn't seem any better.

32.

Waiting for another Fajr prayer in the Prophet's Mosque with Hater Uncle, sitting behind four brothers who read their Qur'ans with soft and pretty voices, a mercy at that hour—

"We should go to Masjid Quba again," said Hater Uncle, "because you know one prayer in Masjid Quba equals the reward of umrah."

"Insha'Allah," I said, hoping to silence him so I could hear the brothers.

"There's no ihram," he continued, "no nothing you have to do, you can't lose." You can't lose, like it's a sale at Wal-Mart. What a deal! But I smiled for him. Maybe I now knew the experience of a born-Muslim teenager struggling to treat his family's religion with tenderness: "Yes, auntie, I read Ayatul-Kursi and then blew on my car keys."

"I like how you recite Qur'an," I told him, nodding to the brothers in front of us as a reference point. "I was listening in the room. You read beautifully."

"Yes, I like it too," he said. "I like it so much, it sounds so good. At my work, the Christian people hear me reading, and they say, 'What is it? It sounds so nice.' When I say it is Holy Qur'an, they don't believe me, they think it must be something else. But I say to them, 'This is the word of your Creator too, your ears are calling you to it!'"

"Mash'Allah," I said. After Fajr we went to the breakfast buffet, and as always Hater Uncle loaded up two plates with a ton of everything they had, but only took a few bites and then went back to the room. "It wasn't my taste," he explained. I stayed and just had tea, hoping it'd help my sore throat. Later I made the bad choice of a long walk at high noon, cooking under my unwashed black hoodie. I needed an Internet café to write to my Muslim girlfriend. Internet cafés were the skeeviest places in Saudi Arabia, with a vibe I've only felt in the massage parlors of Niagara Falls. The cafés were illuminated with strings of dim Christmas lights and filled with teen boys smoking cigarettes and giggling to each other behind the high walls of their cubicles.

"Salam alaikum," I said to a random kifeyyeh-wearing brother on the sidewalk. "Internet café?"

"You need Internet?" he asked.

"Nam."

"What is your country?"

"American," I told him.

"Hajji?"

"Nam."

"Mash'Allah. There is a place but it is too far to walk."

"I can walk, brother." Then I let out what we called the Hajji Cough and must have sounded like death to him.

"You come with me, no problem." His car was right there and he wanted to give me a ride.

We were going off the main road onto a little side-street when the situation finally dawned on me. As dumb as it is to ever get into a stranger's car, I was an American in Saudi Arabia, and the café turned out to be a sketchy little shack that looked dark inside. The car stopped. I thanked him profusely but quickly, then jumped out of the car. He drove off and there I was.

The café was run by an African kid and charged ten riyals for three hours. It came to less than a dollar an hour. I tried to pick the cubicle with the cleanest ash tray and sat there zoning out until they closed the place for prayer.

When the next adhan came, I was on my way across a sand-pit parking lot where the cars kicked up dust clouds in my face. Must have been reasonably far from the Prophet's Mosque, because its adhan couldn't drown out the neighborhood muezzins with their cheap sound systems blending into each other like a symphony from the Mothership. My boiling brain swimming in phlegm and sweat, it felt like a good time to recite Nuwaubian hip-hop lyrics—Nu-wop they called it—*folla the scholas to the Ka'ba where I transmutate my physical state into the form of Chupacabras* (Lost Children of Babylon). *My mind is a replica of Mecca*, the song went, but now I've made the hijra and it's Wu-Tang, peace GZA—*I'm deep down in the back streets in the heart of Medina, about to set off something more deep than a misdemeanor—*

Runnin' through Medina with my glock blastin,' I found my way back to the Prophet's Mosque and drifted through the surrounding markets trying to count all the jewelry stores and perfume stores, even found a Rolex store and right there I lost it—what are the pilgrims thinking? What runs through a man's mind in Medina—*I just prayed at the place where the Prophet led prayers and taught his companions, and I offered salams to his tomb and now what I need is a new Rolex?* I ducked into a supermarket and went up and down the aisles, through the toy department and kitchenware, wanting to know what these people were buying, passing leather purses with pictures of Mickey Mouse and Betty Boop in a polka-dot boostie, her boobs popping out and her shoulders bare, and the whole time the speakers over my head kept blaring ALLAAAAAAHU AKBARU ALLAAAAAAHU AKBARU LA ILAHA ILLA ALLAAAAAH in an unending loop, wherever I went, every corner of the store, ALLAAAAAHU AKBARU ALLAAAAAHU AKBARU LA ILAHA ILLA ALLAAAAAH. For my sore throat I scooped up a wisdom-liter of orange juice, still followed and haunted by that nightmare song beating me

down until I couldn't hold together my thoughts anymore—
ALLAAAAAHU AKBARU ALLAAAAAHU AKBARU LA
ILAHA ILLA ALLAAAAAH over and over and over and now
I've called Allah's Name a nightmare, where did that leave me?
And I stayed away from the Prophet's Mosque surrounded by
Starbucks and KFC and Hardee's, but can we even call it the
Prophet's Mosque? Did anyone really think that he'd want
it that way? When Ali bought Fatima a gold necklace, the
Prophet called it a necklace of fire, so she sold it and bought
freedom for slaves with the money. But the Saudi kings thought
of themselves as heirs to the other enshrined bodies. Abu Bakr
was like Galvatron in the original *Transformers* movie from
1986, who had stolen the Autobot Matrix of Leadership that
once resided in Optimus Prime's chest. Abu Bakr robbed both
Ali and Fatima, and now Muhammad was encased in gold, in
fire. It wasn't the Prophet's Mosque, not anymore. Call it Abu
Bakr's Mosque, Umar's Mosque, Ibn Sa'ud's Mosque, or fuck it,
the Devil's Mosque, Shaytan could claim it as much as anyone.

Allah's Name didn't mean anything, the praise didn't mean
anything, all the beautiful recitations just played over the same
rich-poor selfish sexist racist shit-eating garbage as everywhere.
There were no holy cities. What's a holy city? Cities are
manmade and men are awful. Never in this city or even in
Mecca did I ever want to say, "Wow, this is so much better
than living with the kuffar, I never want to go home." Was
I a Muslim? Not according to the handbook they gave us at
the airport, not in the definition of this place. At the Prophet's
Mosque, I was literally under the Saudis' roof and knew that
I didn't belong there. I was becoming something illegal in this
city, and I'd be dead if my messy notebooks reached the wrong
brother. I'd be like the Shi'a pilgrim put to death in the 1940s,
because someone accused him of smearing feces on the Ka'ba.
Maybe I could only be a Muslim in America, while in Saudi I'd
become an idolater, making shirk to my Muslim Shower.

The winners write the history, and also the religions. The Saudis were the big winners, which by Hater Uncle's standards meant that they were right and exact, having been favored by God. The carpeting at Muhammad's Mosque gave us the royal coat of arms in endless repetition; prostration on that floor was like getting slapped in the face with King Fahd's perfumed balls. But even close-up to royal Saudi genitalia, I found subversion: the crest consisted of a date palm tree above two crossed swords, which some would choose to read—and I did at that moment— as remnants of the goddesses. The swords were taken by Ali from the treasury of Manat, and the X formed by their crossing may have recalled al-Uzza. Herodotus believed Manat and al-Uzza's sister, al-Lat, to be the chief goddess of the pre-Islamic Arabs. If it wasn't for the association with idol worship, we could have taken her name, just the feminine of Allah, and used it for the author of the Qur'an, the One True Goddess of Abraham. In the age of the prophets, women were held in such low regard that the Qur'an mocked unbelievers for ascribing daughters to Allah, since they wanted sons for themselves. Allah had to be a man because the kings were men, and Allah the highest King above them, Lord of All the Worlds, Master of the Day of Judgment, the mightiest and most exalted ass kicker.

I had heard of Five Percenter women who claimed to be goddesses, using al-Lat as a surname to match the men who called themselves Allah, while Five Percenter men typically laughed at the goddess idea as "God in a dress." Saudi Arabia could have used a goddess revival; if not through Allah's daughters, at least bring back the Sakina, or Ibn 'Arabi's assertion that true divinity was female. Since I was already deconstructing God's Word, why not cut off his Big Dick too?

My reactions wouldn't have been so extreme if I was more spiritually mature. You're supposed to thank Allah for the jerks and fucktards, because they force you to grow as a Muslim— the difference between a good pilgrimage and a good vacation.

A better Muslim could have glided through the markets to his rightful place in the desert with a smile, but all praise is due. Good sounds gave me something and bad sounds took it away, I had no steadiness at all.

33.

Mohsin and I were walking to the Prophet's Mosque and I pointed out the teen cop in front of us, his brown uniform hugging him tight—

"Look at his skinny little arms and his hips," I said. "He's like, anorexic with an hourglass figure, almost feminine. He's like a supermodel."

"I heard that a lot of these guards are hermaphrodites," Mohsin replied. "That has to be hard for them."

The hermaphrodite rumor was a distorting of actual tradition, the sacred society of eunuchs who have guarded the two harams since the twelfth century. Originally established by either Saladin or Nur al-Din, the eunuchs—comprised mostly, at various times, of either Ethiopians or Indians—outlasted the Mamluks and remained in the holy cities even in modern Saudi Arabia.

Medieval scholar al-Sabki identified three kinds of eunuchs: the *khasi*, whose testicles were removed; the *majbub*, whose penis was removed; and the *mamsuh*, who lost both his testicles and penis. Because Islamic law prohibited castration, eunuchs were assumed to have undergone the procedure before entering Arabia, in the slave trade.

The eunuchs were border-crossers, like Azreal or Harar's spotted hyena. In the view of Islamic jurisprudence, they were legally adults, having passed the age of reason, but they reached this status without physically maturing. A eunuch was at once adult and child. Al-Subki also considered them both male and female, a confusion of attributes. Eunuchs were jealous like women, he wrote, and leaders like men. They could be loving or vicious, generous to the poor and also merciless to transgressors. A eunuch functioned as both a "kind father and compassionate mother to the *mujawirin*," those who lived around the holy places.

Because of their special religious duty as guardians of the Prophet, the eunuchs also crossed borders of class: they were slaves, but kings kissed their hands. Finding respect among all spheres of society, their network of influence ranged from lowly slaves to royal women, enabling them to rise as a wealthy and connected caste within the holy cities.

As maintenance and renovation sometimes called them to enter the Prophet's chamber, crossing a taboo that struck fear in most men, the eunuchs took on an aura, according to scholar Shawn Marmon, as "superheroes of Sunni piety." The baraka of the Prophet rubbed off on them, making them mystical creatures in their own right. The Wahhabs downplayed the sacredness of the eunuchs; but as recently as 1990, Marmon found there to be seventeen eunuch guards in Medina, and fourteen in Mecca. The use of eunuchs was now rationalized with gender *adab* (manners); only eunuchs could police both men and women without breaking Islamic codes of conduct.

Modern stories depicted them as hermaphrodites, which was easy enough to understand with the challenges of Islamic law and mutilation of slaves. If Allah made them that way, hiring them to guard the holy mosques became a mercy and charity.

34.

"It's too bad about the cops," said one of my brothers over dinner. Because I had been thinking about eunuchs, I wasn't sure what he meant—too bad that the cops are jerks, or too bad that they have no penises?

He looked a few years younger than me, with no moustache and a pointed black beard, like a serious Salafi but he was also from Pakistan and sympathized with the people's need for saints and shrines. "How can they say we're worshiping the grave?" he asked me. "The Prophet's alive in there, that's what we believe as Muslims—and you know, Rasullullah Sayyedna Muhammad *sallallaho alayhe wa salam* is the only prophet who has been granted intercession for us. We just want to say salam to him." I nodded and let him keep going, but secretly the Mystery Prophet stuff got to me.

A story from the nineteenth century had a little kid going into the chamber to retrieve a dead pigeon, only to find Muhammad sitting there with a Qur'an and two angels reading it to him. One of the angels introduced himself to the child as Gabriel, and guided him out of the chamber so delicately that the child had no idea of his mistake—until he attempted to tell the story later and found himself unable to speak.

The chamber holding the Prophet's tomb was once covered with a *kiswa*, a drape like the one over the Ka'ba, which was occasionally replaced in a secret ceremony by blindfolded eunuchs . . . and that freaked me out too.

WHILE THERE WAS a need to figure out the Prophet and how I felt about him because we were in the Prophet's city, I sensed a greater urgency to figure out the Devil because Muhammad was dead and the Devil was alive and Muhammad's ghost couldn't help me fight him. Some Sufis viewed the Prophet and the Devil as both manifesting divine attributes of Allah, Muhammad as Al-Hadi (the Guide) and Shaytan as Al-Mudhil (the Misguider) but that almost sounded like little gods to me. My grandfather the Pentecostal preacher had elevated the Devil to god-status in his house, telling his kids that the Devil would come get them if they misbehaved; the universe as they understood it was just a battlefield for the Devil and Jesus, and God the Father didn't seem much involved.

WE HAD A story about the Prophet and the Devil. It didn't get much circulation anymore. In Islamic tradition, we called it the *qissat al-gharaniq*, the Story of the Cranes. In the West, they called it the Satanic Verses.

The Prophet was a man, and the load that he carried was heavy. God gave him the mission of crushing his people's false religion, tearing apart everything that held Mecca together. Like Allah ordering Abraham to kill his son, Muhammad demanded that people destroy what they loved. When he refused to honor the idols, he embarrassed his tribe and broke his family's hearts. His clan, the Hashimites, were entrusted with providing water to the idols' pilgrims, and his uncle Abu Lahab vowed to guard worship of al-Uzza against the new religion. As Muhammad began to acquire followers, he became something even more serious: a threat to Mecca's social order. Allah's Words to him were dividing households, causing slaves to disrespect the gods of their masters, and calling out the people for their moral corruption, their neglect of orphans and abuse of the poor.

During the early persecutions—when Allah sent verses condemning idol worship, causing Muhammad to lose family and friends and his followers to be boycotted and assaulted— the Prophet hoped to heal the wounds brought on by his mission. That was when, as Muhammad received a revelation before members of his tribe, Allah sent down the verse: *And*

*have you considered what it is you are worshipping in al-Lat,
al-Uzza, and Manat, the third, the other?*

In the tension of that moment, the tribesmen awaiting the
next verse—what would Allah say of their idols?—Muhammad
facing them, himself unaware of what Allah would say but
fearing that the truth wouldn't be soft—the Devil snuck in and
whispered two verses of his own.

*Indeed, they are as high-flying cranes! And indeed, their
intercession is hoped for!*

The tribesmen were thrilled. When the next verse came, a
real one—*Prostrate yourself before Allah and worship him!*—
they happily joined the Muslims. The new revelation had freed
the Prophet not only of the persecution against himself, but the
burden that he bore of the afflictions upon his followers.

That was the Devil, bringing the easy answer. The low road,
the lightened load. But Allah would come back and correct the
Prophet, telling him that every messenger faced verses cast by
the Devil into his recitation . . . *but Allah annuls that which
Shaytan casts and then establishes his signs clearly—and Allah
is All-Knowing, All-Wise—to make what Shaytan casts a trial
for those in whose hearts is sickness and those whose hearts
are hardened . . .*

During Islam's elaboration in the centuries after Muhammad,
the concept of *'ismah*, God's protection of prophets from sin
and error, gained ground and became orthodoxy. Though the
Qur'an itself scolded Muhammad for his rudeness to a blind
man, while constantly addressing his doubts and confusions, the
Prophet's infallibility and perfection evolved into a core tenet
of Islam. By Ibn Taymiyya's time, most scholars were denying
the Story of the Cranes as either based on faulty hadiths or
compromising the sacredness of the Qur'an. To suggest that
Muhammad committed deeds requiring repentence would
tarnish his position as role model for humanity—even more
so for the Shi'as, who extended 'ismah to include not only the

Prophet but his daughter Fatima, Ali, and all of the Imams as the Fourteen Infallibles.

Ibn Taymiyya took a different view: "Repentence is not a deficiency; it is one of the finest aspects of completeness." Prophets were not models because of their perfection, but their continued striving towards perfection—they showed the slave of God how it's done. God protected prophets not from making human mistakes, only from *remaining* in error; a prophet would always realize his or her error and beg God's forgiveness. Ibn Taymiyya took a minority position in his time, one that would be unacceptable today. The Wahhabs are mocked as blind followers of Ibn Taymiyya, but they haven't yet owned up to his treatment of the Prophet.

"Whoever accepts that the Prophet praised idols," wrote medieval thinker al-Razi, "is guilty of kufr," but the cranes were my keys to both the Prophet and the Devil. They showed me what the Devil could do—he even got the best of Muhammad, for a little while—and what I was up against; but they also revealed Muhammad to be a vulnerable flesh-and-blood man who could hear those bad whispers. In his sermon before I left, Dr. Shafiq had warned against worshiping the Prophet, since Muhammad went up on Arafat and begged for mercy like all of us: how could you worship someone who himself cried to his Maker?

35.

Our remaining few days in Medina, I made all efforts to avoid praying in the Prophet's Mosque. If I wanted to join the congregation, prayers were loud enough that I could open a window and follow the imam while in my room. It might have counted. Or I'd intentionally come to the mosque late and join the rows outside. Hater Uncle accepted that I was too sick to go to the mosque, and let me sleep through morning and afternoon prayers.

Sometimes I looked out the window and imagined what Fatima would think if she saw this place. Eternal Weeper, welcome to Saudi Arabia.

I knew that after leaving for hajj on Friday, I'd probably never come back to the Prophet's City. Even if I went for hajj again later in life, I might try to find a tour that didn't include Medina. The Ikhwan Package. But late Thursday night, or early Friday morning, I woke up and knew that it was my final chance to make peace with the Prophet's Mosque, so I got up and brought the rug I had bought for Sadaf, walked over and put it on the red carpet and made my two rakats for Muhammad under the bright lights.

If the story about Abu Bakr and Umar collecting ayats and suras in front of the mosque was true, then this was really the birthplace of the Qur'an, at least the Qur'an that we all knew. I had to make peace with that too. Muhammad first received verses in a spontaneous burst on the Mountain of Light, but the burst came to us filtered through the caliphs and that was just how it had to be.

So much history to the place, I tried to at least appreciate it on that level and see if it brought any jewels. This was where Ibn 'Arabi pleaded with Allah to make him a better imitator of the Prophet, the best of men, and Allah instructed the saint to embark on the hajj. My love for Muhammad didn't have to be broken; I could see him that way too, as the best of men; but first I had to collect the right materials and push out the wrong ones.

Time to pray for the Prophet, and I wasn't sure what I'd say. The saint Muhammad al-Bakri, while on retreat inside the Ka'ba, asked Allah for the best way to send blessings on

Muhammad, and received his answer on a sheet of light: a prayer for the Prophet equal to every glorification of God ever in the universe, equal to reading the Qur'an six thousand times. I hadn't learned it.

Ya Rasullullah, I told the body in the tomb, *I don't know what they've put on your name, and whether this is what it's supposed to be, but you're a human soul and I wish peace for you.* I wished peace for him like I would for the aging Five Percenters that I knew at Auburn State Prison, and then I left Muhammad a prisoner in his blinged-out cage and snuck away from the wicked fortress. This was the day that I left Medina for hajj, my mission to stone the Devil, wearing pilgrim's garb but feeling like a tramp.

36.

In the middle of the night we stopped at a mikat station, going in as tourists and coming out as pilgrims with renewed ihram status. I was already wearing the towels and only had to go in and make my niyya, my intention with two rakats and the labbayk—which I said in English to make it sink in.

Everyone at the mosque was dressed in ihram, doing their individual prayers and making niyya. Deciding that the toilet and shower area was too dirty, Hater Uncle changed into ihram right there in a corner of the mosque, with me standing guard in front of him.

Riding through the darkness, it felt like my old Greyhound jaunts, except for the occasional white minarets dressed in green light. The rest stops were even grimier than on American interstates. At one stop, the toilet was just a hole in a lightless room filled with garbage, and I had no idea what I was pissing in or on. At another, there were no pipes under the sink, so the water went from the faucet straight through to the floor. But they did have mosques.

In the headlight beams of cars going the opposite way, I watched enormous swirls of dust creeping across the road. At one rest stop, the dust blew into my eyes and mouth and I pulled the top half of my ihram over my head as a veil. Some brothers from another bus reminded me in their own language that pilgrims could not cover their heads, and I understood from their hand gestures. *Shukran*, I told them. We were allowed forgetful moments like that; the Prophet had come to make things easy and not difficult.

Our group leader led us in labbayks but I couldn't take part because my throat hurt so bad. First he chanted into the microphone and the squealing of those bad speakers hurt my ears. When he turned off the mic it sounded good, like the Muslims of another time (if the Sahabas rode buses). At one point he told us that we were at Badr, site of the first battle between the Muslims and the idol worshipers—"the *Muslimeen* and the *Mushrikeen*," he said, though it was only darkness out the windows, and the bus never stopped. *Muslimeen and Mushrikeen*, I repeated to myself. The pagans in the old days had their own labbayk, coming to the service of God, with the slight difference that God did have associates, but enjoyed power over them. It even started the same, *Labbayk Allahumma labbayk*.

An imam got on the microphone and spoke to us in Arabic, while the group leader translated. They reminded us to have "good patience for each other, try to be good Muslims as much as we can," and remember that most people did not have what we had, and none of the Muslims of old had what we had. We should be thankful, they told us. And we should remember that no color was better than any other, no Arab better than any non-Arab, all of us brothers and sisters, all children of Adam.

"You get hajj according to your intentions," said the group leader, still translating. "If your intention is Allah, you get Allah. If your intention is show-off, you get show-off." Then he played a tape of an Arabic lecture on the speakers, but it didn't last long. Too many of us were non-Arabic speakers and wanted to sleep.

I WROTE IN the dark and brooded on my spiritual collapse at Medina. Moses the half-original prophet couldn't master the Devil because he hadn't mastered himself, and he even had a teacher appointed by Allah, Khidr the Green Man. When Khidr's ways and actions became too confusing, Moses couldn't check himself and submit, so Khidr left him and the lessons ended. "We wished Moses had more patience," Muhammad told his companions. I was impatient with Muslims. In Pakistan and everywhere else, I was free to take Islam mostly on my own terms, slipping anonymously in and out of shrines and building alone in my own cipher. This hajj group, and hajj itself, forced me to interact with my brothers in closer space, with Islam no longer my private playground but now something we shared. Allah gave me that lapse in Medina so that I could see it, I thought, and recognize that I was still helpless, in his care alone.

For the first time, the question of whether I was Muslim had nothing to do with belief; I didn't know if I was strong enough for this weight.

Hater Uncle was sleeping in the seat next to me. In ihram and so skinny, and still bald from his umrah a week ago, he almost looked like Gandhi.

37.

No more five-star hotels. It was time for Tent City, the endless rows of pointed white huts in Mina. With thirty or more pilgrims to a tent, there were enough tents for four million people. By the time we arrived, an orange haze of sunrise was creeping up from behind the surrounding mountains, with a whitish glow between the orange and blue. There were pilgrims up there, having pitched their own tents on the hillsides. I was jealous of them. On another pair of mountains, we could see the palaces of a Saudi king and his son, the king after him, but fuck their names.

We were packed tight, on narrow mattresses with no room to roll over, but it was fun. Felt like summer camp. We received three meals a day, our group's "restaurant tent" had a constant supply of Pepsi, bottled water, and tea, and I could treat my sore throat with hot water and honey. The Saudis gave us free books: a Qur'an with English translation, a commentary on the last tenth of the Qur'an, and a book on proper worship. I thumbed through the commentary and stopped at Suratul-Asr. *By the Time*, it said, *man is in loss*.

THE NEXT DAY was Arafat, and the Prophet had said that Arafat *is* hajj, the most crucial moment of the pilgrimage. For preparation, a guest lecturer came to address us in English.

Allah's love for us was like that of a mother, the speaker said. He told us of a time when the Prophet and his companions passed a woman who was breastfeeding her baby. The Prophet asked whether anyone could imagine the mother throwing her baby into a fire. Never, his companions answered. The Prophet then told them that Allah had more love for us than the mother had for her baby.

His second story I already knew. The Prophet watched a

mother and her toddler sitting at a bonfire, and whenever the child got up and walked too close to the fire, the mother would pull him back. This made the Prophet weep, because it reminded him of Allah's Mercy.

"Imagine a teenaged son who has misbehaved," the speaker then told us, "and he argues with his mother, and she throws him out of the house. At first, the son is angry, but then you see that he becomes full of remorse. So the son stands outside the house, calling for his mother, and he is crying: 'O mother, I know that I did wrong.' And then what happens? You see the door open, and the mother brings the boy back into the house."

This last story, he told us, was Arafat, the day that Allah forgives us like a mother. On Arafat, all of a pilgrim's sins were removed from her or his record, almost as though Allah had forgotten them, but we had to come with sincere repentence, knowing and understanding that we were wrong.

The speaker suggested that we take some time that night to sit and reflect on our sins. Write them down if it helps. Remember all of the wrongs that we've committed, everything for which we seek Allah's forgiveness. "Don't ask in just a general way," he told us. "Don't say, 'O Allah, forgive me for being greedy.' Think of every specific time that you were greedy. I know that it is difficult. Break it up by years if that helps; try to list all of your sins in the last five years, and then the five years before that. Be mindful of what you've done, and know that no matter how long your list will get, Allah has mercy for you. *Even* you, you are loved by Allah and he will forgive you."

I whipped out my notebook while he was still talking and did a stream-of-consciousness rundown of my sins, starting with girls. The Prophet had said that on the Day that our body parts testify to our sins, our tongues and genitals will do the most talking. I was less concerned with my bad morals than bad ethics, the times when my intentions were wrong, when I was careless with other humans. I've been savage and destructive, and—can

I even say it? Abusive. As one sin reminded me of another and I filled the page, it appeared that most of my sins were against the people closest to me: the ones who gave me so much without my proper thanks, and asked for a lot without getting it. But those were only the sins I remembered, the big ones. I sinned every day, and most of my sins didn't even look like sins to me, I couldn't see them as sins. That was the scariest part.

At the end of the lecture, we got to ask questions. One brother asked if we could beg for Allah's forgiveness in any language. The speaker said no, Arabic is best. If it's absolutely necessary, you can appeal to Allah in your own words, but it would be better for you to find du'as from the Qur'an and Sunna, learn their meanings and memorize them in Arabic. I was too absorbed in my sins to let that bother me.

38.

Arafat lasted from sun up to sundown. To get our full benefit of the time Allah had given us, we arrived before Fajr prayer. The Arafat plain was covered with large tents. My tour group had two tents for men, and I didn't know where the women went. Segregation did strange things. It often seemed that women had ceased to exist, or had gained the power to materialize and dematerialize at random times.

Since we had been in hotel rooms until then, it was only at Arafat that I noticed our group's breakdown: everyone but me was either South Asian or Egyptian. The desi brothers took one tent and the Egyptians took the other, causing an imam to scold us for dividing along ethnic lines. Everyone stayed in their own tents anyway. I stayed in the desi tent.

The Saudis gave us another Happy Meal, consisting of bread and jam, a juice box, and Zamzam water. The package read, "The Establishment of Motawifs of Pilgrims of Turkey, Moslims of Europe, America & Australia," all the white brothers. My throat was hurting, my nose stuffed but I had no tissues. Blew it into my hand during wudhu. I had bought cough syrup at the pilgrims' pharmacy in Mina, but it turned out to be candy; "ivy leaf extract?" I chugged the whole bottle and it did nothing.

After praying Fajr, most of the brothers chose to spend the morning in the tent, but I struck out early to be alone. Cutting across the territories of other groups, I found a gap in an aluminum fence and crawled through. The hills ahead were sprinkled with just a few pilgrims in white. I found a path, and when the path ended I climbed over big rocks to reach other paths. I passed trash and remnants of old and existing camps: blankets, prayer rugs spread out on flat spaces, even some sleeping hajjis. From high up I looked over at the hill across the road, Jabal-e-Rahmah with its white pillar, and a large mosque in the distance with a story that I forgot; and a straight line of large yellow signs just before the horizon, marking the sacred area's border. I couldn't read them, but I knew what they said: ARAFAT ENDS HERE. At the top of this hill was a tent, which turned out to be a station for religion cops.

There were stones arranged into makeshift walls and shelters against the sun or wind, looking like they had been built and rebuilt hundreds of times. Muslims had been coming to Arafat for a millennium and a half, and the reasons for this plain to be sacred were older than Islam, maybe close to the first humans on the Arabian Peninsula.

A British scientist had theorized that all non-Africans in the world were descended from a small band of hundreds who left East Africa seventy thousand years ago, crossing the mouth of the Red Sea and traveling up the Arabian coastline, through the Hijaz. I daydreamed across the Red Sea, back to Ethiopia. Human evolution posed no threats to my faith; the Qur'an said that humankind was made in stages, that we replaced some who came before us and Allah could also replace us with others. We came from the earth, we were mud; I didn't have to believe in the Mystery God literally molding a man out of clay. Adam and Eve had something that their parents did not; the first ones to be responsible for their actions, the first to do wrong and understand, they had crossed a border.

Arafat was what it meant to be human. This land, according to pious scholars, was the start and end of the human story. Arafat was where Adam and Eve found each other after leaving paradise, and Arafat was where we'd all stand on Judgment Day. The previous night's lecturer had told us to imagine that: standing with every human being who ever lived, however many billions that was, including the ones you loved and the ones you heroized or even worshiped, but feeling completely alone.

FOR THIS DAY, the one day when a Muslim's heart was the only jurisprudence, there were no special rituals. Someone had left a flattened cardboard box in the space under a boulder, so I claimed it for myself and lay down. Looking up at the sky, I remembered what sins I could, counting them on a string of zikr beads, not passing a bead until I fully recognized my fault. No defense, no rationalization. It went against all instincts, inviting threats to the self with neither fight nor flight. I was wrong, I was wrong, I was wrong, I was wrong, I was wrong, I was wrong, I WAS WRONG, I was wrong . . .

Ugly people dream of being beautiful, and the weak dream of being strong, and I also dreamed of what I lacked. I only wanted to be good because I knew that I was not. It would have been simple to spit at the clouds and blame Allah for making me imperfect, but that wasn't fair; I had not done the best with what I was given. Going back through my history, I could find decisions made with negative feelings and forgetfulness of Allah, which led to sinful paths, which led to more sins and more bad decisions until sins made sense and didn't even look like sins anymore. It was all me.

A tattered plastic bag, stuck in the branches of a dead bush, fluttered in the breeze. The top half of my ihram felt like a blanket around me, with one hand poking out and clutching the beads. I felt guilt but surprisingly no shame, just the relief of my nafs dropping weight. It was a feeling that the Devil couldn't know, though he also came to Arafat. Sufi tradition told of a meeting between Shaytan and Shibli. When the saint asked the Devil why he had come to the plain on this day of repentence, the Devil replied that since Allah cursed him for no reason, perhaps Allah would forgive him for no reason. In the thousands of years that he has fought the children of Adam, the Devil could never imagine that *he* was the one at fault; his arrogance kept him cursed. A lesson for Arafat. Dropping my defenses, I could only go so far, and there were sins that I could not admit. *Ya Allah, forgive me for them too.*

People started coming out as the sun reached high noon. I descended from the hill to find crowds of pilgrims, and also those working the crowds for money: a man with a decorated camel offering rides, young photographers selling Polaroids, a goat herder selling slaughters, and beggars. A man with stump-arms placed himself on the pilgrims' path, crying ALLAAAAAH, ALLAAAAAH, ALLAAAAAH for the riyals dropped beside him. Three African children saw a white man and rushed him.

"Sabililah," they said, six hands pulling on my arms. "Sabililah, sabililah." For the love of God, they said.

Two boys, one girl. The boys were named Harun and Salman; the girl's name was Hawwa, Arabic for Eve. She wore a torn-up dirty pink winter coat with Santa Claus on it, the stuffing coming out. It looked a thousand years old. I gave them each some riyals. You can't deny mercy at Arafat and then go back there expecting it.

39.

Between two rocky hills, I could look across the road and see Jabal-e-Rahmah covered with pilgrims, the entire hill now white as though it had snowed. Some Turkish pilgrims passed on their way to Jabal-e-Rahmah. They stopped in front of me to manipulate stones, making small stacks of three or four before continuing. When they were gone, I photographed the stacks like they were miniature monuments, causing a brother to approach me.

"You know what this is?" he asked.

"No," I answered. "I just wanted to take pictures, since I know some professors back home who might be able to explain it—"

"Where are you from?"

"New York."

"Mash'Allah! I am Syrian, but I live in Texas."

"Small world."

"Brother, I need to tell you that this is not Islam, what these people are doing."

"The stones?"

"Yes. These people are from Iran, and they are completely ignorant of Islam, they do not know their own religion."

"I noticed Turkish flags, I think they're from Turkey."

"Okay, insha'Allah. They are the same. You see what these people do? This is the reason for the Muslims' condition. If we could follow Allah's Qur'an, and the Sunna that our Rasullullah *sallallaho alayhe wa salam* gave us, that is all we need. The Muslims would be in a better place. But these things that the people do, they follow their own ways and bring down the ummah."

"Do you know why they're doing it?" I asked. "Does it mean something?"

"I don't know, but it is a bid'ah." Innovation. "It is not something that the Rasullullah said for us to do. It is not our religion." He did not notice that ten feet away from us, two Turkish women were making salat, bowing and everything, while facing Jabal-e-Rahmah, even though large signs pointed towards Mecca in another direction.

The Syrio-Texan then told me about a young Christian who had worked for him in Houston. The man was a seminary student, working towards a life in the priesthood, and began to read the Qur'an out of curiosity. With his intensive background in the Bible, it dawned on him that Islam was closer to a genuine Biblical religion than his own Christianity. So he accepted Islam, the true religion of Abraham. "He was a Christian," my new friend repeated, in case I missed that part. "He was Christian, but Allah guided him to the truth, because he had sincerity."

"May Allah reward his efforts," I said.

"People misunderstand Islam," he added. "They say, 'If a Muslim becomes Christian, you kill him.' But they don't know the Muslim way. If our brother leaves Islam, we have to come to him and ask him. We *beg* him to return to Islam, out of love for our brother. And then, if he still does not come back . . ." He nodded at me, knowing that I knew the rest. And then he walked on. I stayed between the two hills for a time, still curious about the stones.

STACKING ROCKS WAS nothing compared to the bid'ah building that I could do. That guy didn't know that I was reading Arafat through the Supreme Wisdom Lessons, Master Fard measuring time in twenty-five-thousand-year units called "Qur'ans." At the end of one Qur'an, the Original Man "renewed" it, planning out his history for the next twenty-five thousand years. It was like Arafat: the chance to start at the beginning again, the power to make your own path. Arafat fell on the ninth day of Dhul-Hijjah, the Month of Pilgrimage; in Supreme Mathematics, 9 manifested the attribute of "Born."

From bid'ah to bid'ah: I remembered the Persian saint al-Hallaj, who stood on Jabal-e-Rahmah and proclaimed Allah to be greater than the praises of "Glory be to you" or "There is no god but God," above "the concepts of those who intellectually conceive of you, over and beyond what your friends and your enemies, combined, say to you." Al-Hallaj pleaded that he had been made powerless to praise Power, all worship and belief falling short; "Therefore," he told Allah, "thank yourself, yourself, through me, such is the true thanksgiving."

Al-Hallaj kept pushing himself out of bounds. "Infidelity is my duty," he said, so he called himself by one of the Holy Attributes and claimed to be in contact with the Mahdi. When al-Hallaj suggested that those who were unable to visit the holy land could perform the rites of hajj in their homes, authorities accused him of Qarmatiyya conspiracies, put him on trial and killed him as an apostate. They might have begged him to recant as he danced to his execution.

40.

One of the cool things about hajj was that you could basically visit any Muslim culture just by stepping into a tent. On the street in front of Jabal-e-Rahmah, these cultures clashed in odd ways. I watched a group of Indonesian pilgrims pay an African woman for the right to take pictures of themselves holding her children; one man took hold of a kid's face and shoved it towards the camera.

A group passed me chanting the labbayk but they sounded so much better than my group, they were *singing*, and I wanted to know their country. Spotting women with the green, white, and red flag on their backs, I followed them until coming to the Iranian neighborhood.

"As-salamu alaikum," I said to a man outside the tents.

"Wa alaikum as-salam."

"Irani?" I asked.

"Yes."

"You speak English?" He shook his head but took me by the hand and led me into one of the tents, where a circle of brothers sat eating lunch. He pointed at one in the middle.

"How are you, brother?" asked the man.

"I am American," I told him, "and I accepted Islam at a Sunni mosque, but I have decided that I want to take shahadah as a Shi'a. I love Ali, I love Husayn, and I do not accept what the Sunni brothers have told me about the Shi'as." And then I just looked at the guy, startled at myself for actually doing this.

"Hajj is a time to bring the people together," he told me. "Hajj is about the unity of Islam. We have differences, but we are all Muslim."

"Mash'Allah," I said.

"Brother, what is your name?"

"Michael."

"Brother Michael, what is the shahadah that you said to become a Muslim?"

"Ashadhu an la ilaha illa Allah, wa ashadu anna Muhammadu Rasullullah." I bear witness that there is no god but God, and I bear witness that Muhammad is the Messenger of God.

"Okay, so all you have to do now is say, 'Ashadu anna Aliyyun wali'Allah.'"

"Ashadu anna Aliyyun wali'Allah," I said. I bear witness that Ali is the friend of God. It was easier to bear witness to a *friend* of God than a prophet, less intellectually complicated.

"Brother Michael," he told me, "you are now a Shi'a." We hugged and then he told me the names of each of the Holy

Imams, starting with the First Imam, Ali, and his sons Hasan and Husayn. Each Imam had his own special quality; one was the best at worship, one was the master of sciences, and so on down the line. The Twelfth and final Imam, he reminded me, was still alive and waiting to appear.

I couldn't really communicate with any of the other brothers, but I exchanged contact information with the one who spoke English, and he explained my story to them. They spoke Farsi, but could at least give congratulations in Arabic that I understood. After tea I left their tent. "Insha'Allah," said the brother as we embraced, "pray for us, that we may have a peaceful situation." I wasn't sure what he meant; was he speaking as a Shi'a in Wahhab Land, or an Iranian addressing an American? But I said I would.

RECONVERTING AS A Shi'a wasn't an inner change, or even a pledge to outer change. I already loved Ali and mourned for Husayn with the Shi'as. Even if I sided with Ali and Fatima against Abu Bakr's thefts and disrespects, there was no way to return to that moment in our history when these were only political disagreements—the time before allegiance to Ali came with an alternate set of orthodoxies, a different school of fiqh and spokesmen for God.

The Shi'as had started out as the righteous underdogs, but however many centuries later, Twelver Shi'ism was the underdog story that beat all the competing versions. To get this list of Twelve Infallible Imams, they endured the same chaos and power struggles that caused the first schism. When each Imam died, it brought a whole new crisis of succession. The claim of Husayn's half-brother Muhammad ibn al-Hanafiyya to the Imamate not only rivaled Imams from the Husayn lineage, but itself divided into numerous subfactions as years passed. After the death of an Imam, Shi'as were often divided between followers of the deceased Imam's son and those who believed that the Imam had not died, but existed in a special state of ghaybat and would return at the end of the world.

When the Eleventh Imam, Hasan al-Askari, died childless, the Shi'a community followed its previous patterns of ghuluww and division. One faction insisted that the Eleventh Imam had not died, but was placed in ghaybat and would soon return as the Mahdi. The Imam's chief agent, Uthman ibn Sa'id al-Amri, rejected this claim and said that he represented the Imam's true successor, who he would keep hidden and nameless. After al-Amri's death, his son Abu Ja'far Muhammad ibn Uthman took over as deputy for the Hidden Twelfth Imam, who was now believed to be a son of the Eleventh Imam, possibly only four years old at the time of his ascension to the Imamate. Ja'far Muhammad ibn Uthman led the community as this Imam's vice president for over forty years, occasionally producing decrees said to be from the Imam. Sometime around the 890s, however, all communication from the Twelfth Imam ceased, signifying his move from the "lesser ghaybat" to a greater one that would last until the end of the world. This "Twelver" sect was the one preferred by Shah Isma'il, first king of Persia's Safavid dynasty, so it became the orthodox Shi'ism, the foundation of modern Iran.

The Twelfth Imam looked like he started out as fiction and then became real, like a character from my novel getting served papers by real-life lawyers. I only wanted to say that Ali was the *wali'Allah*, and I didn't know anything else.

41.

Back in my own tent, I prayed a shortened Zuhr and then Asr right after it. Folding my rug, I remembered a debate I once heard between two teenagers in Chicago. The one kid said that when you finished your prayer, you had to roll up your rug right away, or else the Devil comes and prays on it. And the other said to him, "But wouldn't you *want* Shaytan to pray?"

42.

Then I returned to the hills, bringing some bottles of Zamzam for the kids. Jabal-e-Rahmah and the surrounding land was completely white with the ihrams of pilgrims. I heard conflicting sounds—heated sermons, group chants, and beautiful hymns all mashed together. A fine mist from Saudi-installed sprinklers hovered over them. Someone had told me that the sprays were actually chemicals to prevent disease.

The brilliance of Arafat: given one day to repent for your wasted life, you can look at the sun and watch your time running out. The day was our life, and the meaning was missed by no one. As the sun lowered towards the horizon, the intensity on those hills picked up, Arafat looking like it was supposed to: a performance of the Day of Judgment, a *pre-enactment*. The litter and makeshift shelters made it feel like I walked through the wreckage of my species; it was just like the Day, I thought, except for the mist sprays and helicopters. I walked among figures standing alone on the hills, the sky darkening behind them, some facing Jabal-e-Rahmah, some facing Mecca. Desperate to get it all out before their time was spent, my brothers raised their hands to heaven and cried, or held their faces in their hands. Sometimes I caught myself staring at men's faces, as though trying to climb inside to see why they repented, what sins scared them so much. My sisters were there too, sometimes with their husbands in pairs that would be separated on the Day, or in groups of women, or by themselves.

*   *   *

IT WORKED OUT THAT the setting sun fell between Jabal-e-Rahmah and the direction of Mecca. Finding a place to stand alone, I faced qiblah and began with a regular du'a, my hands open in front of me. I recited al-Asr, stuck in my head from the Saudi books they gave us at Mina:

> By the Time,
>> Mankind is truly in loss,
>> Except for those who have believed and done righteous deeds, and advised each other to truth, and advised each other to patience.

I said it over and over in Arabic, like a zikr, until raising my hands above my head, submitting completely to the Mercy and losing it, terrified of all the time I threw away, an insult of Allah's gifts—*What do I do, what can I do?* It wasn't that Allah asked us to be superheroes, to give away everything we owned and become monks, but he provided us with opportunities every day to do just an atom's worth of good, and I turned most of them down. The Prophet said that even a smile was charity; how many chances did I miss? Now the sun was setting for me. With every breath, the darkness came closer. By the Time, I was in loss and I knew it, everyone on this hill knew his or her loss, and we became so afraid for ourselves that we forgot each other.

ARAFAT HIT ME hard because there was no doctrine to confuse myself over or wars of interpretation, just a clean and simple idea that we're alive for a short time and blow most of it on petty shit. The meaning of Arafat could be appreciated by people of any religion, or no religion. Same with al-Asr, just three verses with no mention of Allah or Muhammad or even explicit reference to an afterlife, just reality as pure as it came. Instead of distinguishing between Mecca and Medina verses, I could just take al-Asr and make it my whole Qur'an, reciting those three verses twenty-five thousand times every day and never coming close to living them out.

ALLAH'S FORGIVENESS OF my sins would make the Devil furious, I had been warned in advance. Incensed at my victory over him, and his own cursed status, the Devil would come at me with everything that he had, his whispers turning to screams. I was ready for him. As I descended from the hills, I looked at my crying brothers and almost second-guessed them with my own prejudice. *They don't know half of their sins*, I thought, *since they can't own up to how they treat their wives.* I did not know them or how they treated anyone, but the Devil did his best with what he had, hoping to rack up my sins again. I ditched those thoughts quick, but feared that it'd get worse.

The first sin that a Muslim commits after Arafat, I was told, was doubting Allah's forgiveness, and that was the hardest to avoid. *Even me?* I kept asking, even on the bus to Muzdalifa where we'd find our stones to throw at the Devil. *Even me? Ya Allah, do you really know how bad it gets in here?*

43.

God told Abraham to kill his son, and the father placed the boy on the altar and grasped his knife. Just before the blade touched the child, God revealed that it was only a test of their faith, providing Abraham with an animal to kill instead. To commemorate the sacrifice, Muslims around the world slaughtered goats on Eid ul-Adha and donated the meat to the poor.

Eid ul-Adha was celebrated on the tenth day of Dhul-Hijjah and marked the completion of hajj; but I had watched a slaughter on Arafat, between the two hills across from Jabal-e-Rahmah. A man pulled one of his black goats away from the herd by one horn, bleating and resisting. He held a knife in his other hand. Two other men took hold of the goat and brought it gently to the ground, lying on its side. They removed the bright green rope from its neck. The man with the knife made sure that the goat was secured, then gripped the goat's face with his free hand, holding its mouth shut. He pulled its head back and then put the knife to its neck.

The blood shot out of it like an ejaculation, the burst reaching far from the wound. Men cut goats like that on purpose, to get the veins. I could see the two places where the blood kept pumping, though it now fell to the open world. It made the gargling sound. The man with the knife ripped the head back more, making the goat look like an open Pez dispenser.

The men backed away from the goat to let its legs kick, since the kicking helped get the blood out. The hind legs kicked up clouds of dust and nearly got one of the men. The front legs did not move. The goat looked like a person that way, like it was running or riding a bike. The kicks slowed down and it looked like the goat was finished, but then it kicked a few more times. We watched it for a while to make sure. Satisfied, the men said things in their language and laughed with each other.

Coming down the mountain, I passed a large stone that was covered in drying blood. Tufts of black goats' hair lay scattered around the stone, and when I looked into the bushes I saw the discarded intestines and the goat's head. I lifted my camera and then noticed a black child's hand in my shot.

He smiled.

"*Masmuka?*" I asked. He repeated it back to me, not understanding Arabic. "*Ismi* Michael," I said, pointing at myself. Then I pointed at him and asked again. "Masmuka?"

"Ishaq," he answered. His name was Arabic for Isaac, Ishmael's half-brother and, in the Judeo-Christian tradition, the intended victim of the sacrifice. Any Muslim in today's world will tell you that it was Ishmael, but that wasn't always the case. In the story as given by medieval scholar Muhammad ibn Abdullah al-Kisa'i, Isaac tells his father, *If you want to sacrifice me, take my shirt off my back so that my mother will not see it and cry a long time over me. Tie up my shoulders lest I squirm between your hands and it cause you pain. When you place the knife on my throat, turn your face from me lest compassion for me overcome you and you fail . . . And when you return, bring my shirt to my mother so that she may find some comfort in it over me. Give her blessings from me, but do not tell her how you slaughtered me, nor how you took off my shirt, nor how you bound me up with rope so that she will not be sorrowful over me. And when you see a young boy like me, do not look at him, so that your heart will not grieve on my account.* Ishmael was the father's sacrifice in the story that I knew, but the Isaac version didn't seem false so much as true in another universe. Seeing it that way enabled me to still bug out that this kid Ishaq popped up in front of the slaughtered goat guts.

The Qur'an never names the son that God wanted to see killed, since the star of the story was the father. Ibn 'Arabi said that it didn't matter which son was the victim. Among the early Muslims, more narrations favored Isaac. Hajar's son only became the choice of "official" Islamic teaching after generations of vigorous debate. The Ishmael narrative served the Muslim community better, because it helped to place Abraham and the sacrifice in Mecca, and the Arabs had already understood themselves as Ishmael's descendents.

Ishaq wanted to have his picture taken, and smiled as I shot him in front of the goat. He looked to be nearly the age of the boy that Abraham laid down on the altar. I knew that if he was my son, I couldn't do it; but I wasn't even strong enough to accept the lesson of the story.

If I pushed my blade into an animal, I'd say Bismillahi Allahu Akbar, because you were supposed to say that; and I'd cut not as the father, but the son. I'd flip the myth and make the goat Abraham. The slaughter would no longer be sacrifice, but feminist justice: *this one's for the women and children terrorized by scripture, the real Muslims in a world that God gave to men.* We acted out Abraham's sacrifice with rituals and goats; but Hajar's sacrifice, the submission of a raped slave woman to the ruling class, was repeated every day in real life. If it wasn't Abraham, it was Thomas Jefferson. *This one's for abused domestic workers, and God loves not the tyrants.*

My first sin after Arafat was doubting Allah's mercy. My second sin was wanting to kill Abraham, to make his throat cum and turn the white beard red. Islamic slaughter was supposed to be done in a merciful way, causing no unnecessary pain; but I would have sliced that goat up, made a real scapegoat of him. Thankfully, I never had to touch a knife, having paid three hundred riyals or so at an office outside the Prophet's Mosque. It was a large operation run by the Saudi government, slaughtering thousands of goats on behalf of pilgrims and distributing the meat to poor Muslims around the world. I knew that I had missed the larger meaning of Abraham's story, but at least the man who killed my goat would have it right.

44.

At the far end of the Arabian Peninsula, in Yemen, they still made pilgrimage to a shrine of the Qur'anic prophet Hud. There was a story of Hud's people praying for rain, and receiving a choice of red, black, or white clouds. The people chose the black cloud, which then destroyed everyone except for Hud and his followers. Of course, the argument has been made that Hud was really just an Islamicized rain deity. I thought of him because we were in the valley of Muzdalifa, everyone collecting their seven stones; and a hill in this valley where

the Prophet had stood, Jabal-e-Quzah, was named for an old
Arabian thunder god. Quzah revealed himself in a fire on that
mountain, like the burning bush that spoke to Moses. It was
hard to prove anything about religion in pre-Islamic Arabia,
but some scholars considered our stoning of the Devil to have
been an ancient call for rain. Before the Prophet came, pilgrims
collected stones from the storm god's plain to throw at the sun
god, or sun demon.

The other theory: men stoned the pillars simply to mark a
passing of the border between sacred and non-sacred land, a
common practice long ago.

WITH FOUR MILLION people on the same road, no one moved.
Leaving Arafat at sunset, we arrived in Muzdalifa at 1:00 AM,
something like a seven-hour ride to travel three miles. The road
was lined with buses, all of which kept their engines running at
least some of the time. Muzdalifa at night was a dusty, exhaust-
fume hell hole covered with litter and people eating food,
people discarding food, people mobbing the flooded bathroom
stalls and wudhu faucets, and people hunched over, looking
for their stones. A father entertained his baby by putting the
stones in a water bottle and shaking it like a rattle. I walked
among them, bent over too, with no idea where most of these
people came from—saw a few Syrian flags, a few Turkish flags.
I had an empty water bottle in my hand and kept my eyes to
the ground. I needed seven stones, each roughly the size of
a chick pea. I felt no religion from it. Dialogue in my group
centered on correct action, not the meaning or what we were
supposed to think about these stones. When you throw the
stones, we were told, do not say *goddamn you* or anything like
that. The Devil's not really there, we're just following the way
of the Prophet. It's only the prescribed action that we have to
carry out.

I complained to Hater Uncle about how nasty the people

were, covering Muzdalifa with their trash and destroying the bathrooms.

"It's the Egyptians," he said without hesitation. "They urinate everywhere, they urinate in the wudhu places, they don't care." He pretended to hold his dick and aim it in various directions. "And they pray where they want, when they want, how they want. When you see the little jamaats, it's Egyptians. Why little jamaats here and here and there? *Big* jamaat to show the power—listen to me, I have twice your age, you do not have the direct experience with these people that I have . . ."

He could have talked shit on the Egyptians all night but I only wanted him to check my stones. They're too big, he said. So I dumped them and found seven more and then sat on the bus by myself, thinking about how the sun played into all of this. We left Arafat at sunset, we joined our post-sunset and evening prayers, we'd leave Muzdalifa after the pre-sunrise prayer, and at Mina the stoning would occur after Zuhr: after the sun god passed high noon, we'd chase him as he retreated. The stopping at Muzdalifa and stoning at Mina used to be seasonal rituals, I had read somewhere, until the Prophet set them by the moving lunar calendar so that hajj could occur at all times of the year. Allah knows best.

The stones were small but sharp. I noticed a hangnail on my left hand but couldn't rip it out or cut it because I was in the pilgrim's state. Fingernails were horns, did you know that? They're made of the same material, a protein called keratin. The same stuff that hooves are made of. No Mystery Devil, we're shaytans ourselves. The Qur'an said that Allah was closer to us than the veins in our necks, but the Prophet said that Shaytan ran through us like blood.

To someone who read the Supreme Wisdom Lessons literally, I was the Devil in real life, Yacub's blue-eyed skunk of the planet. Elijah Muhammad taught that my ancestors had once come to Mecca, but made trouble among the righteous people there, "causing them to fight and kill one another." They were finally driven out by a black god named General Monk Monk.

Why does Muhammad and any Muslim murder the Devil? Master Fard asked in the first Lost-Found Muslim Lesson, and Elijah answered: *Because he is one hundred percent wicked and will not keep and obey the laws of Islam. His ways and actions are like a snake of the grafted type.* Muhammad realized that if a snake is allowed to live, it will sting someone else. It wasn't hard to see myself in there.

IN AN EFFORT to understand, I tangled up secular and mythic histories. Jamarat imitated Abraham's encounter with the Devil, but the historical Abraham—*wait, was Abraham historical?*—most likely did not believe in a devil. The character of Satan, like the belief in resurrection, came much later in Jewish tradition. The early books of the Old Testament just give us an accuser *(ha-satan)* among the angels. He acts as Job's prosecutor before God, the Judge; but he's not evil, only performing the duty that God gave him.

Sitting on a parked bus in Muzdalifa, far from books or the Internet, I lacked any materials to put together a genealogy of the Devil. It was one of the things that I should have researched before the trip, but I at least had some basics. There was the Persian influence: the Jews' captivity in Babylon led to an encounter with Zoroastrian dualism, the good god Ahura Mazda locked in war with the bad god Ahriman. It's only after that encounter, in the post-exile books of the Bible, that *ha-satan* becomes Satan, avowed enemy of both God and man. Christians incorporated the nameless serpent from Genesis into the new character, deciding that he was Satan in disguise; but that serpent had a life before the Bible.

In Canaanite mythology, the god Baal-Hadad killed a serpent who hoped to destroy the Tree of Life. Like Yahweh,

Baal-Hadad was a thunder god. Scholar Flemming Hvidberg argued that as Yahwism and Baalism became rivals, the Eden story was crafted as Yahwist propaganda against worship of Baal-Hadad—who became the serpent. Because people also worshiped Baal-Hadad as a fertility god, it was only logical for him to appear in that phallic form, and appear first to Eve. He promised eternal life, but gave only death and destruction. For ignoring Yahweh and following Baal-Hadad, Adam and Eve were banished from the garden.

Baal-Hadad was often represented with an upright stone, and priests and priestesses used to ritually copulate in his honor. Besides defeating the seven-headed sea god to make the waters safe for mariners, Baal-Hadad had sex with a cow to make plentiful food for the people. He was killed and mutilated, but revived after seven years. "Seven years" probably just meant "really long time," and could have symbolized the changing seasons. Baal-Hadad's cycle of life and death mirrored the cycles of nature. I could understand the storm god as a fertility god, because whatever brought rain to fertilize the earth could also fertilize the wombs.

What makes rain, hail, snow, and earthquakes?
— MASTER FARD MUHAMMAD

If the Eden story allegorized a fight between thunder deities, it would really mean something in Damascus, since the Umayyad Mosque stood on ruins of a Baal-Hadad temple. It also meant that I could never find the Devil's origin, because he'd be as old as human beings fearing the thunder and lightning. Baal-Hadad is said to have derived from Adad, the Akkadian thunder god, and was equated with Ishkur, the Sumerian storm god. And then what? The hard part about genealogies is that you can never reach a true beginning, because there is no beginning. Every generation has parents, and the parents have parents.

The history of gods looks like the history of people. At home I had old black-and-white photos of my father's father, the Pentecostal preacher born at the end of the nineteenth century; I had never met him, and couldn't see myself in his face or recognize the world that he knew. He was gone, but he was also *me*.

Like people, some gods failed and some prevailed, and for the same reasons: social connections, royal patronage, ups and downs of the tribe. The thunder god of Mount Sinai became transcendent Creator of the heavens and earth, worshiped by the majority of the human race, while the thunder god of Muzdalifa was forgotten in his own land.

Though his rituals lived on, I considered why Quzah never amounted to more. Among the gods of pre-Islamic Mecca, Allah was better positioned to become universal. Allah was the god invoked during transactions between clans, and already associated with Abrahamic religion and the Ka'ba. Quzah might have been supplanted by another Arabian thunder god, Wadd, whose name suggests a relation to Baal-Hadad and Adad, or maybe Quzah *was* Wadd; but Wadd couldn't live through the changes either. In a sura called al-Rad, "The Thunder," the Qur'an revealed that Allah was the one who sent rain, and the thunder declared his glory. Allah took everyone's jobs.

SOMETHING STOOD IN the way between me and the rite of Jamarat. I sided with the mother and son against the father and God and couldn't bend my mind the other way, and now we were stuck in this Muzdalifa pit and I lost all the good that I felt at Arafat. Muzdalifa was nowhere, Muzdalifa was a darkness, the lowest circle of however many spiraling darknesses there were. If Allah came to Muzdalifa, it wouldn't be Allah the lofty advanced concept, or even the Force, but Allah's daddy who now embarasses us, Allah's great-grandfather storm god with hands and feet. Allah the man, a real man who lived out there in the dark and sometimes made himself known, walking with prophets and the special elect; the god-man of the Old Testament, a god that you can wrestle; Yahweh, rider of the clouds, who parted the Red Sea with a blast from his nostrils. The Allah described in hadiths as appearing to Muhammad as a young man with short curly hair and a green robe, or long hair, in gold sandals and a gold veil, reclining on a gold carpet. The Allah who placed his palm between Muhammad's shoulderblades, causing him to feel coolness between his nipples ("And from that moment appeared to me all that is in the heavens and on the earth").

Those hadiths have been buried, though the Qur'an still says that the Spirit appeared to Mary as a man. If Muhammad believed in an Allah with a body, perhaps I could find it by kicking around in the Muzdalifa dirt. Muzdalifa felt like a cemetery for dead gods, with hajji jinns feeding the bones to their animals.

I FELL ASLEEP on the bus and dreamed that someone near the bathrooms had cornered a black dog. All the pilgrims from all the countries and tour groups then rushed to circle around the dog with their weapons, and the dog snarled and barked under those dying flourescent lights, vicious and fearless, until a big stone hit him in the right place and he fell, and then everyone swooped upon him with stones and sticks and finally a knife. While I slept and dreamed on the bus, everyone in real life prayed Fajr without me, and when I woke up I didn't even care because at least the bus was moving. Following the Prophet's advice for bad dreams, I turned to my left and discreetly spit three times into an empty Aquafina bottle.

45.

I'm gonna put on an iron shirt
And chase Satan out of earth
I'm gonna send him to outer space
To find another race
—Lee "Scratch" Perry, "Chase the Devil"

Arriving in Mina early in the afternoon, the buses were still crawling so most of us hopped off and walked the rest of the way through Tent City. Reading signs along the road made it seem like a tour through the ummah; we started by the Oyo State of Nigeria, then passed Tajikistan. The sign over one neighborhood's gate declared, for non-arab africans. The section at the end of the road, closest to the Jamarat, was for Arab pilgrims. Our own tents were close too, in something like a VIP section. The Jamarat structure stood plainly visible across the street.

The Devil was originally represented by three stone pillars, but growing numbers of pilgrims made the ritual dangerous. A Persian pilgrim in 1911 had claimed that every year, fifty people were trampled to death during the stoning. Faced with increasing accidents nearly a century later, in 2004 the Saudi government built a new multi-level structure that allowed more people to stone the Devil at one time. Pilgrims now threw stones at three large brick walls, and the stones would then travel down chutes to hit the original pillars below.

The new Jamarat structure looked like a giant parking garage. I entered on the ground level and saw the pilgrims' arms over their heads, thousands of them snapping forward like whips above the crowd. Sometimes they appeared to be in sync. The peoples' shouts were drowned out by the rumbling of crowds on higher levels. I twisted the cap off my water bottle, shook some stones into my hand and almost lost them as someone bumped into me. Everyone forgot each other. Men were jumping around and swinging their arms without any regard for people around them. They acted like this wall—this blank construction with no personality and less than five years old, which wasn't even necessary to hit because all stones went down the chute to the pillars—was the true and living Devil right in front of them, no allegory, and they had to really give it to him good. I saw women in fear and pain, trying to protect themselves from stray pebbles. I got close to the wall and felt the squeeze, wondering how it must have been for small pilgrims, old pilgrims, and the disabled. Three guards were struggling with a man, but I couldn't tell what it was about. Something sharp hit the back of my head. I said Allahu Akbar and threw my stones, one after the other, and then I dropped the bottle and had nothing else to do, so I made my way out of there. I drifted out with the successful Devil-pelters, spotted the Al-Baik chicken place and knew that my tent was nearby. Once in my own neighborhood, I grabbed a Pepsi can from the snack tent and then sat on a wudhu stool but didn't make wudhu, just put my head under the running water and occasionally sipped my Pepsi. Or Bebsi, as they said (there's no *P* in Arabic).

"Can the Devil fool a Muslim?" asks Master Fard in the Supreme Wisdom Lessons, and the RZA on the *Wu-Tang Forever* album. The imam telling us that the Devil wasn't really here was wrong. As tight as it got at Jamarat, the Devil still pushed between us. What a joke we turned out to be; four million Muslims came together to curse Shaytan but acted like animals to each other. Of course the Devil was here, and he laughed hard. He won every year.

WE ONLY STONED one Jamarat wall; but we'd get it again, and the others, over the next two days. Some Muslims believed that the three pillars represented the Devil, his wife, and their baby; in the more popular reading, they symbolized three acts of the same Devil. When Abraham set out to slaughter Ishmael, Shaytan tried three times to stop the sacrifice. He tempted Abraham with compassion for his son, and tried the same with Ishmael's mother, and then tried to get Ishmael to plead for his own life. All three attempts failed, as our three ancient heroes each valued obedience over love.

> The only devil from which man must be redeemed is self, the lower self. If man would find his devil he must look within; his name is self.
>
> —NOBLE DREW ALI

That was my problem here; I couldn't see Jamarat as an allegory for the internal struggle with myself, because in these cases, the ugly lower self was represented by parental love and a son considering whether he wanted his father to cut open his neck. At Jamarat, love was nothing compared to obedience, because we only loved for Allah's sake; love collapsed before ritual correctness.

At Jamarat, the point of the ritual played out in front of me: when God tells you to do something, you forget everything else and do it. If God says to kill, you kill, even your child, and your compassion is the Devil talking. Jamarat might have inspired Muslim soldiers back in the day, when Arabia was wild and Islam was a vulnerable young tribe surrounded by enemies. But here it just looked stupid. I repeated the thought to myself, just to be sure that I was really okay with it: *this is fucking stupid.*

We were supposed to be acting as a collective consciousness, a hive mind like the Borg on *Star Trek*—who traveled through space, incidentally, in titanium Ka'bas with glowing green lights—but I had broken off. I couldn't tell if the break happened there at Mina, or earlier at Muzdalifa, or even Medina, if I was ever connected at all. I couldn't get into Jamarat, the very heart of it. I disagreed with the core idea behind the act, and couldn't bring myself to agree, and that was my fault, my weakness and defeat. The name of the religion is Submission, son. "Resistance is futile," says the Borg.

THE MEN SHAVED their heads again. I had only one razor, a yellow Bic from those packs of a dozen for $2.99, but went to the toilets across the street to see what I could do with it. I sat in front of a wudhu faucet and put my head under the water. No shaving cream. It was clear that this would take a long, long time.

A brother saw me tapping my Bic on the wall, trying to unclog hair from between the blades, and showed me his new pack of unopened razors.

"This," he said, taking the yellow Bic from my hand, "this . . . *bad*."

He cleaned me up quick and I offered to pay him, but he only pointed a finger up to the ceiling—or past the ceiling I guess, to heaven.

Desacralized, I headed back to our tents to take a shower. Waited in line behind some uncles, one with a cane making semi-serious threats of violence to whoever budged in front of him.

"Remember, my friends," he said, waving his cane at us, "we are in the Kingdom of Saudi Arabia, and this is the rule of the Saudis."

"They have changed a lot," said someone.

"*This* much," he argued, pointing to the weapon, "has not changed." Everyone laughed. When I got my turn in the shower, it was the first time I had removed the ihram since Medina. The top half was now a crusty snot/phlegm rag, and the bottom was brown from my sitting outside. I hung them over the door. The water came down at a medium flow and medium temperature, and it was the spout of mercy that I needed and Allah provided. Even for me.

Back in the tent, the newly bald uncles all wore kufis and regular clothes. Hater Uncle looked so triumphant and proud. I slumped onto the mattress, my head pounding, my cough killing me deep in the chest, my nose stuffed up. I also had a terrible under-the-skin pimple on my forehead that my picking and squeezing had turned into an eye-catching wound leaking pus-watered blood; people assumed that I had been clocked by one of the Jamarat stones. My outer condition revealed my inner state, I thought; *look at Hater Uncle, his beliefs are so simple but he lives them out with everything that he has, and that frail old man could probably suplex me over his head right now.* I was missing prayers left and right—Fajr in Muzdalifa, Zuhr in this tent—and now I had fallen apart. Ibn Taymiyya said that rememberance of Allah was for the Muslim like water for a fish, and I could only flop around and suffocate.

Done with ihram, I put on a T-shirt, and under the blanket I slipped on boxers and jeans. Lying on my back, gazing up at the translucent tent ceiling, I asked myself: *After all of this, what are you bringing home?*

46.

While the brothers prayed Asr, I slept and dreamt of Quzah, the old thunder god of Muzdalifa, and a group of Sufis at Jabal-e-Quzah who believed that they could throw lightning bolts from their hands. If such a Sufi order actually existed, I would have wandered away from the buses into that Muzdalifa darkness to find them. In other places, I had found Sufisms and folk Islams that keyed into the area's non-Islamic past, the hyenas and peacocks and pagan caves, integrating images and stories of the past into the new system. Before Islam, the religion of this land was stones, and stones were still the language. We kissed a stone in Mecca, we threw stones at stones in Mina. Beneath the massive Saudi construction of Jamarat, under the clean new walls that we pelted in the big parking garage, the original Shaytan stones remained. We marked sacred borders with stones and erected a Baal's penis of an obelisk to be rubbed where Muhammad stood at Arafat.

Somewhat creepy story from the past, still printed as accepted history in the Saudi books:

During the waves of idol-smashing after Islam's triumph in Mecca, the Prophet sent Khalid bin Waleed to Nakhlah, where the idol of al-Uzza was stationed. Accompanied by thirty horsemen, Khalid destroyed the idol and then reported back to the Prophet.

When the Prophet asked if Khalid had seen anything unusual, Khalid answered that he had not. The Prophet told him that the job was unfinished.

Khalid went back to Nakhlah, and spotted an angry black woman with dishevelled hair running naked among the people. Ignoring pleas for mercy from those around her, Khalid drew his sword and killed the woman. According to one account, the sword blow caused her to become a pile of ashes.

"That was al-Uzza," the Prophet told Khalid. "She has now lost hope of ever being worshiped in this peninsula."

The goddesses Manat and Na'ila were also portrayed as naked black women, pulling out their hair in grief when Muslims destroyed their sanctuaries. Similar stories could be found in the idol-smashing tales of early Christians, who found black-skinned demons at the temples of Zeus.

In both the Islamic and Christian stories, these false gods appeared to exist on some level, and they were not powerless. Paul equated sacrifice to idols as sacrifice to devils. In the century before Muhammad, a Christian named Martin of Braga denounced Greek and Roman gods not as the imaginations of men, but actual demons. Exiled from heaven after aligning with Satan, these demons gave themselves names like Saturn and Venus and tricked pagans into worshiping them.

Modern interpretations always lose the guts, and I had no interest in how today's Muslim scholars would dress up the al-Uzza episode. What did it mean to Khalid? I was on a journey to the end of Islam: not the end of the historical phenomenon, or my relationship to it, just the end of definitions, a postmodern Islam with everything deconstructed. But if someone pushed me to define Islam, I'd call it the tension of Khalid saying "There is no god but God" and then swinging his sword at a flesh-and-blood goddess.

Islam is the tension between Truth and its need for illustration—knowing that Allah is everywhere, but giving him a house. Islam is worship of the Mystery God with no associates, but taking refuge from a Mystery Devil and speaking to a Mystery Prophet in his grave. Islam is Allah having all the power, but delegating tasks to Mystery Angels; and Muhammad asking Gabriel for a favor, but Gabriel replying, "I am only a servant of Allah. Address your prayer to Allah." Islam is smashing idols, but calling the Black Stone the Right Hand of God. Islam is Umar kissing the Black Stone like a pagan, but telling it, "I know that you are only a stone and can neither do harm nor bring benefit. Had I not seen Allah's Messenger kissing you, I would not have kissed you." Islam is me wondering who Umar needed to convince: the Stone, Allah, or himself.

47.

Destroy your Ka'ba.
> —AL-HALLAJ

The Stone was representation, Umar knew, and representation was fiction. Encoded deep within Islam was a critique of itself; you could go so far with tawhid that it liberates you from your symbols and religion, since the Stone can't be God, and our rituals are not God.

The road to Mecca chosen by ninth-century ascetic Ibrahim ibn Adham took him fourteen years, since he halted after each step to pray two rakats. When he finally reached the holy city, he was stunned to learn that the Ka'ba was gone.

Then a voice told him that the Ka'ba had left to meet a lady on her way.

The lady was Rabi'a. The Ka'ba found her in the desert and greeted her.

"I want the Lord of the House," she told it. "What can I do with the House? I pay no attention to the Ka'ba and enjoy not its beauty. My only desire is to encounter him who said, 'Whoever approaches me by a span, I will approach him by a cubit.' What benefit can I receive from seeing the Ka'ba?"

Our Sufi Christ, al-Hallaj, who was executed for compromising the hajj, proclaimed, "The people have their pilgrimage, but I have a pilgrimage to my Love. They lead animals to slaughter, but I lead my own heart's blood. There are some who circle the Ka'ba without the use of limbs; they circled Allah, and he made them free of the sanctuary."

One could easily focus on the provocative statements, forget that Rabi'a and al-Hallaj were deeply religious and even Shari'a-centered Muslims, and just turn them into hippie slouches. I knew better, but they still offered an easy way out if I wanted it.

After missing the first three prayers of the day, I was ready to sleep through the rest. One of the tent imams had given a lame lecture about all the ritual mistakes that could invalidate our hajj and how we should compensate for them, and I wanted to skip Maghrib just to spite that contract-religion mentality. Then I thought about the ugly Jamarat scene and decided that I may never do another regular Islamic prayer in my life, why not throw all the rituals away—did rituals make this a holy place, did they create better people? Would I want a non-Muslim to see this hajj as the essential reflection of our deen? Did we show and prove the truth that we owned? And then I took it further down wicked Islamophobic roads—Shari'a looked to me like everything that the racist white demagogues of right-wing talk radio said it was—and I got up to piss with all this mental piss in my head and spotted another lecturer giving the same kind of lecture. *He's got nothing*, said the whisper in my heart, *and he can guide you to nothing. His religion is dry and spiritless. You have something better. You don't need to pray on a rug, your Islam is better than prayers.*

I listened to the whispers all through my urination and couldn't let it go. No bigger joy than knowing that I was the smartest man in the tents, the most enlightened and maybe even the best Muslim. Imagine that, the best Muslim without even doing my prayers, but the best Muslim because I used my mind and thought it out while these 85ers just banged their heads on the floor and never asked a question.

You can follow those whispers all day, they feel so good. The critique against ritualism and contract religion is valid, but a truth isn't true if your intentions are wrong. Here it came from the Devil because it only appealed to my lower self: my frustration, my arrogance, the need to stand apart from my brothers and above them. Sometimes the whisper can say something true and that's the worst one of all, because you can't argue against it. If the Devil shows up and asks you to say,

"There is no god but God," what can you do? So I washed up and went to the open area that we had set aside for prayers.

48.

Since arriving in Saudi Arabia, I had successfully avoided leading any of my brothers in prayer. It didn't seem like good ethics to serve as an imam for others when I still hadn't sorted out my own religion; I couldn't have them praying behind a kafr, if that was where I'd be placed by their criteria. But as I prayed Maghrib, the unthinkable happened: a man came and stood next to me, putting his hands up to his ears and then folding them over his navel.

His feet were just inches behind mine, enough to make the point. I was imam.

There was no pulling out; I had already started the prayer. Afraid that I'd get distracted and forget something vital, I focused less on my own salat than performing all the motions right and exact—but that's okay, because caring for my brother was worship. When it came time to recite a short sura of the Qur'an, I chose the one that had what I needed, and I hoped that it did something for him too:

> Say: I seek refuge with the Lord of mankind,
> The King of mankind,
> The God of mankind,
> From the evil of the whisperer who withdraws (after his
>   whisper),
> Who whispers in the hearts of mankind,
> Of jinn and men.

"What is your name, brother?" he asked after our du'as.
"Michael," I told him.

"You didn't change it?"

"I think that it's good for daw'ah," I replied. "In America, people see Islam as something foreign that they can't understand. But when they meet a Muslim whose name is Michael, it helps them see Islam as a religion for everyone."

"Al-hamdulilah," he said with the biggest smile I've seen in Saudi.

A FEW HOURS later, I walked to Mecca to see if I'd feel like making Isha at the Haram. It was three miles or so down King Fahd Road. I found the Haram more packed than before, since everyone had to go and make *tawaf az-ziyarat*, their return to the Ka'ba.

The House was dressed in a new, crisp black veil; while we were at Arafat, the Saudis had carried out their annual ritual of replacing the kiswa. As Allah's forgiveness removed our sins from the record, our inner rebirths were matched by the outer condition of the House.

In pre-Islamic times, clans took turns draping the Ka'ba. During the early caliphates, each new kiswa was simply placed on top of the previous one. When the Abbasid caliph Muhammad ibn Mansur al-Mahdi made pilgrimage, he realized that the layers of piled-on kiswas threatened the Ka'ba's structure and ordered that old kiswas be removed.

Throughout Islam's history, kiswas usually came from Egypt, a tradition beginning with Umar's order in 634. As the Abbasid empire broke down, regional rulers sent their own kiswas to the Ka'ba, made in Egypt or Yemen. In the Ottoman period, the kiswa was made in Egypt on behalf of the caliph in Istanbul; as Egypt pushed for autonomy from the Ottomans, Muhammad Ali Pasha took control of the kiswa's manufacture as a nationalist gesture. Every year, a new kiswa was transported from Cairo to Mecca in what looked like a wedding procession—at least until 1927, when tensions between Egypt and the new kingdom of Saudi Arabia led to the Egyptians asking for their kiswa back. Egypt no longer had a hand in the ritual; the kiswa was now made in a special factory just outside Mecca, with each kiswa costing nearly two million dollars. The factory also made the green silks that draped the Ka'ba's inner walls.

It was hard to look at the veil and appreciate that in eras before photography, the kiswa came in different colors. In Muhammad's time, the kiswa was accidentally burned by a woman as she fumigated the Ka'ba, and he replaced it with a white cloth from Yemen. Umar and Uthman used white kiswas. Two centuries later, the Abbasid caliph Harun al-Rashid used a white kiswa, but his son al-Ma'mun dressed the Ka'ba in red. After him, an-Nasir used green for a time but then switched to black. The kiswa has been black ever since. In 1340 gold embroidery was first added to the kiswa, and now people couldn't imagine it any other way.

Long ago, a pair of ancient ram horns hung from the Ka'ba's water spout. Believed to have been from the ram slaughtered by Abraham, they eventually disintegrated. There was also a time when the Abbasids donated sun-shaped ornaments, *shamsas*, to Mecca to be attached to the kiswa, but that wouldn't look right today. I wanted to see what the Ka'ba would look like in the future. Five hundred years from now, we might be making tawaf around a giant Pepsi can.

I TRIED TAWAF on the ground level, but couldn't get into it with all the people and found myself pushed to the edge of the crowd. Giving up on my second circuit, I walked upstairs and just sat against a column, watching the pilgrims go by. I couldn't even see the Ka'ba.

Some Arab teenagers were assembling for Isha and I pulled myself up to join them. Of five prayers that day, I had made two; far from my worst showing.

After prayer I got up and restarted my tawaf, thinking that it'd be easier on the second floor, but it didn't matter. The whole place was packed, and the size of the crowd was getting to everyone. The brothers pushing wheelchairs hissed at us. *Hajji, hajji, hajji*, pilgrims called out to each other, asking for patience when they gave none. *Sabr, sabr.* Pilgrims yelled at each other in different languages, knowing that they could neither understand nor be understood, but still getting into it anyway. When I raised my hands towards the Black Stone and kissed my fingers, an Egyptian brother tapped me on the shoulder and told me not to do that.

"No, no," he said. "Not Sunna."

"This is what my imam taught me to do," I replied. He mumbled something in Arabic to his friend and they laughed. I looked at them like they had simultaneously vomited in my face. These guys were the death of the Muslim Intellect, I wanted to tell them—because we're so hyper-ritualized that arguments about these details take up all our energy, and you'll hear brothers say that "one school of thought allows you to kiss your fingers, but the others don't" as though such things are the concerns of an actual school of *thought*. School of thought? That's what it means to have a school of thought in Islam? That's what our schools and our thinkers are dealing with in the modern world, that's what we give our brains to— whether or not you can kiss your fingers?

I wanted to quit my tawaf but kept at it, and by the seventh circuit—the God circuit if we're still on Supreme Mathematics—I remembered Master Fard's lesson about how Yacub the big-headed scientist made the Devil. Born twenty miles outside Mecca, Yacub was always on the margins. Dissatisfied with society, he went into exile on the remote island of Pelan (Patmos), and it was there that he grafted the weak germ from the strong. I also had a big head, and it tempted me to turn away from my brothers and sisters and retreat to a Pelan of my own.

It's harder to stay in. Allah's servants are so rotten and unworthy, but to pull out would mean forgetting that I was unworthy too. That's the Devil, the refusal to smell your own shit: Shaytan repenting "for no reason." Ali said to hate in yourself what you would hate in others. I could look across the Haram to people on the opposite side, pilgrims on the same floor as me and we were following each other in circles, in *orbit* around the House . . . and then I saw thousands more on the third level and the masses on the ground, all colors and dualities—rich/poor and young/old and male/female—stuck together, and reflected on who has circled this box, pagans who poured sacrificial blood on the Ka'ba's walls, and prophets and patriarchs who cleansed the sanctuary. I was in the footsteps of Abraham and Ishmael, and Muhammad and Ali. And Abu Bakr too, God reward him.

This was where Husayn put his faith in humanity, trusting against precedent that the sanctity of the Haram would be respected, only to learn that Yazid was sending assassins disguised as pilgrims. Kings have always trespassed on God's House. In 802 Harun al-Rashid brought his two sons al-Amin and al-Ma'mun inside the Ka'ba for a meeting, where he named al-Amin his first successor and al-Ma'mun the second. Al-Ma'mun was granted control of the eastern provinces, and al-Amin agreed that if he did not respect his brother's sovereignty, it would render him an apostate from Islam and thus disqualified from the caliphate. Like Harun and sons, the present owners of the Ka'ba used it as a symbol of their privilege, but this was also the Ka'ba of unwritten history, the anonymous peasants and slaves who waited their whole lives to see the House. It belonged to them, and me.

*   *   *

DESPITE THE EFFORTS of ruling powers, there has never really been such a thing as orthodoxy or heresy—even in the modern repressive Wahhab state, this was still the Islam of the world, where Wahhabs walked with the Shi'as, Sufis, Ahamadiyyas, and even Alevis who believed that Ali laid the land upon the waters. Ibn Taymiyya found it hard to make tawaf with a stick up his ass, but he did the same laps as Ibn 'Arabi, who wrote love letters to the Ka'ba. Al-Hallaj was executed for compromising hajj, but he was a hajji; and Rabi'a came here, even if she declared, "Here is the House which is idolized upon the earth, whereas God neither enters it nor leaves it." Guru Nanak came here and put the jewels of Islam into Sikhism. Bulleh Shah said that God did not live in Mecca, but he at least visited the Ka'ba of his heart, so I'll count him as hajji. There were also Sufi tales of telepathic pilgrims, perfected masters who could make the journey without physically leaving their homes. In the mythic histories of American Islam, Noble Drew Ali received an initiation here, and this was the city of Master Fard's birth. Riding a white horse and wielding a high-powered rifle, General Monk Monk drove the devils from Mecca, but Malcolm came here and prayed with devils. Elijah kissed the same Black Stone that I did, and Elijah believed that the Stone represented the black man to whom the world would someday bow. Even if most of these people could not tolerate each other, I at least pretended that they did; and even if they lived in all different eras, I imagined them walking together. And Khidr too, hiding in the crowds every year.

OUTSIDE IT WAS easy to get lost, because there were so many gates to the Haram and I never left the same way I went in. I asked a thick-bearded uncle for directions back to Mina, but he just rambled in Arabic and kept drawing a square in the air with his fingers. I had no idea what he was getting at, but caught him quoting from the Qur'an and realized that he had stopped talking about streets and directions a long time ago.

Allahu Samad, he said. God, the Eternal Refuge—the One who has no father or master, the One who relies on nothing and no one, but as the Saudi books explained, "the One sought in times of difficulty and need, the one depended upon by all existence."

The uncle was laughing and I could only say *al-hamdulilah* to thank him.

49.

Like General Monk Monk orders to chop necks
> —MOBB DEEP, "Apostle's Warning"

General Monk Monk style
Run devils across the desert
> —LORD JAMAR, "Original Man"

Two more days of Jamarat, twenty-one stones each. I picked them from the streets of Tent City. The three days together totaled forty-nine stones, seven acts of stoning, seven stones each time. Islam is Mathematics. The Jamarats were progressively more crowded but I went into them with a lighter heart and practiced holding back bad feelings, and Allah gave me what I put into it. Women were still anxious, but not panic-stricken as I had seen before. Short old men looked adorable as they jumped to hurl their pebbles like Abdul-Jabbar skyhooks and really got into it, their mouths open wide. When people knocked me around, I said mash'Allah but also treated it like a sport. Paramilitary guards barked at us in Arabic but we were Turks, Indonesians, Indians, and sub-Saharans here, and I laughed when brothers threw their shoes at the Devil for added measure. Tossing my pebbles and shouting Allahu Akbar, I smiled—even when catching accidental headbutts and elbows, subhanahu Allah. Since the majority of stoners weren't English speakers, I could curse the Devil like my friend Wesley Willis, the punk-rock legend who experienced demons as audio hallucinations and drove them away with lyrics of bestial fellatio: SUCK A WOOLY MAMMOTH'S DICK WITH MIRACLE WHIP! SUCK A SNOW LEOPARD'S ASS WITH WHIPPED CREAM! SUCK A HYENA'S SPERMY DICK!

Unlike Wesley Willis or Abraham, I have never heard the Devil speak with a real voice. I wasn't stoning the Mystery Devil with the horns, or the sun demon, or Baal of the Seven Thunders, or goat-headed Baphomet, or the Morning Star, or even an allegory for base desires; my enemy for those Jamarat afternoons was the big-headed Shaytan of my separation, my apostasy and withdrawal. He hoped to bring trouble among the righteous, but I'd run him out like General Monk Monk. I took part in Jamarat for the sake of standing with my brothers and sisters. This is how we bind ourselves to each other, this is how we name ourselves. We point at something and yell and throw stones at it until we've worn ourselves out, and then we have tea.

50.

Those last two days, most of the religious vibe had thinned out in our tent. Not a whole lot of Qur'an reading anymore. The uncles just lay around on their mattresses, drinking chai and telling funny stories in Urdu, or having animated discussions of politics. One uncle teased another about the man's Rolex, suggesting that they trade to become "watch brothers." Hater Uncle came over and bragged about his cab fare to Mecca.

"Twenty riyals there, twenty riyals back," he told me. "How much did you pay?"

"I didn't pay, I walked." He immediately turned and asked someone else.

The big announcement came that we could keep our blankets and pillows. They weren't anything special, kind of cheap actually, but the roly-poly, clean-shaven, Rolex-wearing doctor uncles—the ones who might be welcomed as "moderate Muslims" in the United States—all wrote their initials on their pillows and struggled to stuff the blankets into their luggage. The younger brothers, the angry-looking ones with their militant beards, the threats to Western Judeo-Christian civilization, went outside to give their blankets and pillows to families sleeping on the street.

I rolled the words over in my head. *Moderate Muslims.*

It wasn't hard to find someone willing to accept my blanket and pillow; just across the street from our tents, some African women reached out their arms and I gave it to them and then walked back to my gated community. Feeling good and warm inside, I forgot the Whisperer and dropped my guard, just loving myself and the whispers that came: *You're fantastic*, he said. *So much better than the greedy uncles.*

They're too caught up in contract religion to know what real Islam is, the Whisperer told me, but then I shoved him away. I didn't know real Islam. I was selfish and got bratty over small matters, and I impressed myself by doing nothing. I was a loser at hajj. Anything bad that might happen, I had it coming. After washing my soul at Arafat, I already deserved the fire again.

You're as awful as anyone, I told myself.

The Whisperer answered: *No Mike, you're different, you're thoughtful. These uncles go their whole lives without ever considering what they do, but you're so self-aware, you look so hard at yourself . . . That's the difference, and it's enough . . .*

Then I saw Mohsin's aunt in the tent alleys.

"As-salamu alaikum, Mike!"

"Wa alaikum as-salam, auntie."

"How are you holding up?"

"Al-hamdulilah. I think I'm getting what I need from this."

"*I* think," she half whispered, blocking her lips with her hand as though telling a secret, "you'll do better than most of these people here."

I smiled but wanted to run.

51.

Our time in the holy land was slipping away, and my farewell to the Ka'ba would also mean farewell to the graves in the Hijr. It still felt right that the mother and son were buried together at the heart of the world, while the father rested hundreds of miles away in that cave in Israel.

The sacrifice felt like my Devil moment, since I was arguing with God and couldn't see my wrong. I wasn't the first Muslim to have a problem with it. For Ibn 'Arabi, Allah had intended the vision of slaughter as an allegory; Abraham was supposed to slaughter a ram, which appeared in the form of his son to represent his self-sacrifice. Abraham's failure was that he chose to read the dream literally, which smashed my statue of him if I ever had one. I'm not a khalil Allah, but I'd know enough not to kill my children based on a dream. If a prophet could fuck up on that scale, what did it even mean to be a prophet?

Sitting in the tents, thinking about cranes, I found my way around him. Ibn Taymiyya believed that while prophets could fall victim to the Devil, Allah would not allow them to remain in error. The command for Abraham to kill his son came from the Devil, who had all the reason in the world to want Ishmael dead: no Ishmael meant no Muhammad. Shaytan almost had it, first convincing Abraham to abandon Ishmael in the desert, then to put him on the altar and pick up the knife—but each time, Allah jumped in and saved the special boy.

I could at least admit that the father deserved compassion, since God tortured him too. I broke down the whole event as the climax of *Return of the Jedi*, when the pale devil (Emperor Palpatine) shoots blue Force lightning into Ishmael (Luke Skywalker), determined to kill the son, until the father heeds the call of his higher self. When Abraham sees an animal to slaughter instead of Ishmael, Darth Vader heaves his lower self into the Death Star's reactor shaft.

Before returning to the essence, Vader asks Luke to remove the mask. *Let me look at you with my own eyes*, he says, meaning that Shaytan no longer clouds his vision.

The son says, *I've got to save you.*

The father answers, *You already have.*

I didn't want to put my green lightsaber to Abraham's throat anymore, I gave him that much. The mother, father, and son all offered themselves in ego-death, but what a sad family. Try to imagine them sitting together in the years after these things, is there any laughter? Peace be upon them.

52.

One of my Saudi books related the story of a monk who asked the Devil, "Which characteristic of the son of Adam is most helpful to you against them?" The Devil told the monk, "A hot temper. If a person is hot tempered, then we play with him like children play with a ball."

My only goal for *tawaf al-wada*, the goodbye tawaf, was to make all seven circuits without ever getting angry with my brothers and sisters ("Excel to become masters of your circumference," as the RZA says). I almost broke the promise before even entering the Haram, when a religion cop asked to look in my backpack. He unzipped it and I pulled it off to watch his inspection.

"No, no, I am just looking," he said.

"You look at it," I told him, staring that skinny teenager down, "I look at you."

"Okay, sorry, sorry." He zipped it back up and waved me on.

Mohsin and I took the escalators to the third floor, hoping that it'd be less crowded, but the area around the green light was packed. Not only did people stop to make du'as at the green light, facing the Black Stone, but the walkways actually narrowed there and made a bottleneck effect. Our steps were small and shuffling, and no one spoke.

Once we passed the green light, the crowd cleared up and we could walk. Young men started running, ducking in and out between people and racing each other. Mohsin and I followed, but it wasn't long before we were back at the green light and couldn't move.

Men pushing pilgrims in wheelchairs tried to squeeze past us, threatening to run over our bare toes. Husbands walked behind their wives, men's arms up like walls around women. I had heard stories of women being groped and molested in the Haram, so thank al-Lat if they weren't by themselves.

Those times around the green-light corner, we'd be at a complete standstill and even then some guy would plant his hand in the center of my back, pushing like there was anywhere for me to go. I'd stand there and just take it while he kept pushing. Every once in a while I turned to say *Sabr* or calmly wave my hand as though to ask, "What the fuck is your problem?" Seriously, what was their damage? I have been to

WrestleMania with eighty thousand marks, I've been to Buffalo Bills games with masses of the drunk and disappointed, I've ridden crowded New York subways, and I've driven in rush hour . . . and the rudest, most thoughtless people I've ever seen in my life were pilgrims in the holy city of Mecca. I was ready to go home and wished that I could circle the Ka'ba without anyone else around, but that missed the point. If the Ka'ba celebrated the miracle of life, tawaf signaled our commitment to each other. It was something bigger than religion, because our planet also made tawaf, carrying billions of hajjis around the sun, and there was no jumping off.

If the wrong person came to me at one of those moments, I could have lost it and blown my tawaf and perhaps the whole hajj, but Allah never gave me more than what I could bear. The bad feelings washed away soon enough and we kept going round the House. The Prophet said that the strongest man was not the one who could overcome his enemies, but the one who could restrain his anger and I cried thinking about it because I was such a bitch in that way, I was so weak and that became my failure over and over again. Even when I learned that lesson, I'd find in minutes that I failed to live it out, that I kept failing and would keep failing. I saw brothers who tried to follow the Prophet's Sunna by growing their beards a certain way and cleaning their teeth with a miswak; God bless their efforts, but the Sunna that I wanted was just learning how to treat people. It's so hard to be a good person when the human race clearly does not deserve good people.

I wanted to leave hajj transformed but knew that it wouldn't happen that easy. No sense of satisfaction or victory, I couldn't even see the finish line. At least I had this minor triumph: with the crowd so slow, it took us about three hours to complete our farewell tawaf, and in all that time I didn't raise my voice at anyone—though I did come close. At the end of the seventh cipher, I raised my hands and kissed my fingertips and said

Bismillahi Allahu Akbar, surprised that I had actually made it. Then a brother tapped my shoulder to hiss at me.

"No, no," he said, "no kissing your fingers."

The Devil's last wild swing.

I smiled and shared a verse of the Qur'an: *Lakum dinukum wa liya din.*

To you be your religion, and to me mine.

And I was done.

Holy Mosque, Have It Your Way

My original idea for January was to go back to the Shi'a mosque in Queens and beat my chest for Ashura, then head to Washington. First mourn Husayn, then inaugurate Hussein. Or get a flight to Trinidad, where local Shi'as observed Ashura with their own special holiday, Hosay, joined by the island's Catholics and Hindus.

Obama's inauguration was getting hyped like an American hajj, with Obama as the new stone fallen from the sky, and citizens of all colors merging around him to feel like complete Americans for the first time. Experts even speculated hajj-like numbers, possibly four million people coming to Washington. I might have been one of them; but Sadaf was flying to San Jose to visit family and plan the wedding, and bought me a plane ticket while I was in Medina.

In the 1940s, our wedding would have been illegal under California law as a transgression of racial purity, but in the 1940s, the families of Sadaf's community weren't even here. Her South Bay Islamic Association and my Islamic Center of Rochester both emerged in the years after 1965's Immigration and Naturalization Act, which opened the American Borg to increased immigration from the non-white, non-Christian parts of the world.

We wish to improve ourselves. We will add your biological and technological distinctiveness to our own. Your culture will adapt to service ours.

— THE BORG, *Star Trek: The Next Generation*

No one saw it coming, but this act of state would completely transform American religion, creating the exchanges that made culture-mutants like me possible. If I had to name the individuals who most affected my spiritual life, LBJ would be right up there with Ibn 'Arabi.

IT STARTED TO look like our nikkah should be officiated by her sister's father-in-law. He was dignified in the old-fashioned way but still warm with people, and they liked his weddings because he kept things short but powerful—and perhaps because he wasn't an imam, and thus did not speak like an imam. He sounded more like a philosopher who happened to be pious.

"The men think they are dominant," he told me at a family party, "but I tell a young couple, 'Allah made you partners to each other.'" One of his key points was to honor your responsibilities more than your rights. I asked him how he came to perform weddings. The uncle explained that back in the early days of the Bay's Muslim community, there weren't many who could do it. Then I finally recognized that we were in the Bay, which had some secret and strange local Islam of its own . . .

"Uncle, by any chance, did you know a scholar named Muhammad Abdullah?"

"Sure," he said. "Muhammad Abdullah was on the board of directors for the Islamic Center of San Francisco. He came from Fiji. At first, we had some question because he was thought to be Qadiani, you know about them?"

"Yes," I answered. The more heterodox branch of the Ahmadiyyas.

"We asked him about it, and he told us that he belonged to

the sect that does not believe that Ahmad was a prophet." The Lahoris.

"And everyone accepted him?"

"In those days," he said, "the Muslim community was very small, and we could not fight over these things. And he was a good man."

The uncle then added, "We used to call him *Master* Abdullah. He was a teacher."

"I've heard that about him," I said.

"But tell me, how did you encounter his name?"

Somehow I didn't see that coming, and froze for a second. To answer him meant unveiling my full weirdness.

"There are people," I told him with a nervous smile, "who say that Muhammad Abdullah was Master Fard, founder of the Nation of Islam—that he had come back in disguise and helped Warith Deen reform the mosques."

"Really?" The uncle knew who Fard was, but hadn't heard that his friend had been incorporated into the mythology. He said that when it came to Muhammad Abdullah being Fard, he couldn't know one way or another; but he could put me in touch with other local uncles who knew the man better.

Our conversation moved to other things—my opinion of his hometown Lahore, his love of classical music both Indian and Western—but I couldn't pull the grin off my face. As if things weren't already crazy, Allah now willed that I'd marry a Muslim sister from the same Bay where Master Fard put on his final show, interconnecting everything. We were planning a regular Indian Sunni wedding where they'd hold Qur'ans over our heads as we walked out . . . but now I could imagine Fard standing in the back corner the whole time.

ON A COLD and wet afternoon in the week of Ashura, Sadaf drove me to Chapel of the Chimes in Hayward. The cemetery's Muslim section, the Garden of Mercy, contained some of her family friends, and also Master Abdullah. His stone had weathered in the four years since I last saw it. The "Ehsanpur, Pakistan" had become almost unreadable, but above his name it was still clear: PROFESSOR AND IMAM. After fifty thousand miles of ziyarat, this was the last grave.

I built with Sadaf on the basics of his story: Master Abdullah was born in 1908 in the Punjab, and arrived in Fiji as an Ahmadiyya missionary around the same time that Master Fard disappeared from North America. He corresponded with Elijah Muhammad. When he came to the United States, Elijah invited him to teach his son Wallace. When Wallace broke from Elijah's teachings, Master Abdullah convinced the son to rejoin the father, since he was the only one who could lead the organization in the future. After Elijah's death, Wallace/Warith Deen named Master Abdullah head of the Nation's Oakland mosque and the entire Bay Area.

In 1976, after attending a Muhammad Abdullah lecture in Los Angeles, Warith Deen began to suspect that Master Abdullah was Master Fard. In 1981 a Pakistani scholar named Z. I. Alsari made the claim in print. Responding to the rumors, Muhammad Abdullah only said, "It is all right to say I am Fard Muhammad for Wallace D. Muhammad. I taught him some lessons. But I am not the same person who taught Elijah Muhammad, and I am not God." After Master Abdullah returned to the essence in 1992, Warith Deen proclaimed that he had really been Fard all along.

"Abdullah admitted to being *a* Fard," said Sadaf. "Fard for Warith Deen, but not *the* Fard." There were even reports that Warith Deen had recanted the story.

"Fard's a costume you can put on. Anyone can be a Fard for someone."

We stood at the Master's grave and had nothing left to say. My shoes were covered in wet lawn trimmings. Her black Chuck Taylors must have been soaked. We both felt the added heaviness of people who she knew buried in the Garden of Mercy, and also the tombstones of children, some with pictures, some I remembered from my first trip here. For what Ashura meant to me, these graves did the job as much as anything.

For the sake of that heaviness, the Prophet advised us to visit graves, I remembered from signs in the holy cities. The sadness was a good thing. Then I realized that all of the graves were buried with the heads facing Mecca. For some reason I never noticed it at Jannatul-Baqi or the Prophet's own tomb. The farther you get from Mecca, the more necessary these things become.

"DID LOUIS FARRAKHAN ever write back to you?" asked Sadaf.

"No, but I might go to Savior's Day next month." Savior's Day was the Nation of Islam's annual celebration of what they understood as Master Fard's birthday, February 26. "Fard could have been Buddhist," I added for no reason.

A Buddhist named Paul Guthrie had posted videos on Youtube arguing that Master Fard's lessons were closer to Buddhism than Islam. Fard taught that there was no mystery god, and no heaven or hell; those are Buddhist teachings, said Guthrie. Fard said, *Sit yourself in heaven at once!* That's Buddhism. Fard never called his meeting hall a mosque, but the Allah Temple. Fard instructed his Muslims to eat one meal a day, a practice of Buddhist monks that had nothing to do with Islam; and Fard also said to avoid consuming meat like the "poison animal eaters."

Fard told Elijah about a "wheel" that would rid the world of "slavery, suffering, and death"; this wheel, the Mothership or Motherplane, was really the Wheel of Dharma. The Motherplane did not signify a plane as in "airplane," but a higher plane of *consciousness*, and was a mother because it gave birth to the lower planes. The Motherplane would drop leaflets telling Original people to "go inside," said Fard; but according to Guthrie, this meant to go inside the self—seeking the inner transformation that Buddha promised would rid us of slavery (to desire), suffering (from desire), and death (and rebirth). As the Nation saw him, Fard wasn't born Allah; he became Allah by conquering and perfecting the self, just as Siddhartha became the Buddha. Elijah said that Fard was taught and prepared for his mission by twenty-three wise scientists, Fard the twenty-fourth on the council. They ostensibly matched the twenty-four elders from Revelation, but could have been the twenty-four enlightened tirthankaras of Jainism, another Indian religion with cyclic concepts of time and no Mystery God.

Guthrie revealed Buddhism as the secret of Fard's English Lesson C-1. The lesson's degree, "They wanted to go back home, but could not swim nine thousand miles," referred not to Africa or even Mecca, neither of which were nine thousand miles from the American coast—but the Indus Valley, the home of Buddhism.

"If Fard was a professor," said Sadaf, reading the word on Master Abdullah's tombstone, "he must have known something about Buddhism." While humoring my convert mischief about Fard, she did find Buddhism interesting, so the next day we went to the Pao-Hua Temple.

"I don't believe in Fard the way that people are supposed to," I told her in the car. "I don't really believe in the twenty-four scientists or Yacub or the Mothership as 'actual facts.' I don't have faith in the Supreme Wisdom Lessons like people have faith in the Qur'an."

"I'm not always comfortable with that kind of faith," she replied.

"But I still use the lessons and the Math, I do real things with them. And we still use the Qur'an. You still wear Ayatul-Kursi around your neck."

"I think we just do what we can."

At the Pao-Hua Temple, we sat on a bench in the courtyard with free literature and watched people waving incense sticks in front of statues. The literature was okay. "Corporate Body of the Buddha Educational Foundation," it said on the back. It reminded Sadaf of the pamphlets that she used to see at the mosque as a kid, which made it suspect, because one never knew where those pamphlets came from.

Inside the temple, the high walls were lined from top to bottom with shelves of tiny gold-colored Buddhas. There had to be thousands of them, with identical expression and pose. They weren't idols to me, perhaps because there were so many that one couldn't hold my focus. I saw them as representing all the prophets of history, the named and unnamed. Allah has sent us as many as 124,000 messengers, according to some hadiths, teaching 124,000 versions of Islam. Or these Buddhas could have been the same prophet, all Muhammad, but the countless unique Muhammads that lived in our interpretations, or the thousands of Master Fards, whose Islam could even turn itself into Buddhism— but also come full cipher and put me in a Sunni mosque making Sunni prayers, because one of the Fards took it there.

Umar trying to follow Muhammad didn't turn him into Muhammad, only Umar-imitating-Muhammad. Then Umar taught his son how to do as the Prophet had done, which turned the boy into Umar's-son-imitating-Umar-imitating-Muhammad. And so on down the line, putting me at the end of a game of Telephone that has been going on for fourteen hundred years. After all of that, who makes your religion? Master Fard and Bulleh Shah said that you'd never find Allah outside yourself, even if you searched for trillions of years; but I could also say that of the Prophet, since I went to the man's tomb and couldn't find him there. I'm still a Muslim, so I must be the imam of me, the alim of me, the shaykh of me, the caliph of me, the Master Fard of me. The Mothership is my mother's hip, I'm the Mahdi of me. My own gate to the city of knowledge, I'm the Ali of me. Bear witness to yourself. I'm the Muhammad of me.

* * *

WE THEN WENT to Sadaf's childhood mosque, where I met the imam from the hajj DVD and we talked about Mecca. The imam and Sadaf had grown up together, and his dad was the imam before him.

She waited while I made two rakats in the men's section. My thoughts wandered and I reeled them back in, pointing my fingers and toes and brain straight towards the Ka'ba. Sitting after the prayer, I remembered Master Fard's claim that Buddhism was thirty-five thousand years old and Islam knew no birth record. Fard also said that the Earth was home to Islam, and Five Percenters referred to women as Earths, so what did that mean? Maybudi said that when a man kissed his wife, "It is as if he has kissed the pillar of the Ka'ba." I could bring it back to the Sunna, since the Prophet said that marriage was half our religion. According to Ibn 'Arabi, the Prophet said, "The best of you is he who is best to his wife, and I am the best of you to his wife" because of Allah's Attributes that a wife manifested. To me, it all meant that Sadaf and I had to build Islam together in our own universe.

I reflected on more history, but just the history of my Ka'ba growing up in this mosque, my Ka'ba as a little girl waiting for Sunday school to end and the teacher— who was Master Abdullah's son-in-law—to yell, "Snack time!" My Ka'ba terrified of the old lady next door, who the kids all thought was a jinn-lady. The mosque had changed since then, Sadaf noted. It looked cleaner now, and the separate women's area was a recent addition. Years ago at the South Bay Islamic Association, men and women prayed in the same room. Everything changes and it will change again. Look at Mecca, nothing's the same in Mecca. You can never jump in the same river twice; because the river's flowing, it's always new water. And you are water, you flow; so it's also a new you jumping in, a Qur'an expired and renewed.